JUST STARE AT THE WALL!

(Living the Universe from Where You Sit)

by

Mark Blacknell

Table of Contents

Where I'm Coming From (Intro)

Just as a deep spring bubbles through the wilderness for those who are resilient enough to find it—if you found this book through the shallowness of the modern world, it's for you. A spring makes no promises; it moves from its source, offering itself while asking nothing in return. It lives simply, unencumbered by the tragedies and dramas we create, expressing itself the only way it knows how. It's slowly shaped by pressure, patience, and the quiet work of the earth. And those who find such a spring are often shaped the same way: intuitive, weathered by experience, and attuned to things that can't be rushed. As you step into the wilderness of your mind today, let the freedom of the spring remind you that nature unfolds in its own time. Have faith in the living source that shapes you.

A literary agent offered her thoughts on my manuscript, and by "offered," I mean she delivered a beautifully wrapped professional smackdown.

"So let me get this straight," she said. "You tell the reader you probably can't help them, that spirituality is dangerous, that you're not an authority, and—my personal favorite—that they should be skeptical of everything you say."

I sat there chuckling, confident and happy, like someone who already knows the universe is running a long, elaborate joke, and I'm lucky enough to be in on it. She was playful and fun. I enjoyed her presence.

She stopped mid-sentence with a bewildered look on her face. "Wow. You're taking this way better than most. But let's be serious for a moment, Mark. Your introduction reads like an entrance exam for monks. You guarantee nothing, praise the meditative power of being bored, and nudge people toward the nearest blank wall. How am I supposed to sell that?"

For a moment, I thought about explaining the depths of my intentions, but realized there was no point. She couldn't relate to them. Not because she lacked intelligence or heart, but because they aren't built from the usual materials. I offered my thanks and confessed that her willingness to consider my work was an honor.

To stay true to myself, I can't make unrealistic promises. A promise is already half broken the moment it's spoken, because it tries to say in words what can only be practiced. My practice is to keep a steady watch on my intentions and live accordingly. I try to do the right thing. I don't always manage it. When I do, it's not for God or humanity—it's because it makes my life simpler and more fulfilling. I do my best to stay out of my own way and not create extra problems on top of the ones life already brings.

Life isn't easy, and I don't pretend it is. If I do something unhealthy, I'm doing it on purpose, not out of confusion or old patterns. It wasn't until I started meditating on a regular basis that I learned how to be more honest with myself, even when the truth hurt like hell. Most days it wasn't a choice. The practice forced me to. When I invited balance in, it demanded balance back. It didn't let me hide behind convenient narratives or excuses anymore.

Facing things as they are, not as I want them to be, has shown me that the world is far bigger than the stories I cling to. And anything I might chase—escape, pleasure, influence, status—is just another attempt at control dressed up as something meaningful or lasting. Seeing things in a more balanced way changes what I expect from myself. Anything I do well is a small gesture, not a grand solution.

Many years ago, I made a Bodhisattva vow, and this book is one of the fruits that grew from that choice. A Bodhisattva, in plain language, is someone who tries to live with compassion and ease the suffering around them, even in small ways. More often than not, it helps me feel confident, playful, and fulfilled. It keeps my life interesting and focused on what counts.

The vow doesn't make me special. If anything, it keeps me honest. It reminds me that I'm not here to perfect myself or rise above anyone. I'm here to stay awake inside the life I've actually got. Some days the vow feels close, like a steady hand on my back. Other days it's barely a whisper. But that's the practice: noticing the drift, adjusting, coming back to balance.

I've had people say, "You're always talking about balance, but you're not balanced all the time." Fair enough. When they point something out, I take it seriously. They're half right. I talk about balance, and lose it. Then I find it again, and lose it again. I'm not always balanced, but I *am* disciplined enough to return to it. That's the whole practice. I can explain that six ways to Sunday, but it still doesn't matter. I guess mediocrity is only acceptable when it stays quiet.

Usually I *am* quiet. I stare at a wall, mind my business, and watch the wheels go round and round. But today's a little different. I've lived enough life, made enough mistakes, and practiced long enough to trust myself. That's the point. If someone as typical and confused as me can sort through the noise and find a little steadiness, then the whole thing is actually doable.

Part of trusting myself is knowing myself. I'm not the type to bash technology, blame modern society or pin all my problems on the rich. I could care less about conspiracy theories. Even if they are true, what can I do?

I'll meditate in the morning, work with senior citizens in the afternoon, and binge-watch a cult documentary at night—that's balance, right? There's nothing like watching a group of adults hand over their free will to a guy with a goofy mustache, a paranoid prophet, or a linen-pants guru who looks like he got lost on the way to Whole Foods.

So let me save you the suspense: the last thing in the world I want to be is a guru. If you're hoping for an escape hatch—some cosmic elevator or prophet that whisks you away from your routine and into heaven—you won't find it here. I'm just a boring human writing about boring human life. I shop at Walmart. It's all I can afford these days, and honestly, the place teaches me more about being awake than any mountaintop retreat ever did.

I might help a senior grab a box of Shredded Wheat from the top shelf. If it's a zoo that day because the tourists are back, I'll weave through the crowd like I'm on the Schuylkill Expressway—eyes forward, shoulders loose, praying nobody slams on the brakes. Usually, I swing through Walmart to grab what the kids need after I finish my shift at the senior home.

One day, at the home, I started seeing little balls of white foam floating everywhere. Each time there was more of it—on the ground, drifting through the air, falling from the sky like some kind of low-budget apocalypse movie. My mind went into overdrive. Maybe a moving company dropped a truckload of packing peanuts while hauling in a new resident? Maybe the church next door was putting in another memorial? Industrial waste? The citrus industry's pesticides? Angel dandruff? Every day I came up with a new scenario, each one dumber than the last.

Eventually I stopped, took a breath, and looked around. It took a few minutes, but then I saw it: a hole in the awning. Out of the hole popped the head of a woodpecker—completely covered in foam. I burst out laughing so hard the poor thing flew away. When I settled down and shut up, it came back and posed for a picture. It was adorable. Turns out the little guy had burrowed into the building and was flinging insulation everywhere like a tiny, deranged contractor. My mind had built an entire conspiracy theory when the truth was literally a bird with bad boundaries.

So, do yourself a favor, okay? Try not to figure out what I'm up to. It doesn't matter what I'm up to. What matters is what you're up to. Putting your body and mind in a balanced position happens through repetition. The point of all that becomes clear when we least expect it, not when we demand it. It may seem redundant, but if you pay attention long enough and stare at a wall in silence; it will become clear. Maybe not instantly, but eventually. Like the moment a foamy woodpecker head pops out of a hole and explains everything. Moments like that remind me why I practice each morning in the first place.

They say the early bird gets the worm. When I wake up and meditate, the initial wobble and spin settle into a clarity so steady I think, “This is a miracle.” That’s the Coach—the wise one—talking. Then, a warm energy, rising like the sun, shimmers from my belly and settles in my temple. As a loving parent soothes a child, it whispers, “There, there, my love. Everything’s gonna be just fine.” That’s Mother Earth. When our day begins with that kind of gentle reassurance, we are in a good position to trust and appreciate our nature.

And while I want you to trust and appreciate yourself, I’m not your mother. I don’t offer comfort or rules to live by, and I’m not going to scold you for tracking mud across the carpet. What speaks here isn’t authority—it’s the balanced meditation posture itself. It says let your expectations fall away and see what unfolds when you meet the practice on its own terms. We meet meditation when we do meditation. We stop our lives and do it in silence. That’s it.

There’s not much to talk about, but that doesn’t mean if you do it, you won’t end up in a full-blown conversation with yourself. Sit long enough and you’ll meet the entire cast of characters living rent-free in your head. And before you ever reach the Coach or teacher in you, you’ll have to get past the hecklers. They show up first, they show up loud, and they show up convinced they’re running the show.

They’ll throw every tired line they’ve been rehearsing for years. Things like, “You’re no good. This is pointless. It’s too hard. I’m too far gone. It hurts. I need to move. I'm done." And then come the everyday distractions dressed up as emergencies: "I'm hungry. I better eat. Why didn't they call? I should call them. That bill. I better pay it or my credit will be ruined. I'm running late. That work thing. Oh man, I forgot to do that! I better get up."

The mind is dramatic. It storms, it worries, it sulks, it bargains, it whines. It acts like sitting still is some kind of personal attack. It will try everything—anything—to get you to stop meditating.

But here's the thing: all that noise is just like a crowded Walmart. It's the static you pass through to grab what you need and get back to the comfort of home. Balance doesn't shout or panic. It doesn't judge. It waits until conditions just "are." And the only way to reach that quiet intelligence underneath all the chaos—is to stay long enough to get through the checkout lines.

If that steadiness finally arrives, it won't hand you a clean, polished answer. It will show you that truth isn't cut and dry. It's an experiment—trial and error, done wrong before it's ever done right. It's an unfolding mist you move through, not a problem you solve. It isn't meant to be pinned down, mastered, or comprehended. It's meant to be lived.

If you're looking for clean lines, easy heroes and villains, a leader to follow, or a world painted in black and white, you're wasting your time here. I sincerely doubt I'm anyone's leader. Number one, I'm a man; the best leaders are always women. Number two, I can barely lead myself. I don't want you to follow me. I want to help you find the confidence and discipline to follow yourself. Once you do that, you can safely follow a guide, faith, practice or set of principles that may help you along your journey.

If you already find yourself working with an authentic teacher, this book may help you show up well. Consider yourself damn lucky—there are plenty of scammers, fakes, and arrogant creeps out there. If you're already an authentic meditation practitioner or teacher, I hope I can help you adapt your practice to your community, maybe soften your fixed ideas a little, and return to basics. And if you're still sorting out the whole "authentic" thing, welcome to the club. You're in good company. Don't give up.

I don't pretend to carry the universe on my shoulders. I'm one person with one nervous system, one history, one set of guns (biceps). But I also feel the larger unfolding moving through me—the same balance that holds my posture, steadies my heartbeat, and keeps every living thing upright for as long as it can stand. That's the part that feels connected to something more universal than me, something I didn't invent.

I come directly from the Zen lineage of the famous layperson Vimalakīrti, who lived in the time of the Buddha and hung out in bars and brothels because that's where he knew people were suffering most. He didn't hide from the world or polish himself into something untouchable. To say I'm influenced by ole' Vima the bodhisattva is an understatement.

The traditional stories say he wasn't intimidated by anyone—not kings, not scholars, not even the Buddha's sharpest disciples. He stayed in the middle of life and used whatever clarity he had to cut through the confusion. Buddha respected him for it. I'm not claiming to be even a fraction of the man Vima was, but he's the reason I continue to do this work at all. The get ups, rituals, chanting, nomenclature, bowing, discourse and doctrine—all the exotic window-dressing—doesn't appeal to me at all.

I'm just a working-class guy from Philly trying to understand my life from inside my own blind spots. They say you can take the boy out of Philly, but you can't take the Philly out of the boy. In my normal life, I don't talk in a quiet, calm monotone full of cliché New Age terms. Why would I do it here? I speak naturally.

I still bleed Eagles green, Flyers orange, Phillies red, and Sixers blue. Meditation books don't usually mention sports teams, but that's the point—if someone like me can feel connected to the universe, anyone can. You take yourself wherever you go, but you can't take yourself out of where you come from either.

It's not realistic to pretend we're someone we're not. So today, the plan is simple: act naturally, be ourselves, and feel at ease walking side by side on the same road of life. When we think someone's following us or up to no good, we end up constantly looking over our shoulder.

I'm not here to mug you, sell you anything, pressure you or change your mind, and all I'm asking for is a fair chance to prove it. If we crossed paths on the street, I'd say, "Hey, how you doing? Everything alright?" and genuinely be interested in your answer. This is nothing more than two ordinary people in the middle of a typical day, acknowledging each other as they pass.

I'm talking right now, but I'm hoping to hear your story someday. I want to connect with you. In all honesty, connection is what this is all about. This is a little social experiment as much as anything else. Practice is a great connector because that's what balance is about: bringing diverse energies together.

Usually, no matter what we say to one another, we hear it through our own filters. We hear what we expect, what we're afraid of, or what we want to be true. So, if we want a real conversation that cuts through the bull and gets closer to something real, we need to be willing to clear our filters a little.

That's where meditation fits in. It helps us clear our filters—the way you empty a lint trap in a dryer. Do you overthink when you empty your lint trap? You know what happens when you don't clear it: the machine strains, overheats, and eventually forces you to deal with a fire. If only our minds worked that way. They don't. We can ignore them for years. Meditation just gives us a chance to clear things out before the smoke alarm goes off.

When the mind isn't so clogged, there's room for the air to move again. With less static, it gets easier to listen, to address what's right in front of us, and to feel our connection to the larger world we're already part of.

Meditation doesn't give us access to anything special, exclusive, or supernatural. It's not going to give us a direct hotline to God or the universe. It won't enable us to reach financial independence and climb the social ladder straight to success. It's far simpler than that. It just helps us clear our minds and eventually, if we stick with it, trust ourselves enough to trust others.

We trust ourselves when we can focus on what's here in front of us, not the ghosts of what was or the fantasies of what might be. It gives us permission to be a little naive again—not in a careless way, but in the sense of being open, curious, and in awe without worrying that someone's waiting to take advantage of us. With a steadier mind and less resistance, we're not scanning for threats every second.

Consider this a 5K *fun run* for charity. There's no gold medal or prize money—nothing to win by coming out on top. The whole point is to show up, move together, and help each other get through the sweat and pain for a good cause. That's what practice is. Not competition. Not hierarchy. Just people trying to do something honest side by side.

At first, the balanced posture just quieted the noise and put my body and mind in the most stable position they could manage. Things settled. My life didn't feel so out of control anymore, and I could pay attention. Once I could pay attention, the world stopped feeling like something happening around me. It started feeling like something I was inside of.

The bird songs in the morning, playing with my children, the smile of a friend, the sunset, the moon and stars—they weren't just scenes anymore. They were moments I belonged to. It's one thing to witness a sunset or hear a child's laughter. It's another thing entirely to feel like you're part of it.

Once I felt part of things, no longer driven to fix or flee myself and able to step out of my own head, the loneliness and pain began to ease. The old sense of separation started to fall away. It felt less like me *against* the world and more like me *in* the world. I finally felt like I fit *into* my life instead of standing *outside* it. I began to let myself *go with the flow* of the changing world instead of bracing against it all the time.

In that new, lighter space, I sensed how wonderful it was to accept myself as I was—to feel ordinary, not exceptional or broken, just another living being among other living beings. That ordinariness felt like relief, not loss. It made it easier to see I wasn't any different from anyone else. I was just one individual among a universe of them, existing in my own way.

I'd been an anxious, arrogant, frustrated man for most of my adult life, with so much pent-up anger I could have gotten a job at a maximum security, Alabama prison, and no one would have blinked. Suddenly, because I stopped my life in its tracks and put my body and mind in a balanced position, something in me chilled out.

Little by little, my heart and mind opened. Meditation didn't hand me a new universe—it revealed the one I was already living in, right where I sat. Everything felt warmer and lighter. I found people and the world around me fascinating instead of threatening. For the first time in my life, I felt right where I belonged.

My compassion began to grow, a warm, steady care that comes from seeing how each person, being, and system shares a balance that holds together not just my life, but life itself. Believe me, it was weird for a guy like me to even mention a word like compassion. When I first joined a Zen group (sangha), I had to wade through a lot of insecurity and self-consciousness before I could feel remotely comfortable expressing my feelings. I was too cynical.

Cynicism felt like strength back then. It kept me sharp by keeping me separated. But cynicism is its own kind of exclusion. It shuts the door on connection, keeps people at a distance, and convinces us that caring is a trap. It's a stance that says nothing gets in, even when something in us is starving for contact. By taking a hard look at myself in meditation, my cynicism started to look less like toughness and more like weakness and self-protection. It wasn't clarity. It was distance. And once I saw that, even a little, my whole disposition began to loosen.

Fast forward fifteen-twenty years, and I realize that I have a life, a family, interests, a point of view—and so does every other living being. Every individual feels the way they feel about their life just as strongly as I feel about mine. Mine isn't more important than theirs. If I were them, I'd be them; I'm a boy from Philly, so I'm me. It's all a matter of circumstance. Those kinds of inclusive feelings took root in me the way a seed settles into fertile ground.

We don't choose where we're born or to whom, yet that determines everything. If my parents were birds, I'd be a bird. I'd experience the world as a bird. I'd chirp and dig up worms and poop on your head to give you a bit of good luck. Despite their terrible etiquette, I have profound love and respect for birds. To me, the sky is one thing. To a bird, it's *everything* including a bathroom. I often stop and listen to them sing. Their melodies carry me away.

Being human doesn't mean I see the world better than a bird—it just means I see it differently. When we open our hearts and minds—and invite more of the world in—something shifts. We start paying attention to more than ourselves. We balance ourselves out with everything else. We appreciate the connection between our lives and the fuller range of life around us.

Even though I'm not from central casting—and other Zen teachers might not appreciate my style—meditation still makes me feel less like I'm standing alone in my own shoes and more like I'm standing in something larger. Not just in the shoes of birds, or you, or my spiritual lineage, but in the shoes of the whole universe. Birds don't wear shoes like we do, but in a way they do—their feet are both feet and shoes at the same time. That alone should tell us birds are far more evolved than us.

Part of this is imaginative. I can't actually experience what you, or birds, or the universe experience. But part of it is real. It's a feeling of empathy, a warmth cultivated through the balanced position. I feel part of something much larger than myself. And it's up to me to feel this way. When I walk out my front door and stroll through my neighborhood, I'm always saying hi to my neighbors. Not because I'm putting on a show, but because I actually feel like their neighbor.

I feel like a neighbor of everything in the universe for the same reason. I practice balance so it feels good to see it all around me. It gives me the confidence to know for sure I'm on the right track. All life shares a balance that's built into the basic conditions of existence. Even the planet itself is the result of endless energies and matter coming together in just the right way. The sun and Earth formed through a relationship so precise that if either had been too far or too close, too big or too small, too old or too new, none of this would have worked.

Balance brings diverse forces together. Gravity pulls, heat pushes, motion spreads—each doing its own thing. A star survives because inward gravity and outward heat match. A planet holds its orbit because motion and pull line up just right. Molecules form because attraction and movement meet in a narrow range where they don't fly apart. We're built inside that same narrow range. We're part of the slice of the universe where balance is possible.

Balance is the meeting point where independent things hold one another in place long enough for anything to exist. Not everything in the universe is balanced—most of it is chaos, collapse, explosion, drift. But anything that lasts, even for a moment, lasts because some set of forces found equilibrium. That's the connection between us.

All life and everything we recognize as real emerged from a meticulous balance. The planet is the master of that balance, not us. A human master isn't a master at all, and we'd do well to remember that. We are simply the universe—God, nature, whatever name we give it or refuse to give it—expressing itself, not a person holding a title.

All we can do is *be* the conditions we already are. That's not very original, since those conditions were shaped by forces far more complex than any one person, and yet it is original in its own way. It's no small thing for a limited human being to return to balance and appreciate it with any consistency. The person that practices balance, that intentionally goes back to it in body and mind, is wild and wonderful.

We're not held together by the whole universe, just by the balanced pocket we were born into. I'm doing my best to create a pocket like that today for us, but I'm no expert in any of this. In fact, I often warn about the dangers of pseudo scientists merging things like physics and spirituality.

Although I'm influenced by the wild ideas of some pretty cool academics, like Mary Evelyn Tucker and Brian Swimme, I'm not pretending to understand ecology or cosmology on any deep level. I find them interesting because I feel connected to other people who appreciate balance as much as I do. Since the whole world and everything in it are forms of balance, they make sense to me. I see me in them. It's pretty miraculous when I think about it.

Staring at a wall convinced an adrenaline-addicted Marine who spent a little time in the slammer to finally slow down and connect with a universe of possibilities well beyond his comfort zone. It blows my mind, man. How? I don't try to figure it out. But sitting there long enough, steady enough, brought me in line with the broader world, and the connection became obvious. Because I feel it, I can live it.

I feel like I'm living the whole universe where I sit because of the meditation posture. Putting my body in a balanced position brought that connection all the way out of me and into the real world. When the mind settles, it can step out of its own world and enter the world of whatever it brings into awareness. Then, it can *feel* outside of its own world.

If I'm thinking of the eternal universe, I can't suddenly be it or understand it with any degree of intricacy. But when I'm steady, I can feel the balance I come from holding my body together. I can hear it directly in my heartbeat—steady, patient, unforced. I can feel it in the way my breath evens out, in the way my spine finds its line, in the way my muscles stop bracing for problems that aren't there. My body showed me that I exist in a balanced pocket of the universe long before my mind caught up.

I can't know the origins of that balance or the cosmic conditions that shaped it, but the intention to return to equilibrium keeps me oriented—a little more at home in the body I belong to. The world feels like home now, and that feeling of inclusion helps me carry a quiet warmth, care, and humor wherever I go.

My life was already forming its shape long before I ever meditated. So, when I talk about practice, I don't just mean sitting on a cushion. I mean paying attention to the whole thing—the habits, the reactions, the stories, the conditions, the parts of myself I used to overlook. When I finally started seeing more of it together, something clicked. My life made sense from the inside. *I* made sense. Everything that had happened before felt less like a mistake and more like the path that brought me to the realization that I was at a balanced point in my life.

Our bodies, emotions, and thoughts all move through the world, but the instrument we use to meet all of it is the mind. Practice is studying that instrument. We study it in meditation, and that's where we find ourselves in balance.

At first, I was just sitting there, doing nothing, and my mind naturally drifted and filled. There was nowhere to run. And then, without trying to analyze or script or figure everything out, things simply came into view. The noise settled, the clutter dropped, and what was real became clear. I didn't need to protect myself or run mental simulations so much anymore—I just paid attention to the moment I was in and started to appreciate it.

You don't need to be a Zen master, psychiatrist, or neuroscientist to study your mind. You don't need to understand the universe or God that formed you to see the universe or God working in you right now. As soon as you make a conscious effort to stop, go still, limit your sensory stimulation, and turn your awareness toward yourself, you'll start to get a feel for balance. Then all you need to do is get out of the way. It sounds easy, but it isn't.

Awareness is simply where we place our attention in the present. The mind is the larger field that awareness moves through. They're made of the same stuff, but they function differently: awareness is the part we can guide; the rest moves on its own, shaped by forces we can never fully understand. You're using your awareness to read this. Reading takes focus, and your mind might already be slipping in and out of it. Just notice what's popping up—little thoughts, sensations, aches, the impulse to drift.

If your head hurts or your attention keeps scattering, it might be time to pause and follow the simple meditation instructions in the back. You'll learn more from your own silence than anything I could tell you. Why would you fill your head with more information if you *aren't* fully here?

Thoughts, feelings, and sensations interrupt our presence, but they're also what enable us to feel life fully when we *are* here. Meditation doesn't dull or stop any of it—it just slows things down enough that we can work with what arises instead of being pushed around by it.

From the vast, spinning universe that gave rise to everything, back to the breath we're taking right now—awareness is the one part of the mind we can direct. It cuts through everything that moves on its own. It pierces it. Our attention is the only steady point inside all that endless motion, the only place where our choices appear. Meditation sharpens that point in ways that are hard to explain without doing it.

Through years of practice, I began to notice that when I stood up and started moving, I could direct my attention with a little more clarity. My thoughts and feelings weren't getting in the way of my experiences so much. I could actually be where I was, doing what I was doing. I saw more of the bigger picture around me. I could consistently put things into a healthier, more positive perspective.

More than anything else, the main change I started to feel was that my pain stopped being the center of the universe. I could finally see through it. For years it had kept my world small, everything narrowing around it, but once it loosened its grip, my mind could show me what else was there.

I realized the mind is far larger than anything I can grasp. It revealed how limited, temporal, and biased I am, and at the same time it showed me how I'm connected to a timeless potential. My practice lives somewhere between those two truths.

I feel that the real value of meditation is that it helped me think myself so far out into the universe that I finally saw the whole exercise was futile. I didn't find some hidden meaning waiting out there—I realized I could create my own. Meaning wasn't scattered across the stars; it was right there *in* my mind *with* the stars, in the life I was already living.

Our minds hold the whole universe from the beginning. That may not make sense yet. Give it time—meditation has its own way of showing you. But that doesn't mean I understand the complexities of the universe. It's way beyond me. To the great cosmic unfolding, my understanding is a joke. I can't even know the complexities of my own life with any accuracy.

It would take me as long as I've been alive to re-live every moment that led here. And every single one of them led here. I'd be a hundred and ten years old before I finished. Even if we could recreate every moment since birth, it still wouldn't give us an accurate picture. It wouldn't even begin to account for the countless forces that had to come together from the beginning of time just to get us here (X). (X) marks this precise spot in our minds.

I see my life and life itself as one ongoing, infinite formula that can't be solved. **(X)** = ∞

At some point, I had to accept that anything I think I am and know—or anything I think happened—is always far more than I'm capable of grasping. Our awareness isn't just the accumulation of information. It also comes from emptying the mind enough to see what's right in front of us.

A mechanic needs to know a lot about vehicles, but they also have to focus on the one sitting right there in the shop. Sometimes they run into a problem that isn't standard. That's when their knowledge meets their ability to pay attention to the specific situation and solve it in a creative or intuitive way. Being a good mechanic takes a balanced mind—because a vehicle needs to be balanced to run smoothly and safely. When the mechanic and the vehicle are *ONE,* you've got a good car and a good mechanic.

Much of this is hard to talk about. These are the private moments you face alone in front of a wall. But I share what I can, because it might help you. I'm willing to tell my story, but to get anything from it, you should understand that it's no longer the center of my life. This is and isn't about me. For me, it was ALL about me—until it wasn't. Now it's about you. I'm trying to show you a way into your own mind, so you can learn how to stop torturing yourself like I did.

I might not know much, but I don't torture myself anymore. I'm less anxious now, and a more compassionate person, even when I'm so full of pain I can scream. I don't question my pain or try to figure it out. I try not to hand it to anyone else. The world I love doesn't need to carry it. I sit with it in meditation, face it directly, do my best not to run, and somehow that makes it manageable. I accept its place in my life. Even my pain finds itself in balance.

I can still focus and appreciate my life despite the pain I'm living with. When I'm in pain, I take care of myself. I know when to lay off the gas and when to hit the pedal, so my speed is just right. We can't be compassionate with anyone else until we learn to be compassionate with ourselves. I talk about compassion a lot, but my outlook obviously isn't "kumbaya." It was shaped by pure grit, not gentle teachers or steady tradition. I learned the real value of compassion by acting like a jerk—through my big mistakes, the people I hurt and left behind, the dark stretches of my life, and the people and situations that scared, hurt, or disappointed me.

I had to live on the edge to learn how important it is to step back. I'm damn lucky to be alive. I don't say that lightly, and it's the reason I'm willing to share my practice with you today. I think of it as payback, not a *payday*. I'm still the person I've always been, with a distinct personality, but I take very little personally anymore. What matters is that, despite the odds, I'm still here, and I have something to offer that might help someone else stay here too.

If you're in pain, there's another way to live with it—but it starts the same way: by actually looking at it and admitting you're in it, instead of letting it run your life from the shadows. The wall makes pain so simple to face. There's nothing to think about. It's a body thing, not a mind thing. I don't call it mindfulness; I call it ***bodyness***. *Bodyness* is just a matter of meditating, sitting still and quiet no matter how bad it feels, acknowledging our pain, experiencing it and letting it play out naturally. The balanced voice or Coach in you will eventually come to the surface and point you in the right direction.

Whether you identify as spiritual or not, whether you feel like a master or a beginner, real learning rarely arrives in a tidy form. It comes through the unexpected—the moments we'd never choose and couldn't plan. If we're open and paying close attention, we may learn in the simplest ways we didn't even know were possible.

I'm not offering a pinpoint map to buried treasure. What I've got to give is more like an arrow—a weathered mark on an old-growth tree pointing toward your original nature. And like nature, the path it points to isn't always predictable or inviting. Sometimes it's wild, painful, or just plain scary.

Meditation is the discipline I trust to find my equilibrium in this fast and furious universe of ours, but it isn't the only way to find it. It's easy to mistake a spiritual practice for something fixed. No matter how wonderful it is, when we cling to a particular practice, we end up clinging. We try to control what can't be controlled. Something inside goes tight, and that tension transmits to others. We go out of whack.

You might think, *why is this guy so fixated on meditation?* I don't blame you. It can look a little extreme—like I'm two steps away from opening my own commune. But honestly, staring at a wall is simple. After going through hell and back, simple started looking pretty good. It's hard, sure, but you don't need to be Einstein. Maybe that's why it works for me.

I'm just a Jarhead from Philly who's blown more fuses, literal and metaphorical, than any electrician has ever seen. I've tried almost everything, and silent meditation just… works. At this point, I can't even clearly recall how it all unfolded. It's just my ordinary, everyday life now—the least dramatic "extreme" thing you could imagine, and that's good enough for me. I'm safe, happy and fulfilled.

Once I sought mental-health treatment and became relatively stable, meditation was the thing that kept me pointed in the right direction. And if it can help an old, salty Devil Dog like me, it can help anyone. I've helped a lot of troubled people start a practice and stick with it. I didn't charge them a thing. I did it because it kept me out of trouble. I guess trouble draws trouble, but not always the way we think it does. We all have a niche. This just happens to be mine—something I fell into and could do naturally.

I spent years in a meditation group and learned within a specific tradition, but it has become clear that this is something I need to do on my own. Stillness, quiet, balance, and a reduction of stimulation aren't techniques or traditions so much as conditions—ways of stopping long enough to watch ourselves on a basic level. Any practice that settles the body and clears the mind puts us in a position to receive that broader perspective. You don't need to be Buddhist, spiritual, educated, privileged, or anything else to do it. You can be yourself. But you *do* need to be patient.

So go slower, settle in, and decide whether you're here for real. This kind of pace mirrors the practice itself: repetitive, inconvenient, uncomfortable, and a little boring at first. If you can't stay with me for twenty pages, you're definitely not going to stay with yourself for twenty minutes each morning. Nothing in nature hurries. Things don't reveal themselves right away; they need room to unfold. Trust your nature. Whatever led you to this book is real.

Some of this may feel strange in a world built on speed, but slowing down shows us what's real. We are nature itself, even if we forget. The pages ahead are an invitation to rediscover who we are and where we come from—not through information, technology, culture, tradition, or academic study, but through the living history carried quietly inside each of us. The intention is to guide you back to yourself, so you don't need people like me.

The one thing we truly control is our focus, so today we turn it inward—toward the original nature unfolding within. Our original mind is the unforced, unpretending awareness that's been here since the beginning, the part of us that doesn't need to become anything to be whole. It lives outside the roles we play, outside our beliefs and cultures, outside the personalities we've hardened into something we call "ourselves."

Touching even a trace of that nature takes effort, but the effort is only part of the story. The conditions have to be right. We can set some of them—by settling the body, quieting the senses, and easing the mind out of its usual stream of stimulation—but the deeper conditions were in place long before we arrived. In a sense, we're simply learning how to sit in the right place at the right time.

The first thing this book can teach you is to appreciate the simple fact that you're here reading it. If you're here, it means you've been given enough space in your life—even if it doesn't feel like much—to reach for something that might open your mind. You may be hurting and lost; you might think you're too broken to bother, but you're still here with the ability to pause, breathe, and learn. That alone is a kind of privilege; a quiet blessing many in human history will never know.

And you—the person sitting here with this book in your hands—you're more of a miracle than you may realize. Not in some Hallmark way, but in the plain, physical truth of it. You're a living spark in a universe that spends most of its time collapsing, exploding, and tearing itself apart. Yet somehow, in all that violence and chaos, there's this small pocket of balance where life can exist… where *you* exist.

Your life is a brief, impossible opening in an endless night—and the fact that you're here, awake enough to look inward, means something. It means you matter. It means you're not done yet. It means there's still something in you worth tending. Do you understand how rare that is? How rare *you* are? Stop and look at yourself. Really look. You're beautiful inside and out.

In a technological world, this is a kind of anti-technology—not because I think technology is evil or steering us toward the apocalypse, but because it grew out of the same era that made speed, notoriety, wealth, and social influencing feel like the whole point of being alive. Technology is the reason this book even exists. I'm a product of my world. The fast world pulls us in one direction; this grew out of my natural pull in the other. It's balance at work.

Extremes can feel scary and out of control, but they always end up turning the world the other way. Push far enough in one direction and something in us, or around us, starts pulling back toward center. Not enlightenment. Not transcendence. Not some perfected version of ourselves. Just the original mind that's left when the noise falls away.

When we pause and turn attention toward ourselves, we open a small space to see what binds us and what releases us. In that shift, attention may stop running after thoughts, sensations, and emotions and notice the field they appear in. And in that field, we might glimpse that our attention, though personal in this moment, is not separate. It belongs to everything.

If we sincerely stick with a silent meditation practice, we might start to feel part of something bigger than ourselves. The way it unfolds is beyond anything we can plan or imagine. So, there's no point thinking ahead or filling your head with big expectations. Just act naturally and it will unfold in its own time like everything else in nature.

Meditation is the practice of acting naturally. I trust it because it keeps me grounded. If you let it in, even a little, it can help you find your own ground too—one breath at a time. So that's our "message to self" today—the voice of the wise life coach in our heads, the whisper from God or the universe, our self-help slogan, our tagline, our mantra, our hashtag, whatever language works:

#One breath at a time.

Chapter One

Evolving Practice

I'm learning alongside you—not above you—just another person trying to live a more honest, grounded life. My practice keeps changing. It builds on mistakes and on what works, equally. Most shifts are small, barely noticeable until they make themselves known. Fixed ideas close the mind and turn the world rigid. I try not to mold my practice. I let my practice mold me. Meditation gives me one steady thing to return to. The bodily posture is fixed, but the mind inside it isn't. That's balance. Whatever life brings, I carry it into stillness, and in that stillness it becomes clearer. Movement enters the quiet, and the quiet follows me back into movement. I reshape what I do as life reveals itself. Everything I share comes from lived experience, not theory.

I only have so much time and energy, and most of it goes toward keeping myself steady enough to be a good family man, partner, friend, and member of my community. That's my real practice.

In my neck of the woods, churches outnumber meditation centers, about ten thousand to one. For years, people have come to me by word of mouth. Despite my best efforts to stay low-key, my community is small, and word got out about a wild man staring at the wall. Although I have the credentials, I don't call myself a teacher. I meditate with people, and if they're serious about it, help them develop a routine. When they stick with it and respect my boundaries, we usually become great practice friends.

I'm not here to judge; we all gotta start somewhere, but when people find out I am encouraging them to stare at the wall, alone, for the rest of their lives, with no promise of reward, they usually run.

My practice isn't sexy or glamorous. It's hard work down in the dirt, so I focus on those who are willing to get their hands dirty.

The seed of meditation doesn't grow right away. We need to plant it first. We practice patience and consistency, even if we previously told ourselves we didn't have them. We become more aware of and less influenced by old, habitual, fearful, defensive, or insecure voices. We care for the seed.

We plant ourselves and let nature run its course without fighting it. We stop running from our problems. We face ourselves in boredom that transforms into nourishment. When you do nothing, and it doesn't feel boring, you know your life is rich.

We get down on the ground in front of the wall each day to put our bodies and minds in a stable position. Only then does the seed of practice have the conditions to slowly grow within us and extend out to nourish the rest of our lives.

If we don't mess with it too much, our practice can unfold and reach maturity. We mess with things in our minds. For me, the point of meditation is not to sit alone and ponder my existence. The real point, if there is one, is to do as much as possible to help myself and my community appreciate life.

When I first started working in my area, I found myself getting too involved. Over the years, I have learned to be more careful about what I say and do to try to help people. In most cases, I repeat the voice in my head out loud, "Simplify your mind! Just stare at the wall!"

Folks say they come to meditate, but really, they come to me hoping I can solve their big problems. Like everyone else, I have my own and don't need any more. I'm not obsessed with fixing the world. A person like that either has no problems or refuses to face their own. No one can solve our problems. We solve them when we're good and ready, not because someone else tells us we need to or can.

Most problems I encounter in the community are self-induced and minor. Meditation can help us with those. But some are beyond my expertise and require professional help. I can't diagnose your medical issues, explain why you may have anxiety, PTSD, panic attacks, OCD, depression, or ADHD. Those are questions for health care providers to address.

Meditation is not a substitute for legitimate treatment. Our first spiritual practice may be seeking professional help. On the other hand, if you lack the focus or resources to get clinical support, I know how desperate it can feel.

It wasn't all that long ago that the only relief I found from my physical and mental anguish was getting shit-faced drunk. Of course, my symptoms came back even stronger when I sobered up.

A meditation book helped me turn my self-destructive cycle around by inspiring me to get down in front of the wall. It reminded me how important consistency is. Everything changed after I committed to daily meditation, but not in the way I had expected. I didn't have mystical experiences where Buddha came and laid healing hands on me.

On the contrary, meditation helped me look at my situation clearly and take practical steps to address my issues. Only then could I deal with them based on my actual circumstances, not superstition, wishful thinking, or hearsay.

Unless strong biases prevent us from doing so, we already know that meditation is good for us. We also know that adopting healthy habits, such as regular exercise, maintaining good oral hygiene, eating a balanced diet, and saving money, is too. Our unhealthy habits don't require a lot of consideration. We do them because they are easy and don't take much discipline.

The trick to meditation—and anything else worthwhile—is to consistently do what we already know is best and avoid what we know isn't, especially when life gets depressing, boring, stressful or overwhelming. It's simply sitting—doing it—and fighting off fearful, complaining or self-defeating voices. Why do we meditate? No intent. No expectations. Just do it and see what happens.

The only way to fail in meditation is to stop meditating. Every person is different, but if you continue doing it each day—for maybe six months or a year—you may experience a profound change in your life. Or more accurately stated, you may finally notice, accept, and appreciate that everything is changing. Instead of fearing the torrent of time, you will go with it. Both good and bad days will be perfect times to practice.

Our practice is about avoiding harmful habits and focusing on sustainable ones in a fast-paced world full of distractions. If we commit to it, a meditation practice can help us trust ourselves enough to find stability within, right here at home, rather than everywhere and anywhere else.

Your "go-to" habit might be to use AI for self-diagnosis or endlessly surf the internet for techniques, books, or videos to heal yourself. Or maybe you binge-watch streaming television, troll exes, shop, work, gamble, fall into porn rabbit holes, doomscroll, make plans that aren't realistic, or get wasted to escape reality for a while.

Your old habits and narratives, along with everything inside of you, may be telling you to run. But I'm here to tell you that unless you find yourself in a violent situation where you are completely vulnerable, you can face your issues today. You can stop thinking you need to "get better." Meditation is doing better. As soon as you do it, you are already in the best position possible.

All you gotta' do is get started and trust it, and meditation will take care of you. You will directly experience its value. No one can force you to do anything, let alone make significant changes in your life. If you're stubborn like me, you will appreciate that practice is a gradually stabilizing force. You don't need to make big changes to change big-time.

When I first started meditating, I was like a ten-year-old practicing soccer alone against the wall. I repetitively experienced the racing thoughts, habits, inner voices, and overwhelming emotions that were symptomatic of my issues. I watched them come and go like bouncing soccer balls. That's how I learned to handle them. Repetition is the heart of practice. Our bodies practice balance before our minds and emotions can stay balanced when we get up and walk away.

I practiced my problems—or, more accurately, they practiced me—until I realized that most of the big ones were gone. One day, I woke up and they were gone. Where did they come from? Where did they go? It really didn't matter. Things just came and went naturally. My life became a blank canvas no longer painted by the colors of past disappointments, fears, and traumas.

I never thought a simple guy like me could find a peaceful place in the universe. Or the universe could find a peaceful place in a simple guy like me. I didn't even know such a thing was possible until I shut up, sat down, and practiced mental health instead of just talking or reading about it.

I'm telling you to sit in silence, yet here I am blabbing away. That's why I'm super cautious when speaking highly about my practice. To remain realistic, I often emphasize the limitations just as much as the benefits. Sometimes, I'm not a very effective spokesperson for meditation.

While it helped me develop the focus to determine which of my problems were real and which were imaginary, it is not a quick cure or treatment. It's not a supernatural miracle either, and I'm far from a healer, preacher, or priest. Practice is simple biology, not mystical ideology.

To be physically fit, I work out. To be emotionally and mentally fit, I meditate. If meditation is our core, life is a sweet apple. The seeds and nutrients are in the core. Without them, there is no fruit.

I don't work on commission, nor do I expect to earn spiritual currency with the heavenly father for referring you. My practice is first for me, then for my family, and if there's anything left over, it's for you and God.

Leftovers are often better the next day. All those savory flavors have time to soak in. Open the fridge, take this out and pop it in the microwave for a minute or two. Smell it first, to make sure it's not spoiled. My intent isn't to poison you, but when it comes to religion and spirituality, unfortunately, it's possible.

While it may appear miraculous how much more stable, calm, appreciative, focused, and fun I've become by trusting the balanced posture, there's nothing "woo" about me.

I know how much work goes into maintaining my stability, and how dizzy I can get if I drift too high into the clouds. Those closest to me can tell you how low they feel when I get too high and mighty. Romantic partnerships and family are often the most challenging yet fulfilling practices.

I'm not out to enlighten you or myself. To me, enlightenment is stumbling upon a bleeding alcoholic passed out in a piss-soaked alley and seeing myself. I've been there. I may not be able to help the alcoholic or you, but still, if the situation isn't too hairy, I'll try. That's my vow in a nutshell.

There are no levels of enlightenment. Enlightenment is understanding that no one is more enlightened than another. It is seeing everything as equal and interconnected and living in accordance with that realization. Yet, when we meet someone honest, welcoming, kind, and comfortable in their own skin, we may be drawn to them. If they earn our trust and respect, we may call them enlightened, but we do this only because of our inner need for authentic connection.

It's difficult to say, "I'm sorry, I can't help," to some of the desperate people who come to me searching for stability. I know the grueling climb that lies ahead of them, and the serious consequences that follow if they fall.

If we continue to abuse ourselves as we age, each fall becomes harder. Every obstacle feels higher. If you're past forty, you probably realize it's not going to get any easier. For many of us, it's stability and healthy living now or never.

If it feels like I'm talking to you directly, I am, but most of the time, it does no good to pressure ourselves or rush into things. At its most fundamental level, a meditation practice is a careful, gentle approach that means being present and compassionate with ourselves and others.

When we're running out of toilet paper, we are more careful about how much we use. The same goes for time and energy. As much as I'd like to show them the healing powers of a tender hug, sometimes I distance myself from troubled people because I know how much goes into helping and being helped.

We need to be ready to help and be helped. If we aren't careful and try to push it, helping our fellow citizens can go terribly sideways. My most cherished spiritual ancestor, the old, crooked cucumber, Suzuki Roshi, whose wisdom still inspires me to practice, brought an unstable student home who brutally murdered his wife. Like so many of his lessons, I keep that one at the back of my mind. *(1)*

Truth seekers may not like to hear that, in certain circumstances, so-called spirituality can make our lives worse. If I suspect someone might be more than I can handle, I give them brochures of relevant community resources and send them on their way.

Turning ourselves into little "do-gooders" can be overwhelming if we don't manage it properly. We can hurt people with the best intentions. We can hurt *ourselves*. Spirituality is like a loaded gun. We need to pay close attention when handling it.

I've been around long enough to know I can't promise anything. I learned the hard way to establish firm boundaries. Unfortunately, I learn everything the hard way. To me, students are pains in the asses because they take me seriously. Being seen as someone who knows something doesn't work for me. I'd rather be known as someone who knows nothing.

Speaking out like this is a risk. I may offend you or, worse yet, impress you. Even though I'm just trying to help, power has a will of its own that I can't control. If you ever read or watched "The Lord of the Rings," you know what I mean. *(2)*

A longtime meditation practice, pursued with patience and realism, brings many joys. More clarity may appear. Fear and anxiety may slowly lose their hold and make way for a playful warmth. The cultures and circumstances we once took as fixed may loosen their grip. We may begin to feel natural again—part of something larger, woven into a living whole.

If we take the time to learn how to let balance live in us—as itself—we begin to see that clarity rises from countless conditions, not from our efforts alone. From that understanding, we become steady enough to share what we've learned. And with that sharing comes a new challenge: the subtle power we may hold over those still shaped by fear and internal conflict.

This is delicate ground. We can harden around our insights, cling to our methods, and forget the openness that made learning possible in the first place. Any influence we carry must serve only one purpose: to help others find their balance and learn to teach themselves, so their fulfillment arises from within rather than from us.

Without warmth, humility, and a constant eye on our own intents, even our clearest understanding has the potential to become another form of harm. When we're trying to help someone who's vulnerable, we need to remember that our understanding of the whole picture is highly limited.

In my limited experience, few come to practice because their lives are going smoothly. We tend to gravitate toward spirituality because we are vulnerable and seeking answers outside ourselves.

Most meditators crawled or fell into their routines. I nose-dived into mine. I was a mess. I had to be grounded before my practice could take root. Finding a spiritual home was like my experience with mental health treatment. It took a lot of trial and error, sleepless nights, and anxiety to find the right fit.

I help people who are suffering because I can relate to them. I made it through the neighborhood bullies, a traumatic enlistment as a grunt in the Marines, twenty moves, several nights in jail, far more close calls with the law than I can count, divorce, dozens of failed relationships, I can't tell you how many jobs, and a VA outpatient substance abuse program.

It's exhausting and risky to talk about my past. I relive the trauma in my stomach, muscles, and nervous system, and you might not trust me. That's OK. If even one person learns to trust themselves because of my openness, it is a risk well worth taking.

I woke up trusting myself for good when I stopped running away from my problems and admitted I needed help. I went to VA counseling and took meds for ten years, then exercised, ate right, and meditated for another three years straight. I did everything as right as I could.

I sat on my cushion and felt balanced, but it took another year for me to believe it. It took longer than that for others to jump on board.

Everyone thought the same thing as me, "Mark is stable? No way! When's the bottom gonna drop out?"

Once the change was "official," I had to fully process the guilt associated with all the people I hurt. For me, it's easy to forgive others, but it's a grueling practice to forgive myself. If I ever hurt you, I ask for forgiveness. In many ways, this book is an opportunity to make amends.

Now that my shit's been together for a long time, I can help you and still have enough space to man up to my responsibilities. I look back and see that my mistakes play an essential role in my present situation. I learn from my mistakes, turn them around, and use their powerful energy to move past them.

Everything that happened previously, even the bad things, makes complete sense. Although I work hard, the whole experience is quite mysterious. It's not easy to put into words, and that's because it's not about words. It's about action. By getting into a quiet, balanced position, we signal to our nature that we trust it.

My current position has less to do with my efforts and more with favorable conditions. The conditions for me to grow exist so I can grow. The universe, nature, or God, however you prefer to call it or not call it, put me in a position to free myself from the shackles of the past.

We can't free ourselves unless the potential for freedom is in place before we are born. Many people, living beings, and cosmic forces far greater than I had to come together to make the ground I sit on so fertile. I can take credit or give it. Today, I give. That's all.

When business-minded individuals force crude oil to wake from its hundred-million-year slumber, the gases in the ground scream and cry like a child snatched from their mother's loving arms. A violent force tears the liquid apart from its sacred bosom, causing it to cough, spit, and roar in fear. It knows better than to leave its natural state.

Practice is not about forcing our way to success or gain. It's focusing on what we can do to be a stabilizing force, no matter how unsustainable it feels around us. With endless wars raging all over the world and the planet reeling from our impact, it's easy to feel small, unsure of what any one person can do.

I wrote this book to offer something—however modest—to the great turning of things. I knew it was finished when, on a day everything in my life felt "off," it still felt "on." That's the balance of nature at work. The worse I feel, the more focused I am when meditating. When I feel good, it's harder. It took years to notice, but this tells me all I need to know.

In the stillness and silence of meditation, we learn to listen to the Earth again—to feel its pulse beneath our own. In that listening, we remember it's not separate from us. It's everything. Nature's balance is ours. So, we find skillful ways to act in its interests, which are no different than our own. We get down and do balance each day. That's how we develop unwavering confidence amidst injustice, instability, and uncertainty.

Silent meditation is a non-violent protest in its most basic form. Authorities invent threats and use the heavy hand of so-called justice to quell them, but they can't react against rebellions they can't perceive. Even those of us who do it day in and day out, year after year, can't conceive how stopping to do nothing makes a big difference.

In terms of peace and sustainability on Earth, doing nothing may be the most important thing any of us can do. In my mind, it's time to start a new social movement: stop. Just stop! For God's sake. For the entire planet's sake. For our sake. For your sake. For the sake of our children and the children still alive in us.

Through our faith in nothing but our original nature, we can regain the vigor, openness, and creativity of a child. We may find an awe-inspiring quality in our mature loneliness that helps us play and love again. We can know *then* what we know *now* and know *now* what we knew *then*.

I'm privileged. Only a privileged person could think and feel like this. My life feels more like a situational comedy than a violent, dark tragedy. Most folks aren't so lucky, and that's why I pass on the gift of silent meditation practice for free.

I've meditated with seniors in assisted living homes, veterans, grieving widows, middle and high schoolers, sports teams and athletes, prisoners on death row, and various individuals and groups in my community and beyond.

Without a doubt, I've helped many people into stable positions, but I don't keep track. I've been unable to help just as many. I gave up on measuring myself. Nothing I do is ever enough to pay back the gift of life.

I practice for myself, no one else. Just knowing I need to get up at 6 AM to meditate keeps me from getting too carried away. When I don't get up, I know I'm slipping. Sometimes, people join me for morning meditation. In that case, I always get up. Showing up for others is showing up for ourselves.

Usually, there's no exchange of money in my practice. I never understood it, but some people don't take me seriously because I don't charge them. Maybe this book will help address ill-advised cultural misconceptions like that, but I doubt it.

We can't focus on practice until we meet our basic needs and are relatively stable. In a monastery, everything's regimented, and all of the monks' needs are taken care of. Distractions are few. I am far from a monk.

Money is essential where I live and work. Without it, I can't take care of myself or fulfill my responsibilities. Distractions are everywhere. My time is limited, and my focus is worth something. So, I accept donations. Even monasteries have overhead.

Someone has to pay the bills, but if I considered meditation instruction a service or product rendered in exchange for cash, what would my practice look like? I probably wouldn't act naturally because I'd be too worried about pleasing you, the customer.

In business, the customer is always right, but my teacher and practice were hard on me. If I were a customer, instead of a committed student, I would've taken my business elsewhere. The back and leg pain alone would've chased me away!

Just because something is difficult or I don't like it doesn't mean it isn't valuable.

One of the first lessons I learned after becoming interested in spiritual practice was that if it's too good to be true, it probably is. Money, authority, and spirituality are a dangerous mix. If we think our practice will protect us, or give us good fortune and status, we may be disappointed.

Be on the lookout for the well-intended, but ill-informed, or the ill-intended but well-informed. They're equally as dangerous. Writing a book and showing people how to meditate are not urgent public-safety issues. There's no need to take it so seriously.

I'm not an authority figure asking for your help in capturing anyone or anything. It's impossible to capture the essence of practice. If you think you are an important person who has done so, you may want to reassess your situation.

This book may or may not help you get unstuck from your fixed ideas, but I'm just a regular guy who appreciates silent meditation and encourages people to value it too. I don't own it. No one does.

When the balance of the universe speaks, I do my best to listen, regardless of who, what, or where it comes from.

My message is simple. No matter how experienced or new to it, when you meditate each day, you give yourself the best chance to address your problems and appreciate the intrinsic truth of transience. For me, this broad and adaptive perspective provides just what I need when I need it and is a gift from the ever-loving universe, but I make no promises to win converts or friends.

In the end, staring at a wall may not do diddly squat for you. All it did was convince me to do little things, such as cleaning up after using a public restroom for the next person, fulfilling my responsibilities as a parent, family man, and community member, and appreciating water when washing my hands because it's sacred.

I'm unread. I stopped filling my head with more information and emptied it.

I'm not a scholar. Theoretical discussions about Buddhism or any other topic no longer interest me. I've studied hundreds, if not thousands, of Buddhist books, texts, and scriptures. I learned sutras, koans, precepts, rituals, and paramitas. Most of them, I can't recall in any detail, but I acknowledge that Buddhist posture and sensibility have ingrained themselves in me.

I'm ordained as an entrusted layperson in the Soto Zen lineage of a wise and well-respected priest who does not appreciate this. Because of this book, and the contemporary ways I choose to carry out my vow to help people, he pushed me away from my tradition.

Although I help people establish meditation routines, I remain a lifelong student of Zen, a beginner at heart. I respect tradition and give all credit to mine, but my practice is to live it and, in doing so, keep tradition fresh and alive. I don't care who will be the next dharma heir, or what I should call myself or my practice. Maybe I am practicing Bodhidharma's way? Maybe not?

Typically, I don't talk about meeting people where they are; I meet them. That's why I don't use fancy or exotic terms. My people talk like me, and I sound like them. We don't use words like dharma, Buddha nature, or visceral. Is Hinayana vs. Mahayana a big football rivalry? If so, what are the odds on the game?

The Zen purists out there may think it's heretical to turn people of all cultural, religious, economic, and political positions onto zazen practice. Who am I to think I am qualified to do such sacred work or tell ordinary folks it's OK to meditate alone in a chair? Do I lack discipline and respect?

To me, purism is heretical. I've heard all the talk about pure religion I need for one lifetime. I learned discipline as a Marine with my ass on the line. Extreme Buddhism is just as imbalanced as any other extreme belief system. It's time for me to do the Buddha's work, right here, right now, where I live, and as I am, or shut the f**k up.

I can take the heat for using profanities like f**k in a spiritual context. I was a member of the Teamsters Union under Jimmy Hoffa Jr. and a low-level bookie for the Irish Mob before joining the Marines. And when I got out, I was so confused and angry that I came dangerously close to making my dream of becoming an outlaw biker a reality.

I'm not in an exclusive club, like the Pagans 1% Motorcycle gang, nor am I inviting you into one, but you are more than welcome to have a cup of coffee with me. I'm not a tea drinker. We can sit at the same table as equals and chat for a while. The conversation won't be all that engaging, because I promote radical simplification and raw appreciation at the molecular level. I break life down to its bare essence.

I just stare at the wall. Today, I invite you to as well!

The One-Minute Wall Sit (A Tiny Baby Step)

If you've got sixty seconds, you've got time to start a meditation routine. A little pause can go a long way. Even a tiny baby step in the right direction is one.

Find a wall. Sit or stand. Face it. Don't overthink the angle or the distance—just close enough that it fills your view.

Now breathe once, like you mean it.

Try to relax. Be aware of your body. Really try to be aware. Where are your hands, arms, feet, legs, head and shoulders? Watch the sensations, thoughts, and feelings swirling around. Notice how wobbly it feels.

Let the wall be the wall.

Your job isn't to *do* anything about your feelings and thoughts. Just notice that they're there, like weather. They come, they go. The wall stays.

If you get bored, congratulations—you're already doing it. If you get restless, also good—that's the practice showing up.

Stay here until you've counted maybe ten slow breaths, or until you realize a minute is longer than you thought.

Then stop. That's it.

No bowing, no bells. Just carry that tiny bit of stillness with you into whatever's next.

If you actually did that—if you just sat there for a minute and stared—you've already done the hardest part. You stopped. You looked. You didn't check your phone. You didn't fix yourself. You just let the moment be the moment. That's the seed of the whole thing. Meditation isn't about tuning out or chasing bliss; it's about noticing what's already here before the noise starts back up. Once you realize you can touch that quiet on purpose, even for sixty seconds, you may start to see that peace isn't hiding in a monastery or the wise words of a guru somewhere—it's hiding in plain sight, usually behind whatever's right in front of you.

Chapter Two

Search the "You Net"

Silent meditation is a simple yet challenging practice that, with genuine effort, can lay a foundation for overall well-being. Sitting in stillness, facing a plain wall, can help us develop focus and appreciate the wondrous details of daily life. Overthinking is exhausting. In a busy, information-saturated world of distractions, meditation offers a simple and authentic way that doesn't need to be complicated by spiritual jargon, theory, culture, or authority. It's the closest thing I've found to searching the You Net—that quiet and free inner network where the real signals of my life finally come through. In meditation, we may realize that the You Net is connected to the U-Net (Universe Net), but practice is about taking one small breath at a time.

I'm past the stage of analyzing the past to death. The point isn't to complicate anything—it's to simplify. All I'm really doing is acknowledging and accepting whatever I can, after years of counseling, labeling, and dissecting myself like a science project.

Psychology says people who grew up without consistent affection often develop traits that look like strengths—hyper-independence, reading a room before anyone speaks, minimizing their needs, bracing for things to go wrong—and I can see plenty of that in me.

Silent meditation didn't make me analytical; it led me away from accumulating more information. It gave me a way to sit still with myself and observe instead of trying to solve every problem. It simplified everything.

So, if any of this appeals to you, there are reasons for it—reasons you likely feel in your bones even if you've never named them. Establishing a meditation practice may not be appealing for the same kinds of reasons; it isn't convenient, and it can feel counterintuitive. Your bones may say, "This isn't for me." But do yourself a favor, stick with it for a few months, no matter what you tell yourself. If it still isn't for you after that, fair enough.

The form is simple enough to learn, but maintaining it is work. It's not disposable, like a plastic bottle you use once and toss aside. Convenience always has a price. The You Net doesn't load instantly; it asks for presence instead of speed, which is deeply inconvenient for anyone in a hurry. Sit with it long enough and you start to realize the search you're running is intuitive, even if at first it feels like a bad fit, a waste of time, or the spiritual equivalent of assembling cheap Amazon furniture without instructions.

Each morning, when I get down and stare at a blank wall, I am recycled into something new. It's surprising how stopping to do nothing helps me accept that while my mind changes slowly, life changes fast. In those moments, I'm not scrolling through the world—I'm scrolling through my real-time experience as relaxed as possible at that moment.

Sometimes, I feel ridiculous sitting there still and quiet. A critical voice born and raised in the hurts and disappointments of the past asks, "What's the point of sitting here doing nothing?" "Just shut up and stare at the wall!" I respond without thinking. It's one thing to tell myself I don't need to meditate. It's another to think it isn't helpful anymore.

My old, habitual voices and feelings are less influential. They're still here, but through years of self-study at the wall, I call myself out on my own bull. I can't easily capture the experience in words. Still, I try. Why? To encourage you.

My cat, Porkchop, loves to sit on my meditation cushion. For him, it's just a warm, comfortable place to rest. Usually, when I finish, I put my cushion away to save space. Some days, I leave it out for the cat. Other times, I leave it out for myself. Today, I leave it out for you. That's all.

Having no clue where it would lead, I sat for thirty minutes, facing a wall, doing nothing every day for what seemed like forever. Then, I don't know precisely how or when I developed the focus to make better decisions and live up to my responsibilities.

I could pay attention for the first time in my life. Once I knew how to pay attention, I started appreciating all the little things that make up the big picture. I'm grateful to be alive.

I used to overthink everything. Every sit turned into a courtroom where I was the judge, witness, and the accused. The practice wasn't winning the argument. It was noticing the noise and returning to my focus anyway. Once there, I could finally learn to hear my original nature. The Coach or teacher in me didn't speak up right away because I wasn't listening. He took his time and knew pressuring someone as stubborn as me wouldn't work.

Taking time out of my busy schedule to do nothing frees me up to put things into perspective. I don't feel stuck anymore. I'm exactly where I'm supposed to be, doing exactly what I'm supposed to do. I don't need anything more. I live simply and can just be myself.

I wouldn't deny myself the joy of looking forward to things like travel, a hike in the woods, meeting a good friend for a cup of coffee, or a savory meal, but I generally don't daydream about what I want to gain or experience in the future.

Notions like "It would be nice to own a house by a stream in the mountains" still occur to me. It isn't reasonable to think I can control what arises, but I can direct my reaction by acknowledging it. Meditation taught me to stop and pay attention.

My practice is to be aware of my desires so they don't generate unnecessary feelings, such as jealousy, disappointment, or ambition, that may cause me to lose focus. Because I carry a simple mind, I let go of what I don't have to appreciate what I do have. Whatever I have or don't have is enough.

I've gotten proficient at letting go, but if, in the future, someone presents nice, desirable things to me that are presently unattainable, I might want them. I'm constantly changing, and so is my idea of who I am at this moment.

No matter how enlightened we may be, there is no such thing as a perfect human being. We all suffer and face similar challenges. It's essential to consider my limitations in my understanding, especially as an advocate of silent meditation.

When you respect life, you appreciate all of it, especially the complex diversity that makes life beautiful, interesting, and possible. You understand your limitations and allow the broadest perspectives possible to arise. You give the vastness of nature a chance to influence you. You learn to search your own inner network before assuming to understand anyone else's. You judge less and pay attention more.

An influential thinker in the 17th Century spoke for the individual, "I think therefore I am." *(3)* A humble man who rose above his terrible conditions to inspire the world spoke for the universe, "I think, therefore, I am not here." *(4)*

Sometimes, all we need to do to initiate radical change is nothing. For example, if we want to help stop big businesses from exploiting the world, we do as little business as possible with them.

Even though they may be too focused on work to see the irony, businesspeople pay close attention to silence. When we stop buying, they listen. Nothing can say a whole hell of a lot. So can something.

I'm careful not to judge others. My shit smells like everyone else's. None of us chooses our parents, how they raised us, or where and when we were born. Far more than we can imagine brought us here today, but it's safe to say that the people closest to us bring out our best and worst. They're the ones who unknowingly help us map the *You Net* inside us—our triggers, our blind spots, our strengths.

Some may think that doing their best means tilting the playing field in their direction. My best is to stay out of their game and spread the word about nothing. I don't know what that says about my family and community, but my approach feels balanced in a dog-eat-dog world run by short-sighted, quick-buck artists.

After meditating every day for about six months, I didn't feel so different. It was business as usual. I didn't expect people to see a change, and that's probably why they saw one. My friends and family were the first to notice.

They said things like, "Your vibe is different." "What's going on with you?" "Is there a new romance in the picture?" "I've never seen you so calm." "Is something wrong?"

I knew I wasn't out of the woods yet. So, I didn't get too excited about my new practice. If I preached about how wonderful it was to stare at a wall, people would've assumed I stopped taking my meds or joined a cult.

It's best to keep practice to ourselves until we have no choice. Confident and playful people naturally attract others. We want a little shot of what we think we don't have. My job is to help you realize that you already have everything you need. God or nature provides everything I need. So now I'm free to help others.

The people I know who may be genuinely enlightened, like my former teacher *(5)*, don't claim to be. I may have learned more from his mistakes than he ever has. Authentic leaders are self-effacing or unafraid to show their "stupid human" side. They don't take their position so seriously.

Rather than accomplishments or titles, they emphasize their big mistakes and funny little habits. More so than anyone else, they are humble in their realization that myriads of things, limitless and innumerable, brought us here today.

I'm not channeling God or the universe. Then again, I am. We all are. Everything is. I am careful not to think deeply about God. God's too big for me. If I believe I have God figured out, I may make the big mistake of thinking "little me" is enlightened or special. I don't have God figured out. God has me figured out.

It's perfectly natural to wonder about our origins and purpose, but it took a lot of overanalyzing to realize that God or the universe is too big for my little mind to comprehend. If we sit still long enough, the silence shows us who's who and what's what. It takes us further than ourselves. For me, silence is the word of God. If I try to explain how silence works, I break it. God doesn't say much to me anymore unless it counts.

The deepest, most profound thing I can tell you is to skip the rest of the book and follow the meditation instructions in the back. Maybe you aren't ready, so I'll keep talking, blah, blah, blah.

There's no way for anyone to teach you how to meditate. It's something we teach ourselves once we assume the basic bodily form. Like the foundation of a house, the form is not a preference. If we prefer to build a house without a foundation, it won't last long.

Maybe I need to say "no" more. Helping others establish a stable foundation is hard practice. I voluntarily bring instability into my life. I should be careful what I ask for. My meditation practice is more like a job and responsibility than a hobby to get my mind off things.

My purpose is my function and identity. To me, there's no line between practice and life. If I am taking out the trash, that's who I am at that moment. I'm trash. When I meditate, I am nothing but space. Now I write, so I am words. All living beings do something, and I'm just a doer, no different than any other. What I do is me. One of the things I do is meditate with my community. It's that simple.

People come to me to learn how to stare at the wall. I don't invite them. They invite themselves. Once we sit down face to face, they often say, "I want you to guide me, not just sit there silent." "I put my hands like this, not your way." "I keep my eyes closed, not open like yours."

"Why come to me? You already know everything." I reply. My intention isn't to belittle them. I mean it! Maybe they think I'm condescending and never come back. Then, I'm a worm off the hook, free to bury my head in the earth.

All this spiritual stuff takes me away from my kids, who need my attention. Helping them establish a stable foundation is my primary responsibility.

I'm divorced and share custody. I'm one of the fifty percent who couldn't make it work. I don't beat myself up for being a failure or talk trash about my ex. That's not going to help my kids.

When the children are with their mom, I'd rather spend my free time teaching AI how to be more honest and compassionate or standing by the railroad tracks, watching the long freighters chug by. People say tornadoes sound like trains, but in my head, the whole clumsy, clanky movement is the theme song for the Industrial Age.

I appreciate the showy graffiti on the boxcars. In my hood, the authorities call it vandalism or defacing property. I call it making the world brighter. It warms things up and brings cold steel to life.

Through years of focus, I realize my art is to help you build a stable foundation in the simplest way I know how, but only if our tracks cross and you want it. I'll do whatever it takes to encourage you to do nothing but be your conductor or guru. I'm no master. My job is to help you be your own.

Generally, we aren't interested in what people say unless it confirms what we already believe. Nothing scares me more than a vulnerable person thinking I know something they don't. That's why I keep pointing people back to their own *You Net*—their own inner circuitry—because that's where the real guidance is.

I do everything I can to make it clear I'm just a typical dude. Even if peers or teachers believe it's inappropriate, I find it necessary to use casual words. It feels more authentic to speak naturally, not how others expect me to. I learned that things like expectations and assumptions pigeonhole me. I'm at my best when I'm just being myself. If not me, who could I be?

I say, "It's lonely at the bottom" because I have an odd job that's often all guts and no glory. I'm a doctor of nothing. I closely study nothing and show others how to do the same. It sounds a lot easier than it is.

I can say, "There's nothing right over there next to the wall. It might be nice to sit down and listen. What do you have to lose?" But it's up to you to make the acquaintance.

A silent meditation practice is hard to establish because it's simple and may appear dull. Until we commit to it, we can't conceive that sitting there doing nothing is major. If we go to college and graduate, we get a degree and hopefully a job. If we stare at a wall, what could we possibly expect to gain?

Meditation will help in ways you can't imagine, but that won't help you establish your practice. Big expectations get in the way of the little steps needed to keep going.

I am comfortable saying that if someone as screwed up as me can keep it together in a fast-paced, misinformation-driven world, you can. For me, meditation is the key.

Ask anyone who knows me, and they'll agree I'm better off now than before. My mother isn't so sure. She doesn't quite get it.

She says things like, "I don't know what he's calling himself these days. I think he's Muslim, or is it Hindu? All I know is he's not Jewish anymore."

Over the years, we put each other through hell. Luckily, time and memories pass quickly together. The calendar takes care of everything. With parents and loved ones, it's always a good idea to remember they won't be around forever. We won't be either.

In ancient times, a curious man went to a famous rabbi and asked him to predict his future.

"Worm food!" said the laughing rabbi. "Our future is worm food!"

Family is an excruciating spiritual practice, but the most fulfilling. We can dump our closest friends and even our spiritual tradition, but we can only dump so much blood without causing permanent damage to our hearts and minds.

No matter how unstable our background is, if a partner or leader tells us to cut our connection to our family, we should cut our connection to the controlling person, not our family. Cutting our connection to our family is cutting our connection to ourselves. It's like throwing your internet router out the window and wondering why you can't get online.

In the case of abuse, violence, and trauma, it may be necessary to cut ties. If that's our situation, our first step might be to find a legitimate mental health or law enforcement professional to help us stay safe. Our practice is building a solid foundation without judgment or shame and using all available tools.

To talk ourselves into a meditation practice, we take our own word for it, not anyone else's. I've meditated long enough to know I am as peaceful as possible in the posture.

Inner peace doesn't always feel good, but it's a stable base to let things settle. The proof is in the experience. For me, it's simple. Sit peacefully in a balanced position and be it. For you, that may not make much sense. It's a peace beyond understanding in the sense that I know longer analyze it or try to attain it. It's beyond my grasp. Peace is possible in the universe, so I get in the best position to receive it. When peace feels comfortable enough to come, it comes. We can't force a thing like peace. Peace is the opposite of force.

I searched the term "inner peace" and was inundated with the following advertisements: "Stop worrying! Start believing in truth!" "End your suffering forever!" "Find inner peace at the Inner Peace workshop. Enter discount code INPEACE."

Searching or asking your AI assistant won't help you live in peace. We experience things like peace directly in our daily lives when we trust our nature. Searching the *You Net*—your own lived experience—is the only search engine that matters. It's the only news we can guide.

Peace is more than a symbol or slogan. It's an intent that takes practice, focus, and effort. It's a gentle feeling, a clear state of mind, and a comprehensive experience beyond words. It's something warm and soft we come back to that feels like home.

We can't pursue peace without directly experiencing conflict. When we know what we don't want, we know what we want. Sometimes, it's good practice to accept the things we don't want in life because they are part of it. Then, what we don't like doesn't disproportionately influence us. As much as possible, we move past it and help others cope with and accept what they can't control.

Unless we become a victim of things like domestic violence, regional conflict, violent crime, or terminal disease, we usually get only what we want. You may think your mind and emotions drag you down and around, but that's impossible. We're the ones who follow them. The same thing happens when we're aimlessly scrolling the internet—we don't get pulled in by force. We walk ourselves into the distraction, step by step, thought by thought. To take back our focus, we walk ourselves out the same way.

My mind used to pull me all over the place. It was mercurial to say the least. I thought I was following it across the world, but really, I was running from it. I was unable to manage my emotions. They managed me. Now, I am my own life coach and part of the broader solution. I don't feel like I have any significant problems. If I have issues, I know I am the cause. I know I need to sit in a balanced, peaceful position and let things settle. Sometimes, all we need to do is get back to basics.

In meditation, we cultivate a new narrative—an alternative voice—that eventually wins us over because it works. It teaches us to be more confident, flexible, compassionate, and accepting. We do meditation to let meditation do us. How can we know what something does without doing it?

Thinking about doing something in the future and what it's actually like when doing it are two very different things. Sometimes we plan to take care of our responsibilities, but usually what we expect doesn't match what happens.

It never feels like we thought it would. What doesn't? Everything.

I can't tell you how many times I've heard, "I have ADHD. No way." "I can't sit still for more than a second. No way." "I would like to learn how to meditate, but I don't have the patience. No way." "I've been doing it for so many years, I no longer need to. No way." You know better than that.

Yes, way!

If you tell yourself you are in the perfect position to start or re-establish a silent meditation practice, you are. Gurus, shamans, religious traditions, teachers, politicians and experts don't know you. AI, YouTube, Facebook, TikTok, or Google can't either. I certainly can't. Only you can.

Chapter Three

Meet the Coach

We can develop an inner voice or "Coach" through meditation. This voice guides us and provides stability like a sports team manager who prevents players from taking themselves too seriously. Meditation is insurance—not always required, but necessary from experience. The essence of meditation is equally accessible and free. It's beyond laws and regulations. Beyond income and social status. Beyond culture and tradition. It's beyond words. When we trust it, we become our own coaches and insurance. We don't need anyone else to keep us straight and protected. We find freedom within. We become as disciplined and practical as possible. Then, we are truly free.

The Coach is the steady voice in you that says what needs to be said and nothing extra. It doesn't perform. It doesn't scold. It just calls the next play: sit still, breathe, pay attention, return. That's usually all the Coach ever asks. Practice won't make you perfect—it makes you present. One breath at a time.

It all begins with cultivating a simple inner voice. "I'm exactly where I'm supposed to be." It might feel nice to tell yourself something like that and wholeheartedly believe it. So, I caution you.

Spiritual practice is highly emotional. Please try not to take me or my practice too seriously. Regardless of how long I have been practicing, I constantly remind myself of that. Even the Coach needs to be kept in check sometimes.

All these empty words are worth it if you ignore them and just stare at the damn wall. Then, I'll feel like I did my job. I'll keep talking if you want, but you don't need to learn anything new to start doing nothing.

I don't have any answers you don't already have. My life is like yours. It's an even flow of ups and downs. I have just as many problems as you, or maybe even more. I can be difficult. I have bad habits that I'm constantly working on.

I make all the typical mistakes. I try to take short cuts sometimes. There's nothing extraordinary about me. I'm an old-fashioned, cheese-pizza type of guy. Fancy toppings may add variety, but I don't need them.

I speak plainly and directly to keep you from getting excited. I don't use flashy terms to capture your sense of adventure. Exotic customs and ways can easily take us away. We can't forget that our practice is establishing a stable foundation at home. That way, we don't feel the need to be anywhere else.

When it comes to building a stable foundation, excitement leads to mistakes. When we're all worked up, we miss potentially vital things. Have you ever fallen madly in love with the wrong person?

Today, one of our intents is to hear our inner voices clearly, not take them so seriously. If I say something that gets you going, please pay attention. Why are you so excited, and how does being excited feel? That's the Coach tapping you on the shoulder, asking you to look closer.

Silent meditation practice is more than what we agree or disagree with. It's how well we listen. The wall listens unconditionally. We don't listen for any particular reason. If we listen for a reason, the reason will be all we hear. Not expecting to hear anything, we listen.

I'm not impartial. Sometimes, I think I'm Judge Judy. *(6)* I need a good coach to remind me that there's a big difference between doing nothing for nothing and nothing for something.

Without a doubt, meditation is second nature to me now. It does me. I don't do it. Like a football player repetitively practices their kicks, passes, or ball control, I practice sitting still, stable, and quiet. That way, when I'm running around getting knocked down in the heat of the moment, I'm ready for anything.

Most good football coaches played the game. They know what a mistake it is for a player to take themselves too seriously. A big personality disrupts the team.

Time sitting still and quiet helps me follow the Coach's direction. His strategy is always team-oriented. The Coach is the stable voice in me. We all have one.

Silent meditation is more about "less" and less about "more." More accurately stated, it's right in the middle of more and less. It's space.

Do you think the space I illustrated is wrong? Did you try to fix it? Do you have it all figured out? It's intentional. It's space, representing nothing more or less. I know it's just right. Do you? Or are you still hanging on to the past?

Can you let go and follow me back to the beginning?

A simple practice is the most realistic and authentic one. Less fixing, calculating, opinionating, dreaming, expecting, assuming, teaching, talking, and more doing. If we patiently meditate with focus and faith, everything else may fall into place. That's the Coach's way—fewer speeches, less theory, more practice.

Birth, health, life, sickness, death, and no death may feel perfectly natural. It might all make sense, even when it doesn't. I wrote almost every day for thirty years, but this is my first book. Now, I know why.

I wanted to write something real, but couldn't figure out how. Once I stopped figuring, POOF! Out of thin air, here's my book. It wrote itself. Like magic, it appeared because of my hard work and experience.

By meditating, I tap into something bigger than myself. How is a way of thinking, feeling, and living transmitted out of the endless universe? I stopped wasting my time trying to figure it out. Meditation feels balanced and reliable. The Coach doesn't over-explain. He just nods and says, "Practice hard. Pay attention! Keep going."

Some call the Coach—God, nature or the universe. Whatever we call or refuse to call it, it is telling me to stop writing and practice, and you to stop reading and follow the instructions at the back of the book. I don't always listen. Sometimes I exert my God-given free will and encourage others to do the same.

I have developed a certain mischievous satisfaction knowing that ambitious, business-minded individuals, governments, and organizations will never turn "nothing" into a commodity they can buy, sell, regulate, tax, or fight over.

Who in their right mind wants to control nothing? AI may be helping the rich and powerful dumb down and manipulate the populace, but even the highest technologies can't conceive the power of "nothing."

With AI taking over the world and a camera on every corner, nothing may be the only thing left with enough elusiveness to combat authoritarianism. When we pause the fast-moving world dead in its tracks and do nothing for a while, we can't help but see things differently. The Coach inside can only help when we're open enough to be coached.

If we start acting like we're the star player who doesn't need practice or feedback—the guy who thinks he's already got it all figured out—then Coach has one move left. He benches us. Not to punish, but to get our attention. To remind us we're still part of the team, and the work is never over.

And if we still don't listen, forget about it—the Coach will throw us off the team and spread the word. Before long, every coach we meet is giving us the same message: *slow down, change your attitude, and maybe I'll give you a chance to start over.* Coaches talk. They compare notes. And when they all start saying the same thing, it's usually because we need to hear it.

Maybe they pass it along through some kind of cosmic spinal telephone—who knows? It doesn't matter. We don't need to worry that our houses are bugged. It's just the same message coming through different mouths, all pointing us back to the work we already know we need to do.

In times of trouble, people say, "Even walls have ears."

The ancient warning is more relevant than ever, but I don't worry. What can the authorities hear in my silence? Tyrants have always done what they do. I do what I do. The timeless view watches it all come and go. It quietly listens and only speaks out when it can make a difference—just like a good coach who's in it for a love of the game. To Coach, it isn't a game at all. It's an art form.

Organized "spirituality" can become a hierarchical business that works hand in hand with the establishment. Silent meditation in its most basic form is no such thing; it's just that, "silent" and totally under the radar. The Coach tells me that's the way it's supposed to be—focus on fundamentals and develop your skills through hard work down in the trenches.

Although people form groups to study and practice, and it's essential to accept honest feedback, the essence of meditation is free and independent. It's something we do alone. It's not about becoming special or part of an exclusive club. Once people realize this, they tend to give up.

We face ourselves and the world in a balanced posture. To casual observers, we're either meditating or doing nothing. Whether we're doing nothing or something isn't the point.

The point is whatever the point is or isn't. *(7)* The point is ours and no one else's. No one can take away our point. It's free. The Coach doesn't argue—he points us in the right direction. Whether we listen or not is up to us.

We may practice for a particular reason, but that will change. If we hang on to our present point in the future, we might quit practicing. We might not see the point anymore.

If we stick with meditation, we may incidentally penetrate the heart of a perpetually transforming reality. But only if penetrating the heart of reality is NOT our point.

Yes, it's true. We can't force the truth. The truth is NEVER forced. Through discipline and faith in our balanced practice, we embody it. Then, we realize it was here all along.

Someday, with enough sincere effort and focus, we may feel perfectly stable even though everything we know as real is reconstituted dust. Then, we can laugh at God's comic irony or the universe's sense of humor at play. The Coach laughs *with* us and at himself but never at anyone else's expense.

We may start our practice so seriously, but the more serious we become, the less serious we become. Our piety, too, is nothing but dust. If we stay serious, we may have missed the point. We may be stuck in our own ideas of practice.

Enlightenment could mean showing people how to be fun, open, considerate, light, appreciative, happy, and positive when appropriate. If we don't live this way, why would anyone believe us when we claim such a life is possible?

Helping people means being a steady force in difficult, stressful times. If we know we built our house to withstand its unique environmental conditions, we don't need to worry about the next big storm. How can we help anyone else rebuild if our house gets blown away?

When kids build and knock down houses out of cards or blocks, they know what they're doing. Play is the practice of living. These days, maybe they play on electrical devices, but kids are kids no matter their historical circumstances.

Cute babies say, "Dadda, momma, goo-goo, gah-gah" long before they say, "Mom. Dad. You just don't understand what I'm going through!"

Meditation helps us play again. For this reason alone, it could be the ultimate tool to change the world. But we don't need to go that far. If our practice helps us and a few others have a little plain old fun in this big, serious world, that's more than plenty. And the Coach inside us—steady, simple, unpretentious—would call that a win.

Chapter Four

A Feeling of Home

When we limit our sensory stimulation and sit still, our attention turns inward. The usual inner dialogue shows up—the noise, the doubts, the habits—but if we stay with the posture long enough, things begin to settle. A blank wall can steady us and help us meet ourselves on a basic level. Meditation can feel like home because it lets us see our true nature and accept ourselves as we are, without all the extra commentary. We may realize that our bodies, lives, communities, and this planet are the only home we really have. None of this is guaranteed. Practice just puts us in the best position to feel that sense of home wherever we go.

With limited sensory stimulation and nothing but a blank wall before our eyes, our focus naturally turns inward. Once quiet and still, we may see what's stirring about. Then, we can teach ourselves to be supple. A feeling of home begins here—not in a place, but in the quiet familiarity of our own presence.

We lost a lot when humans built the first wall, but the walls we build around ourselves cause the most loss. Our emotional and intellectual walls inspire us to create real ones. So today, right here in our homes, we take a fresh look at what stands before us.

Do you ever take the time to appreciate your walls? Until losing them to misfortune, we usually don't.

If we convince ourselves we need to open things up inside, we might devise a plan to knock down a few walls. We may swing a sledgehammer and hit a load-bearing wall. Then, things crash down around us. We may want more space, but it might not be how we envisioned it once we get it.

Sometimes, we knock down the wrong wall and, in the process, must rebuild the whole house. With that in mind, we don't want to tear anything down too quickly. Home is fragile when we don't consider its structure.

It's nothing but trouble to convey a spiritual teaching without practicing for a long time, but today, it's commonplace. On the internet, a slew of inexperienced gurus, healers, teachers, and coaches knock down walls without realizing the dangers.

Rushing to become famous, respected, or rich from spirituality is unnatural. It's not what it's all about. Spirituality is about acting with stability and authenticity. Today, that's what we are trying to do. We are already finding a warm feeling of home together.

Like an olive seed knows how to grow and become a fruit-producing tree, our bodies and minds know what to do if we let them be. In meditation, we stop and put ourselves in the best position possible to grow from whatever nature provides.

We start fresh to see what a little space or pause offers. We don't continue searching for answers from people we don't know and sources we cannot validate. We know ourselves best. So, we surf ourselves for a change.

We don't try to stop our thoughts and feelings. We limit our sensory stimulation and allow ourselves to observe what's happening. We can't see what's right under our noses until we stop and focus on what's under them.

We might be surprised by how many things we step on or miss when we're not paying attention. Some people call this "being in the moment." I call it (X).

(X) = right here and now, no matter what we call it. It's a pocket of time when we no longer jump ahead to what's next, behind to what was, or even analyze what's happening now.

(X) is complete immersion, a state of being fully engaged in what we're doing, observing, or experiencing. It isn’t an altered state, and it doesn't always feel good. It can be painful, and it feels different each time we experience it.

Once seated in front of a wall, the only information we need is already present at home. We don’t need to go on the internet, somewhere more sacred, or into the pages of a book to find ourselves. We don’t need anyone else. We can be totally off the grid.

You might find this appealing if you have a little anti-establishmentarianism in you, like I do. Whatever it takes to just stare at the wall will do. As we age and grow, our intentions naturally change anyway.

We may notice things like the electricity coursing through our bodies if we pay close enough attention. In that case, the electricity is ancient, but our awareness of it is new. Silent meditation is like electricity, a time-tested certainty in a world of change, distraction, waste, violence, and social disparity. It can bring us back to our original nature—back home. But, just like a real home, it takes resources, time, skill and patience to build.

It’s a lot like planting a fruit tree from seed. We can't plant a seed and expect it to feed us in an hour, week, or month. It takes years. The olive tree, a universal symbol of peace, takes around sixty years to yield a stable crop.

We can’t watch a couple of videos or podcasts, read an academic, spiritual, or holy book, disappear into the wilderness, catch a class, take a hallucinogenic drug, go to church on Sunday, or attend a retreat, expecting it to magically improve our lives. I should know. I’ve done all of them.

Spiritual practice is a long-term partnership solidified mainly in the privacy of our homes. It’s a lot of what we do and intend when no one is watching—a daily routine that requires work and attention to detail.

No matter what's happening in my life, how shitty it gets, I drag myself back to the wall, often kicking and screaming. I am committed to a routine that is beyond debate because it unquestionably works. It feels like home.

If we sincerely commit to our practice, its presence may begin to feel reliable, warm, and safe, like our loved ones, hometowns, or the sofas in our family rooms. Once it feels familiar, we can trust the wall to help us be ourselves. Then, our meditation will hold us upright, give us respite, and reassure us even in the most uncertain times. It will help us weather the storms. It will be part of us and do us as much as we do it.

When we leave the house to run an errand, pursue a hobby, or go to work, the walls are typically right where we left them when we return. They sit stable, silent, and flexible, holding up our most private spaces, where we feel warm and secure.

I don't meditate to get high or take a vacation from my real life. I do so to try to accept reality right here at home, no matter how confusing or painful it gets. That's why blank walls represent so much more to me than meets the eye.

Sometimes, a situation is intense, and I cannot accept it easily. I need to be careful not to get stuck behind my own walls. I get stuck when I tell myself stories. They take me away so easily. It's like a good drama series starts playing in my head, and I'm compelled to binge-watch.

My doctor calls and leaves a message that she needs to talk to me tomorrow about my blood work. She doesn't say why. Is there a problem? Is my iron low again? Do I have cancer?

I sit in front of the wall, and it answers all my questions. Coach tells me what to do: "Go to the doctor's tomorrow and pay attention.

Good news? Bad news? Have compassion for yourself and be ready for anything. That's best." In moments like this, the wall becomes my refuge at home—the one place where I can think clearly without sugar-coating things.

Compassion is a gentle feeling that keeps me calm, flexible, and balanced. It helps me see situations more comprehensively and consider the other person's circumstances as much as possible before acting. Compassion includes empathy. It's a warm feeling like the one we get when we're relaxing at home.

We can feel compassion toward ourselves, other living beings, and even inanimate objects. How do we show compassion toward our kitchen table? We keep it clean and appreciate all the good times we've spent hanging out around it.

Last week, I ate in a new "mom and pop" restaurant called "Giorgio's." The owner was friendly and eccentric. He was so proud that his ingredients were not only authentically Italian but organic. Giorgio's whole family worked there. They helped us feel at home.

His adorable, curly-haired son, Little Petey, who couldn't have been more than ten, kept filling our water glasses. He wore a black bowtie. He was a "chip off the old block" and so happy to keep us hydrated. We had a lot of fun.

Everything was perfect, but there was one thing wrong. My friends and I were the only people in Giorgio's restaurant on Saturday evening.

"How is he going to stay afloat?" I thought. I felt for Giorgio. So, I wrote an excellent review for him online, using Little Petey and the lack of crowds as selling points. That is a simple act of compassion—a small way of helping someone else feel at home in their own life's work.

No matter our specific circumstances, if we sit in front of a plain wall long enough, we can't help but recognize that we are vulnerable, struggling, and in pain. Mysteriously, we might see that everyone is sitting at the same table.

We may realize that life is suffering for EVERYONE, which produces compassion and balances the more protective or aggressive instincts of our nature. In simple terms, if suffering produces compassion, it's only half bad.

I need to be careful saying things like that. I don't wish it upon myself or anyone else, and I don't downplay the fact that many living beings in this world are suffering unnecessarily. That, too, is the balance of nature at work in my mind.

When we pause in real time to consider compassion above our preferences, moods, cultures, and authorities, we are living a spiritual life, no matter what we label it. To live a life as fulfilling and warm as this, we need to feel stable and open right here at home.

In terms of spiritual progress, a compassionate mind is home, but our life is our life, even when it doesn't feel warm and fuzzy. Sometimes we need to take care of ourselves, which means establishing firm boundaries that others may view as insensitive or aggressive. If someone barges through our front door uninvited, they can't expect us to be hospitable.

Being compassionate doesn't mean we are always running around trying to be a good person. It's just a base that we return to when possible. It's not always possible, and we need to remember that. Otherwise, we can become overly critical of ourselves and others. A person who beats themselves up may not realize they are beating us up as well.

We have limitations and suffer like all other beings, but nature also endows us with the freedom to interpret and change the world. Where every other being on the planet is sure of its balanced purpose in the big scheme and compelled to live it, we may be confused about what it is or feel that we have no purpose at all. The world might not feel like home.

We are odd creatures, especially me. I say that in good fun. Are you having fun yet? If not, why? If so, don't get too excited. Follow the instructions at the back of the book. You know what they say, "Work hard, play hard." I say, just stop and stare at the wall so even hard work feels like play.

Chapter Five

One Cool Cat

While being a compassionate person is ideal, we also learn to accept our limitations in meditation. Compassion, much like water, can be both nurturing and overwhelming. If we value it but don't feel it, we might become overly rigid or drowned by rules. We might box ourselves into practice. How do we stay warm and open? A meditation practice helps us be patient and see the beauty in simply being present (what I call the cat-bird seat), even when it seems pointless or we don't feel like it. Ultimately, we can embody a seed-like faith in nature, letting go and appreciating the transformative power of our experiences, as they are. That's the beginning of becoming a cool cat—steady, curious, relaxed, and unbothered by any extra noise in our heads.

At its root, we gravitate to various spiritual practices for a clearer sense of purpose and to feel more at home in the world, but once we find something that works, we may become protective of it. No matter what brand of spirituality we practice, we are like little sparks that can easily turn into out-of-control wildfires.

We should be careful when playing with fire. Otherwise, we'll burn down our home and maybe even the whole neighborhood. If we live in a fire-prone area of the world, we know that some of our fires even take out entire regions.

Once a wildfire starts, every strong, sensible being in its proximity with the power to do so rushes away. Unfortunately, not everyone has the means to flee. Such fires always go out, but not before leaving a trail of charred destruction behind.

When the embers cool, life returns to the burnt land and works with the nutrients left in the ash to bring everything back to balance. Then, the area flourishes again, but in every thriving individual and community, there are traces of destruction. Even a cool cat carries a few singe marks from the past.

It's never a good idea to rebuild in an area prone to fire. Sooner or later, it will happen again. We can view our own lives the same way, but we need to be careful.

Sometimes, we're in a lush place where wildfires are nearly impossible, yet in us, they seem very real. The embers are still burning and have not yet turned to cool ash. Every cat has some *scaredy cat* in them. It's alright. That's nature's way, but there's a time to be cautious and a time to relax and appreciate our lives. Spiritual practice is knowing the difference. If our practice makes us more worried, we're doing something wrong.

Typically, it gives me great solace to realize that, at my core, I'm nothing but a pile of cool ash. Other times, it brings me down. I mean, what's the point? It's good to keep a close eye on our point because, ultimately, we go in the direction we point ourselves.

When we become too sure of our point, we risk being consumed by the fire of authority and custom. In our commitment to compassion as a practical way of life, we can become careless and callous. We can get lost in our heads and become pious assholes, sticklers for rules and theories that have no tolerance for other modes of thinking and behaving.

We can go through the motions of practice or let authority figures (many of whom we don't know personally or are long dead and have no conception of the world we live in) make decisions for us. Then, anything that doesn't conform to our way will bother us, and eventually, our pent-up aggression will flare, spread, and burn. There won't be enough compassion or practical wisdom left to put it out.

Compassion and water share many similarities. So long as we have an empty container, we can fill it up and carry it anywhere. It is practical, but we can drown in a flood of representations of compassion without being able to apply them. We might value it but not feel it. Then we will beat ourselves up for not living our values, and they will drown us in bitterness. There's nothing sharper than the claws of an angry cat.

Once we heavily invest in something, it becomes harder to let go of it. For example, we might believe our purpose in life is to carry a bucket of water to thirsty people. How do we practice this? If we try to do it by wandering around a desert wilderness, we will get desperate, drink the whole bucket, and leave nothing for the future.

Our emotions and real-life predicaments are far more forceful than our theories. We can get weighed down by ideas of practice that don't correspond with reality. We can get stuck behind our own walls. Especially if we stop to see things as they are, deep down, we will know something's off. We won't feel so good. We'll feel more like a feral cat with fleas than a cool, relaxed one.

That's why it's so important to pace ourselves and let nature play out. If we step back and give it time, nature will distribute our spiritual practice into our lives in a balanced way. Then, we don't need to worry. We won't need to be appreciated. We will appreciate ourselves. We can play it cool. We can wait and be thankful for our lives instead of forcing ourselves into bad situations or making ourselves feel worse. That's the cool cat approach—curious, focused, steady, unhurried, completely trusting their nature.

We can't go from an anxiety-stricken, bitter person to a calm and compassionate one in a matter of weeks or even months. Compassion and calmness take time to grow. Our job is to let them without injecting self-doubt. To believe in the balance of nature is to trust ourselves.

As an expression of my practice, I serve seniors at an assisted living home. *(8)* I fell into the position. I started the job ignorant of what went on in there. I intended to offer free meditations to senior citizens a few days a week, but ended up finding one of my niches in this world. When I first walked in, I couldn't imagine that nature was taking its course, and I was ready to bear fruit.

Now, I do far more than lead senior meditations. I show people how to have fun. I spent nine months teaching an old chord banger with dementia how to play the guitar again. I wander around the facility being my goofy self. I bark high-pitched like a little dog. Then, deep like a big dog. I purr and meow like a cool cat. I pretend I'm an opera singer. I also perform music, call bingo, hang out and drink coffee, teach painting, and drive a huge bus!

A ninety-three-year-old "good ole' boy" at work named P saw me leading a meditation class one day. He asked, "Say, Mark. What was you doin' in there with all those folk?"

"We were meditating."

"Ha, intrestin'. What yawl do when settin' there all that time doin' nothin'?" asked P.

"We watch it all come and go," I replied.

P loudly chuckled and slapped me on the back. "Man. That's cool! Down South, we call that the cat-bird seat. You in the cat-bird seat, my boy. You are one cool cat!"

No matter where the practice originated or leads to, what we call it, and how it may or may not work in a cosmic or scientific sense, I'm in the cat-bird seat when sitting, which is the best position to see. See what? As much as I can from my limited position.

Like I don't know how a cat knows how to act like a cat, I haven't the faintest clue how staring at a blank wall can expand my perspective, clarify my decision-making, and open my heart to new opportunities.

It makes no sense, but I'm eternally grateful that some cool cats throughout history thought it was a good idea to experiment with nothing for a change. They'd probably be shocked if they saw how their practice of nothing has grown into something.

Even when I don't practice this simple form, I remember how to do it. Its value is clear. No authority can talk me out of it. Not even my own. I trust nothing more than something. I mean the authority of doing nothing. Sitting still. Letting things unfold in their own time. Not forcing a moment to arrive before it's ready. That inclination didn't start in adulthood; it was there long before I had words for it.

My father Bob tells a funny story about my childhood. He says he would get frustrated with me because I didn't want to learn how to ride a bike. He'd run behind my brand-new Sears and Roebuck BMX and try to get me going, but it always ended the same. I'd lie on the street and cry, and he'd yell for me to get up and stop acting like a sissy.

One day, he came home from working the midnight-to-eight shift at the factory, and there I was, zipping up and down the street like I'd been riding my whole life. When I wanted to ride a bike, I rode one. It's that simple. My father couldn't believe it.

If you stare at a wall long enough—with courage and sincerity—believe me, no one close to you will believe how doing nothing has done so much for you, but we can't ride a bike without jumping on one and finding our balance.

Staring at a wall is like riding a bike. We find our balance through doubts, fears, and falls. Once we learn how to ride one, our bodies don't forget. If we overthink it or question the balance of riding a bike, we might get wobbly and hurt ourselves. We just need to jump on and do it—cool, steady, and unforced, like a cool cat following its own natural rhythms around the house.

In the silent meditation posture, we nurture ourselves and the world by creating the most balanced conditions possible to cope with what we don't control. We don't control the balance it takes to move freely and comfortably on a bike, yet finding it is required to enjoy the ride.

We grow within the parameters set by our conditions rather than fighting them. We focus on what we can and cannot realistically do right here and now. We eliminate unnecessary things that may complicate or confuse our situation.

There's enough pain in this world. It's not a good idea to impose it on ourselves. We aren't ascetics out to deny ourselves life's joys, and we don't beat ourselves up when we are unable to live up to the high standards our disciplines place on us. In spiritual practice, it's very easy to fall into that trap. Cool cats aren't walking around judging themselves all the time. They know how to keep themselves safe and amused. So long as they have a litter box, some food and water, and a couple of toys, all is cool in their world.

There's no strict guidance or commandments to tell us what's extra. It's all trial and error, and mistakes are just as important as getting it so-called "right." In Spanish, there's a good saying, "Perder es ganar un poco." "To lose is to win a little."

In silent meditation, we plant ourselves like seeds in hospitable enough conditions to facilitate growth. We find the best space available. We are not alone. No living being chooses its ecosystem. We are all equally thrust into the world. Cool cats are cool because they weren't born feral. A feral cat is always on guard, hungry and ready to fight for their lives.

We may see that we're all equal, even though sometimes we're not. If we're privileged enough to have our needs met, we should appreciate it. If we have everything and want more, it's our choice. Our choice is always in our minds. If we are poverty-stricken and oppressed, we might have no choice but to focus solely on survival. An alley cat is never a fat cat.

The first thing we do before meditating is stop and assess our actual situation. We bring our focus to our mat or chair and brush it off. We observe things as they are, not how we want them to be. Based on our interpretation of our unique environment, we prepare the ground for growing to the best of our abilities.

We prepare the ground with a simple cushion and pillow or an armless chair. Then, we sit still and silent, staring at a wall. We watch nature do its thing in us. We act naturally. We let ourselves grow. We begin to see how we get in the way. We may marvel at the power and cleverness of our self-destructive sides.

I'm not sure how staring at a wall helped me become more careful, courageous, and comfortable in my own skin, but that's one of the most reassuring outcomes of the practice. I don't need to know where it came from and how it works to trust nature's subtle ways. A cool cat never questions its purpose. It knows its place. Seeds do too.

If we place a seed in fertile soil and care for it, it will move through its various growth stages. It intuitively knows what to do. I can't tell you how seeds know how to act like seeds, and cats act like cats, but today, we will try to be more seed-like and cat-like.

Hopefully, we will realize what a privilege it is to transform calmly and with composure in real-time. We will learn the value of pain by facing it. Then, when we experience it all around us, we won't be intimidated or afraid. No matter what happens or who does what, we can remain relatively upright and strong—cool housecats unphased by the complicated world around us.

When we encounter a person in pain, we'll see them for what they are. We won't pick on them or point out their weaknesses. In typical situations, there's no need to take a suffering person who's acting out so seriously. We can tell when they are suffering enough on their own.

If there's room, we can show those in pain some kindness, which may or may not make a difference in their lives. If there's no opening, it's OK to distance ourselves. So long as we do our best, the result doesn't matter. We only have so much time and energy to distribute.

Sometimes the best spiritual practice is not to practice, and the most serious action is not serious at all. Most of the time, when I'm focused, I find it impossible to take practice seriously. In my practice, it's about taking things less seriously to appreciate the little things in life. We take things seriously at the wall and leave them there. It's not easy to sit in silence for thirty or forty minutes without moving.

I know I'm in a good place when chasing my tail feels perfectly cool. Still, I had to learn this the hard way by being too earnest and set in my ways. I had to be around other people who were too. For example, I've been to more than my fair share of meditations where people walked around somber, defensive, and critical of others who didn't know the rules.

"Bow here, before and after this. Say this. Don't say that. Eat like this. Be quiet! Don't move! Act like me!"

Imagine sacred sanctuaries—peaceful oases amid the deafening chaos—lacking compassion and being unwelcoming? How is it possible? Theoretically, it shouldn't be, but in reality, it is. I understand why there are rules in a zendo. Without them, everyone would drift into doing whatever they pleased, and the whole thing would fall apart. But there's a way to keep order and still be compassionate. Structure doesn't need to mean stiffness.

I find that stiffness doesn't do much to help people become more aware or balanced, but humor and kindness usually do. Stiffness shuts people down; humor and kindness open them up. They make room for honesty, for mistakes, for trying again without shame. They keep the practice human.

Many longtime meditators who spent time at the San Francisco Zen Center in the 1960s and 70's told me they would have never continued their practice if it weren't for a man named David Chadwick, who made them feel at home. *(9)* It never ceases to amaze me. I mean, how many people did this guy influence?

Legend has it that David was a wild party type who broke all the rules, yet was the teacher's favorite because he made everyone who wandered in feel equal and welcome. I know David and admire him greatly. He's far from perfect, but David is one cool cat.

If, like David Chadwick, we practice compassion, we also find a home within ourselves, free from extremes. The entire universe, with its mix of darkness and light, unjust rules and freedom, love and hate, joy and sorrow, warmth and cold, nature and toxicity, magically transforms into a welcoming place.

We can't always be welcoming, but a silent meditation practice, respectful of (yet cautious of) authority and focused on practical application, gives us the best chance to return to our original nature.

When we return home, our minds and bodies send a signal out to nature or God that we welcome its presence in our lives. With God and nature welcome inside, how could we not grow strong and free? Sure, some rules are necessary, but we don't welcome them until we accept our own natural limitations and boundaries.

If you practice long enough—three, five, maybe even ten years without giving up or expecting gain—the heat of idiomatic purity may suddenly drop away. Then, you'll see the forest for the trees, and it will feel cool, alive, and magical. You will get creative with your practice. If you're young, you'll feel like a tiger, running free. If you're a little older, like me, you'll be perfectly content frolicking around the house without too much worry. Everything will be taken care of.

You don't have to worry about who takes care of things. Maybe God? Maybe Buddha? Maybe nature? Maybe the universe? Maybe nothing? It doesn't matter what name we give it. What matters is that, at a certain point, you begin to feel how everything balances itself, and you have a place in it. You stop trying to control every outcome. You stop trying to force life into shapes it was never meant to hold. You just know, in a way that's deeper than thought, that things are unfolding the way they're supposed to.

Then, you will know for sure that you are free to have fun. You can play it cool. But only this time, you'll be careful where you step. You won't get carried away and forget your obligations. You will be aware of extremes because you appreciate the fragility of balance. You will compassionately realize your limitations. You'll know that when we restrict nature's potential to be itself, we ultimately limit our own. You will accept that your pain is perfectly natural.

Chapter Six

The Value of Pain

Physical discomfort during meditation can be a transformative experience. It helps me face pain instead of running from it. It doesn't always relieve the pain, but it changes my relationship with it. Sitting with discomfort shows me that suffering isn't a personal flaw—it's a universal part of being alive. That shift makes it easier to be compassionate toward ourselves and others facing their own struggles and disappointments. That's the value of pain: it teaches us what matters and reminds us we're all here together trying to do our best.

At first, I didn't see the point of sitting in front of the wall. It hurt like hell. My back, neck, and legs, particularly, screamed out for mercy, but in time, I settled into the form, and the pain eased up. Physically, it isn't so bad for me, but some people need to lie down or sit in a chair to meditate, and that's perfectly fine. At the end of this book, you'll see a few simple ways to do it.

The lack of sensory stimulation made me feel most uncomfortable at first. My discomfort was less physical and more emotional. I had to face my raw feelings without falling back on bad habits or trying to escape. I grew up in front of a television. As an adult, I still wanted to grow faster than the flow of nature and garner admiration like the fictional heroes on the screen.

Patience was a challenge in those days. Stopping to face myself didn't make sense. Ambitious, educated, and successful, I lacked something. I felt I was racing against time, fearing aging without achieving my goals and worrying about my image. I pressured myself like an overbearing parent, wanting quick success.

Happiness seemed to be grabbing whatever I could and running with it. The world felt like a wall I had to break through. I didn't see the value of pacing myself.

"Seize the day! Or lose it forever!" was my mantra. In a way, I was onto something. After Zen meditation retreats, we ceremonially shout, "Don't squander your life!" Yet, this pronouncement is a delusion. Reality lies between the self and everything. It's not just "our" life we experience and contribute to, but the eternal movement of life itself. Mysterious perspectives that give us a sense of the big picture are one unintended consequence of staring at the wall. Some people feel like they're talking "to" walls. I feel like I'm talking "for" them.

Before I found this practice, my mind spun like a roulette wheel. Round and round he goes, where he stops nobody knows. At times, it felt like I couldn't lose. Then suddenly, I couldn't win. When the wheel clicked just past my number, I convinced myself it was antagonizing me. How could a wheel antagonize a person? I antagonized myself. Impractical feelings feed into the notion that life isn't fair. Disappointment gave me an excuse to be angry and frustrated. I easily justified my carelessness.

I beat myself up and wanted to be someone else, anywhere but where I was. I was uneasy and worried in my skin like I didn't belong. Depression, anxiety, and insecurity defined my disposition. My habit was to believe I wasn't living up to my potential. I wallowed in the tears of regret.

I hoped changing jobs, relationships, and physical locations would help me feel better. I found temporary relief in sex, traveling, long periods alone, adrenaline, and substances. I searched for solutions everywhere but at home, hurting people close to me. I couldn't see that I was already standing on fertile ground.

Meditation helped me be more grateful for the conditions I was born into. The Coach talked some sense into me. I am a product of my time and place. I have just enough privilege to keep me from being spoiled, and not so much that I lose touch with reality. This middle—this balance—is a gift from God, from nature, from all the beings and people who placed me here. They say the middle class is dying. It's either poverty or wealth. I sure hope not. That's extreme.

I realized that all my inner discord and thus, the broader discord of the world, had a purpose through meditation practice. I could only see pain as an essential part of who I was after it stopped being a tyrant. A tyrant is extreme, forceful, and blind to the bigger picture. The world revolves around them, and they try to project the images in their own mind onto everyone else.

I couldn't have survived the tyrant of pain without leading it in a new direction. Once it trusted me, I took it somewhere quieter and more inclusive. I sat with it, listened to it, and talked it into being more compassionate. But I wasn't really talking to pain—I was talking to myself. It's hard to describe. Meditation lets us do these strange, almost impossible things, like having a direct conversation with the part of us that hurts.

When we sit still long enough, the noise drops, the inner dialogue becomes clearer, and we can finally respond instead of react. That's how we lead our suffering toward the light instead of letting it pull us deeper into the dark. And that's another value of pain—it shows us how to be our own teacher and guide.

Suffering opens a path to freedom, but only in the right measure. I had to seek professional help and really commit to healing to reach a point where my pain wasn't overwhelming or trivial—it was just enough to help me grow. I'm reminded that I didn't do all this by sheer effort or insight alone. I was helped by forces far beyond myself. The potential for that kind of transformation existed long before it ever took hold of me.

I let myself transform in meditation. I learned how to get out of my own way. My mind got in the way. It had a habit of trying to run.

Now, I sit, sensations like pain bubble to the surface, and I experience them on a fundamental level. I get used to them. I focus on them and invite them in. I don't panic or dread them. My feelings about pain have changed because I sit on my cushion facing the wall and don't move. I sit with it. That's my part and the part we can play.

We calmly sit and feel it out. Feel what out? Anything and everything. We stop trying to escape our situation and start getting into it. We try reality on for size. If we stick with it, pain stops feeling so overwhelming. We may see that the way out of pain is to go into it, and that it has a place in the balance of nature and in our own lives.

When we're in pain, there's always a reason, even if we never figure it out. We don't need to devote our lives to solving it. We just need to accept it, take care of ourselves as best we can, and not unleash our pain into the world.

When we start sitting, we stop running into all the things we use to avoid ourselves. We run into silence and it stops us cold. We settle into nothing. Boredom transforms into gold. Then, it no longer feels boring. It feels like a blessing.

We stay put long enough to see what's actually happening. We see change—constant, unstoppable change. It's the root of our suffering because we keep trying to fight it. Powerful people even get elected on the promise that they'll turn back the clock to better days. They are talking directly to our pain. Pain wins elections.

But sitting shows us the truth: we can't change *change*. Once we accept that, something shifts. Things seem less painful. We have space to look within and then, look around. We can breathe easily again. We breathe into our pain and stop treating it like an intruder. We see it more as a helpless person on the ground that could use some CPR.

We start taking care of it, the way we would a loved one lying in a hospital bed. We see it for what it is. It's in bad shape and needs our compassion. We give it a place to rest. In that rest, the mind begins to clear. Our suffering comes out of hiding, and we finally address it. We give ourselves a chance to talk to it and get to know it. The Coach might ask, "What can I do to help you feel better?"

The whole inner world settles the way cloudy apple cider settles in a glass—the heaviness drops, and the rest becomes clear. Meditation is that kind of rest. We rest our bodies, we rest our minds, and in some quiet, mysterious way, the universe or God, or whatever name we give the great balance, gets to rest in us too. We give our pain a good vacation.

When I first sit down to meditate each morning, everything's spinning. I used to put my hands on the wheel and spin it even faster. My hands look like hands, but they're really extensions of my mind. The puppeteer is the brain. A wheel already knows what to do—it's built for balance. Sometimes our wheels make life easier, sometimes harder. I don't worry about spinning out of control anymore. I only gamble on sure things, like staring at a wall.

To let everything settle inside, I closely follow my breath. Everyone breathes uniquely, and we can find our natural rhythms. Facing ourselves in silence sets the stage for subtle realizations. I experimented with various breathing techniques and found one that helped me accept my pain. It's not relieved, but it's more manageable—and that, too, is part of the value of pain. It can teach us how to stay still and balanced no matter how much it hurts inside.

Even enlightened or successful people suffer. Our efforts alone aren't enough. My pain persists. It has a life of its own, but sitting still and silent puts it into perspective, making it less personal. I transfer my personality into pain. It becomes more of a character while I become less of one. Every living being suffers, even if mine feels like it's from a physical or personal issue. Cultivating that kind of expansive perspective really helps. But ignoring or downplaying pain that may indicate a real problem is the worst thing we can do.

The value of bringing our full awareness toward pain isn't that it disappears or that we rise above it. It simply stops being the center of the world. We have the room to see our actual situation through the pain instead of the one we wish we had. We stop dreaming about stuff that's unrealistic. We begin to see which pains we create ourselves and which ones are simply part of being alive. The best we can hope for is to be comfortable in our skin right where we sit. Sitting puts our lives back into perspective. Even a life in pain is still a life.

When we're busy running from ourselves, from our entire planet, we forget we're finite beings with finite so-called resources in an endlessly spinning universe. Turning toward pain reverses that. It reminds us of where we sit and what's real. We may not view things as resources to be exploited anymore. We may view them as lives to be cared for. We might treat them as we'd like to be treated. Life is full of pain for all things living.

It's not healthy to keep delving into the big picture. We can get stuck there. It has its place, but BIG thinking can get in the way. Sometimes, it's best to focus on the little things. The littlest thing we can actually experience is our sensations. People are always asking me, "How do you feel?" I say, "I don't know, how do *we* feel?" Sometimes, they laugh because they know me. Sometimes, they look confused.

Meditation directly brings physical sensations to our attention. They are one of the most basic, primordial experiences any living being can have. They bring us straight back down to Earth. In fact, paying attention to them helps us borough into the earth like roots. When we root ourselves, we feel stable enough to trust nature. We stop trying to figure out how to grow. We believe in the present.

That doesn't mean we ignore our responsibilities. Even being in the moment must be practiced in moderation.

Our little lives may flash before our eyes on the cushion. Residuals of the past are always sprouting up. But when we stop, we start to notice that our minds, bodies, and emotions are all connected. We might understand that the past, present and future are all coming together in us.

I see this directly when my back and neck pull on my throat and create a sinking feeling. I used to dread it. Now I address and accept it. It gets my attention alright. That crap led me to meditation in the first place. It was fertilizer. We don't usually think of pain as something that keeps us in the moment, but that's only because most of the pain we feel is the kind we invent. Real pain doesn't let us drift. It holds us right where we are.

In the morning, I focus on any sensations of pain present, whether from the past, a bad dream, or sleeping on the wrong side of the bed. Instead of trying to figure it out, I feel it and let it tell me if it's real. Over time, it lessens. I know it's no longer a problem when my mind drifts and the pain loses its urgency. These types of pains in the asses typically come and go. If it comes and goes, it's not a problem. If it comes but doesn't go, it is.

In meditation, nagging soreness comes out of my back and neck and into my mind. My upper body pain literally feels like a heavy pack filled with all the tension and disappointment of my past. I pay close attention to it. Once I do that, a little time passes and it usually doesn't feel so heavy. It lightens because I'm back in the present. I can't put the soreness down completely, but I can empty it out as much as possible on that particular day. I know it's as good as it's gonna get when balance and flowing air whisk around my body. It's a refreshing sensation that carries forward into the rest of my life.

The calm voice of the Coach tells me, "This pain has its place. There's nothing wrong with it. It's perfectly natural." That's the value of pain; it can become an ally instead of an enemy.

It's quite mysterious. I don't pretend to understand it. If I tried to figure it out, I'd just get in the way. We can get in the way of our own healing by filling our minds with information. It's important not to self-diagnose. Unless we have real physical problems, we are usually the one weighing ourselves down.

If you were drowning and two things were the same distance from you—a rock and a life vest—would you go down to the rock or up to the vest? Up toward the light or down toward the darkness?

Now, I meditate even when I am not meditating. I'm always staring at walls.

I know my suffering led me to become interested in so-called spirituality. I dabbled here and there, reading this and that, doing such and such, until finally, I found a home in front of a wall. Then I realized I was home all along. Why do we long for a feeling of home at home?

At first, I didn't know what I was doing. I felt unsure of myself, but now it's natural. It's something I do and need, like breathing. I don't overthink the air coming in and out unless I'm sick. I appreciate the living systems that provide my air, how they make me feel, and what they inspire me to do. How could anyone think it's perfectly OK to get in the way of the planet's air supply? How could they think they own it?

Trying to outrun our own natural limitations is where the trouble begins. We can't be pain free and still be alive. When powerful people fall into that kind of delusion, the consequences ripple across the entire living, breathing planet. None of us are innocent. We were all handed a way of life that pushes us faster than we can see, but we don't need to be atmospheric experts to know when something is out of balance. The key to balance is remembering the simple things—like air—so we don't unnecessarily or disproportionately destroy the people and things we rely on. Many of the things we rely on our inside ourselves. If we smoke, we destroy our lungs and the very air we breathe.

That's where expansive thinking comes in. Not the kind that tries to dominate or control, but the kind that widens our view just enough to put our personal pain into a more universal perspective. Sitting in front of a wall does that. It stretches the mind without force. It opens it without demand. We see what we can direct and let the rest go. We pay attention. It gives us a little more room to notice what we usually rush past. It brings us out and in at the exact same time. It's perfectly balanced like air.

How sitting in front of a wall expands the mind like hallucinogenic drugs or science, while at the same time narrowing our attention to what's right under our noses, I honestly don't know. I don't pretend to understand the mechanics.

All I can say is balance works. The mind loosens. It opens. It settles. What needs to come forward comes forward; what needs to fade fades. Thoughts and feelings rise and fall, sensations appear and disappear, and we let them. That alone is enough to keep us from collapsing into a haze of pain and worry.

So, I leave my mind alone, the same way I try to leave air alone. I don't try to control it or improve it or make it behave. I just appreciate it. I respect it. I impact it as little as possible. I understand it as best I can. That's all I can do—stay out of the way of the natural processes that keep me alive and try not to inject more imbalance than the world has already.

The universe doesn't need to mimic my personality. It needs less of me, not more. My personality is already fading. I don't really see it living on. Once I'm gone, Mark is gone. It's simple balance. That's just my mind thinking it knows something. I'm not here to judge people who believe in eternal life. I'm here to help. Maybe I can? Perhaps I can't? Each of us lives our way for a reason. Our life experiences—highs and lows—and stirrings within lead us here and there.

Pain can bring us back to ourselves. It reminds us how much we missed. I once asked a senior in a wheelchair, "What would you do if you could do anything right now?" I expected something big. He said something small: "I'd walk wherever and whenever I wanted."

Being with so many seniors on their deathbeds, I've noticed one thing: whatever they can still see out their window is beautiful to them. It doesn't matter if it's a city street or a patch of woods. They appreciate the world moving outside. In the end, the smallest bit of life is enough.

Fundamentally, we focus on what we need, but when life gets hard and the world beats us down, we miscalculate. We get confused. We lose our balance and fall. We take things for granted. We lose track of who we are. That's alright. A human being losing track of themselves is perfectly natural. Sometimes pain is the very thing that brings us back to Earth. It's a wake-up call.

Chapter Seven

Further Practice (Aka Big Mind)

Further practice involves meditating on the go. It's when we take what we've learned in stillness and silence and apply it directly in our lives. It's street practice (10). Most of us can't live like monks in peace and solitude. We navigate our spiritual practice amidst the chaos of everyday life. Meditation can help us realize that everything is interconnected and that each moment, even the most mundane, has the potential for insight. My practice helps me be present for others and fulfill my responsibilities while also embracing and appreciating the uncontrollable complexities of life. This is Big Mind—the mind that includes everything, not just the parts we prefer or understand.

I can't sit there like a monk in front of a wall my whole life. While many practices originated in the monastic setting, and I'm eternally thankful for them, I'm not in a place where everything is quiet, regimented, and provided.

From what I've seen, monks are just people. At a Vietnamese temple retreat I once attended, some fell asleep or arrived late to meditate. They were more aware of the rules, but people like me from the outside were more careful to follow them. "Temple Life," I thought, "would make a good reality show."

When I was younger, I used to say, "Maybe I'll run away and be a monk." Now I know better: the whole planet is my monastery. Big Mind doesn't need a temple—it needs us to focus on practice in our ordinary lives. If our ordinary lives are in a monastery, Big Mind needs it.

Life provides plenty of practice material. I'm not saying monasteries don't have their own drama—they do—but the real world is saturated with drama and stimuli of a different order. Some people look at the life of a monk and think, "It's too hard and too regimented for me." I look at it and think, "Man, they have it easy."

A powerful holy man sent into exile to a monastery because of a disagreement with a king shared my sentiments long ago when he said,

"Lord, what do you really want me to do? Remain here a poor monk in simplicity of spirit? The path to holiness in this monastery is effortless. I think it would be too easy to buy you like this. Bargain price." *(11)*

In a legitimate monastery—not a cult—the balance is built into the structure. The environment itself keeps you upright, even if it comes at the individual's expense. Out here, there's no such guarantee. If your practice is imbalanced, you feel it immediately. You get tossed around. You grow up quicker or you don't grow at all.

That's why a practice that survives in the middle of everyday life is so beautiful—and so rare. It has to hold its shape among ordinary people doing ordinary things, surrounded by noise, personalities, responsibilities, and the constant pull of the world. When a practice can stay steady in all that, without robes or rituals or gates designed to protect it, it becomes something real. Something earned. Something alive. It becomes street art for all to see. It becomes this book.

For most of my adult life, I was trying to figure spirituality out. I was always searching for big ideas that led to big improvements. I couldn't stay aligned with any tradition or authority for long—something always raised a red flag, some belief or behavior that didn't sit right.

It felt like I was wandering a maze, guided by a feeling I trusted but couldn't yet read or express. I kept thinking, *If I can't relate to the spiritual people, how can I be spiritual? They can't all be wrong.* It isn't that I didn't take ideas and practices from different traditions—I absolutely did. I just couldn't see how to put everything together and live it in a little way that made sense in my environment.

My mistake was believing there were big "spiritual things" on one side and "the little real world" on the other. I didn't understand that everything is spiritual—that everyone and everywhere is connected. I couldn't imagine an ordinary person seeing things this way.

Experience has taught me that choosing a particular brand of spirituality can be limiting. We may not need a single tradition, authority, or identity—but sooner or later we *do* have to choose a practice to actually practice spirituality. It's like a talented athlete playing every sport under the sun; if they're serious about making sports their life, sooner or later they need to pick one. It's a fine line, something to be experimented with. If we try something and it doesn't work out, we haven't sinned. It may simply lead us to something that *does* work for us. So long as we don't invest too much in a practice that turns out to be extreme, it's easy to pivot.

I just needed something that was balanced and honest enough to satisfy my inner nature. It doesn't mean we have to be a solitary monk or wander off on our own without guidance—it's something more in the middle. It's paying attention and trying our best. It might seem small, but doing our best and not beating ourselves up when we fall short are huge. Those two habits change the whole tone of life. They keep us moving instead of tightening up, learning instead of hiding, and growing without turning every mistake into a verdict. What looks "little" on the surface is usually the stuff that makes the mind wider and the days easier to live.

When I first started meditating, I did it to feel better. My mindset was achievement, but it isn't anymore. I achieved "achievement." When I am present, I help people appreciate the balance of nature we embody. We embody it whether we know it or not. So, there's nothing to achieve.

Our original nature is beyond achievement, but if we make an effort to follow it, it may achieve us. Everything in nature expresses our original nature. When we realize this, we know we didn't do anything alone. Anything we achieve, everything achieves, and there's nothing to gain, nowhere else to go or be but here (X). That's Further Mind—the mind that doesn't divide the world into "me" and "not me."

When we're busy trying to be better, do more, or become some upgraded version of ourselves, the mind tightens around that goal and everything gets smaller—our attention, our patience, our sense of possibility. We start measuring instead of noticing, comparing instead of living. But when we're willing to be who we are for a moment—not as a final verdict, just as a starting point—the heart and mind expand.

Acceptance gives us more room to see what's actually happening, more room to move, more room to grow without the pressure of becoming someone else. It's mysterious, but the minute we stop squeezing ourselves into "better," we finally have the space to change.

When I stop and closely watch my cat Porkchop, I see a sacred statue in motion. He's not trying to become better. He's *better* in the flesh. He leaves me in awe. I don't take him for granted. Even when he bites through a cord or scatters kitty litter all over, I'm happy to have him around.

It takes discipline to have a cat. He has his routine, and I have to adjust mine to take care of him properly. I need to know my own nature and preferences to appreciate his. I can't judge him by human standards. That would be ridiculous. That's the thing about judgment: it's always too small for the world we're trying to fit into it. When I judge him, I shrink him down to my size. When I notice the judgment instead of believing it, my mind gets a little bigger. There's more room for him to be a cat, and more room for me to be a person who enjoys having one.

Judgment limits us. Awareness of judgment frees us. It doesn't make us saints—it just gives us a wider field to live in.

Sometimes, I'm like Porkchop. He wakes, patrols, and reacts to the smallest movement. Whatever grabs his attention is his life. His focus is total and fleeting. Watching him reminds me how to be present without overthinking. Some ancient biological computer system in him does much of his thinking and feeling. He knows no other way. He's just a cool cat and accepts himself as he is.

But, if I took Porkchop's lead, I'd kill for fun, not necessity, and neglect everyone else. He's easily distracted and lacks compassion. I grow fresh catnip for him. When I put it in the bowl, he's worse than any addict. He incessantly licks the area and rolls around for at least ten minutes after it's gone. His focus is perfect until the next thing grabs his attention. He's all over the place. His senses, moods, and instincts exclusively move him. So, Porkchop as a teacher is limited.

A mother with a litter is as close to a human master as a cat can get. But we can't forget she'll still eat a sick or wounded kitten. We don't like imagining our furry friends doing something so brutal, but it happens. That's nature without a filter—life responding directly to life. And the purity we see here may not look anything like the purity we imagined.

We love our pets and consider them members of our family because they help us to feel better. They open our hearts and minds to unconditional love. I know what Porkchop is capable of, but that doesn’t take away from his cuteness. He’s both cute and a natural-born killer, kind of like me.

Only my current obligations prevent me from acting like Porkchop all of the time. I'm free but elect to stay within boundaries. Freedom *is* boundaries. It's understanding what we can and can't realistically change. It’s trying to minimize the harm we inflict. It’s not unnecessarily impeding the freedom of anyone else, human or non-human. Freedom is discipline. That’s following the big mind—not impulse, but clarity.

We can run, but we can't hide. I learned that from authentic teachers who admitted they abandoned or neglected their children, families, health, and/or material interests (for so-called enlightenment), only to pay for it later. Sooner or later, we pay for our big mistakes. The idea is for us to include the obvious ones in the price of living.

Through hard work and focus, I earned faith and confidence in the simplicity of my meditation practice. It helped me appreciate my ordinary life and realize I had taken it for granted. Not that there’s anything wrong with it, but I don’t need pomp and symbolism. I don’t need to escape to a peaceful ashram or Zen Center in the mountains either. My cat’s big enough for me.

Which brings us closer to the point: the actual moment is life with no subjective filter. But we also know we can’t ever see it that purely. Recognizing this means acknowledging the limits of our circumstances, feelings, thoughts, and responsibilities. Even priests, masters, and monks have their niches, duties, preferences and blind spots. Our mistake is thinking that they don’t—that in some way they are bigger.

Monks work in silence; we don’t. We inherit our own set of conditions—noise, speed, responsibility, and the constant pull of other people’s needs. Our problems always feel bigger out here. More than the monastery relies on us.

Out here, silence isn't built into the environment. It has to be brought into the mind. It took me a long time to accept it. Just plain old silence became a miracle in itself. I felt like I didn't deserve it. I didn't have any space for it. I still don't understand how I found silence in my chaotic mind, in this chaotic world—but somehow it found me when I finally listened. I gave it space to fill me, and eventually it did, slowly and on its own terms. Silence is way bigger than my noise.

My mind emptied until it could absorb again, like a dry sponge. I had to find a different way to practice than the one the monks and priests of my tradition passed down. Out in the noise of everyday life, a unique kind of silence began to form in me—not the silence Zen masters worked in, but the silence that develops only when you stop in the middle of everything and your mind becomes open to more than just what you can control.

I stopped trying to keep up with tradition and all the fast pace around me and started paying attention to what was happening in me instead. I practiced nothing. I slowed things down. I simply followed my own unfolding the way the sky clears—clouds shifting on their own schedule, not mine. Watching my mind unfold without analyzing or judging it, changed how it unfolded. I accepted that my mind was a whole lot bigger than me.

The stillness I cultivate doesn't stay at home. It moves with me into the world. Confidence grows from nothing—something we'd never discover without trying it. I trust myself to do and say what's best, nothing heroic, just what's appropriate and helpful. Sometimes the best thing to do is nothing at all. I don't always get it right, but that's part of the process.

If you're ready to practice nothing rather than just talk about it, forget all this and follow the simple instructions at the end. What's the point of reading about nothing?

Whether I'm silent on the mat, providing you with instructions, working in my community, relaxing at home, or walking through a mangrove forest, the practice of nothing helps me become a gentler, more appreciative, more loving person. It's pretty mystical when I stop to consider it. That's exactly why I don't spend much time considering it. What's the point of trying to figure out nothing? It's more truthful to do it and let it shape things on its own.

Nothing is the biggest mind of all because it isn't cramped by our usual noise—no opinions, no labels, no judgments, no self-improvement projects, no story about who we're supposed to be. When the mind drops all that for even a moment, it becomes wide enough to hold whatever shows up.

"Nothing" isn't a void; it's the absence of squeezing. It's the space where we're not chasing, fixing, defending, or performing. In that space, the mind isn't small and reactive—it's open, steady, and able to see clearly. Nothing is the biggest mind because it leaves room for everything.

I have to be open enough to let nothing show up in ordinary moments. It might seem irrational, but really it's practical. Earlier today, for example, a difficult co-worker said something rude, and a wave of irritation hit me. Right in the middle of it, I recognized the emotion, gave it a little space, let it pass, and returned to the present (X). I didn't react. I practiced nothing. Despite being triggered by someone else's behavior, the irritation itself was literally nothing—just a passing ripple in my mind.

Some people would say, "There's no excuse for someone to act rude," but the co-worker in question has three kids, no family support system, two baby daddies in prison, and a generally tough life. She's suffering enough. I don't need to add to it. I've been rude plenty of times.

I may as well have been sitting on the floor in front of the wall. I was meditating off the mat and on the fly. I tinkered with my irritation right there in the moment—no ceremony, no Asian ritual, no theory, no moral obligation, no hesitation, no nothing—and responded appropriately. I just nodded my head and went on my way. I was the bigger person because I had the luxury of better conditions. It had little to do with me.

It happened so fast and spontaneously. I didn't plan anything. Whatever it did, it did me. It took me further. I can barely remember how it went down, but after I caught myself, the irritation quickly changed into nothing and passed. I've done this so much, it's just part of me now. It also helps to remember how small I felt when I was the irritating one.

My co-worker irritated me. So what? So-called successful people are always talking about big deals, but I know only I can make a big deal out of nothing. My co-worker's a far more complex being than Porkchop, but the feeling was the same as when he does something that gets under my skin. He's just being a cat. My co-worker was just being human.

Later, when she cools down, I'll bring her a can of her favorite soda, even though I'm always joking that it's basically poison in a can. Big mind doesn't flinch at that. Big mind accepts poison, soda, cats, and humans—all of it. It doesn't sort the world into "good" and "bad" before it lets things in. It just sees what's there, responds to what's needed, and moves on. The small mind wants everything to fit its standards. The big mind knows the world is bigger than our preferences, and it makes room for the whole mess without losing its balance.

It wouldn't make much sense to take my cat personally, as if he were a person. And honestly, it's not always wise to take a person personally either. Most of the time it isn't personal at all. It's usually something far more complex—something bigger we can't see, don't know, and may never understand.

These are the kinds of subtle realizations that grow out of doing nothing in silence—things we never could have imagined or anticipated. Expansive thinking and compassion develop out of nothing (we can conceive). They develop on their own, in their own time. All we can do is give them room to grow. If we over-analyze them, we stunt their growth. A big mind isn't a full one. It's an empty one.

Each of us has our own set of natural characteristics. We might be funny, nervous, sharp, cautious, bold—or all of the above. But none of these traits started with us. They're bigger than we are. Humor existed long before we were born, which is why we can be humorous. Fear existed long before we arrived, which is why we can be afraid. Every trait is a character in its own right, part of a cast that's been rehearsing for hundreds of thousands of years.

All of them live in our minds. It might be nice to have a big party and invite them. In a way, we do that every time we sit down to meditate. Everyone shows up. The whole cast checks in—the anxious one, the funny one, the stubborn one, the tired one, the hopeful one, the peaceful one. Meditation doesn't create them; it just gives them a place to gather so we can finally see what's living in us. I always pull peace aside at the party. She's the friend everyone goes to when they need to talk about their problems. Her mind is always open.

There are two sides to nature: the violent part and the peaceful part. That's balance. But there's nothing violent about peace. We all want peace. We all talk about it, but peace is really about listening. When we truly listen—without trying to fix, judge, or get in the way—love flows. We see the pain in our friends' and neighbors' eyes, and at the very least, we offer a smile or an encouraging word. We don't make anything worse. We don't feel the need to fill a world full of endless potential with our little personality.

People talk about original sin as if we have no choice, but they forget that compassion is human nature too—our nature, the original nature. All living things work for the betterment of all other living things, even when it looks violent to us. That's nature's purity. It includes everything.

Our purity looks different. But purity isn't what we're after. If we look for purity, all we'll see is grime. If we look for grime, all we'll see are things to clean. If we look for nothing, nothing finds us—and it's as unlimited as the universe itself. Somehow, we have to sit long enough to stop sitting to heal ourselves and start sitting to accept ourselves as we are, good, bad or indifferent.

I talk about nothing and emptying the mind a lot, but it defeats the purpose. So, I'll say something empty that says nothing. It's pointless to explain these things, because until you actually experience nothing— an empty mind, even for a breath—it won't make sense. And even then, it still doesn't make sense in the usual way. That's the wild thing about meditation: it makes a whole lot of sense, but not the kind that fills us with more information. It's the kind that fills us with trust in balance, in our own nature, in the exact pocket of our awareness (X) in an otherwise endless universe of chaos. It's the kind of sense that lets us know, without a doubt or understanding how, that we are the stable universe right where we sit. And what could be bigger than faith in the whole universe?

I learned how to settle my mind during those long days sitting in a silent position. Once I was calm enough, I noticed I was really suffering. It's hard to look back. I was in so much pain, but over the years, it eased up and I was able to feel it out without ruining my day. I was able to check it out on the fly which made things really interesting. My practice kept going further and further into my life off the cushion.

I wasn't looking for patterns or to rid myself of pain, but the more I examined my mind in action, the more I saw that I was like a bloodhound on a scent. It ran madly forward, sniffing this and that. It was noisy. If a mind can slobber, mine certainly did. Some days it felt like it even had fleas. Whenever I felt uncomfortable or threatened, I howled and snapped. I showed my teeth. Anything in my way risked being bitten. That was the small mind—reactive, restless, convinced every rustle in the bushes was a crisis.

At first, all I could do was notice that this was how I behaved. I judged myself, too. I was surprised by how aggressive I was, and a little ashamed. I thought about all the people I may have hurt. But I pushed through the strong emotions. I kept watching. Again and again, I watched myself behave on the fly and my understanding of who I was watching expanded.

Eventually the judgment softened, and self-compassion and understanding slipped in—quietly, but strong enough to change me. I didn't think my way into becoming gentler or less reactive. I practiced my way into it by being aware of my aggression as it happened. I studied it like a scientist that had no thesis or publications to worry about. My feelings about my feelings changed. I felt better about the bad ones. I found them far more interesting than the good ones. That's balance.

These days, the way I handle things is more like an old hound on the porch. It takes quite a commotion to get me barking. I've been on one too many frantic hunts to fall for every noise. I'm a dog that knows better now—a wiser mutt who's learned when to lift his head and when to just feel the breeze on my nose. I let things come and go without getting in the way. I guess even an old dog can teach *themselves* new tricks.

Since I'm the owner of my actions, I can practice catching myself when I'm uncomfortable or irritated. It's a choice. Once I could stop and do it, again and again, it became a habit like any other. Like a dog slowly learns how to roll over, I practiced letting my mind ease back into a broader, steadier frame of reference. From there, my feelings made more sense, and I understood what it meant to respond instead of reacting. That's Further Practice—shifting from the small mind of "my irritation" to the Big Mind that sees the whole yard, the whole day, the whole picture.

I don't always get it right. Sometimes, I start howling at nothing, but I'm aware of my own behavior and that's close enough. When I howl, I laugh. Hopefully I don't startle or annoy anyone. I'm always studying my mind and refining it. Hey—every dog has its day, and I guess today is mine.

When I first started catching myself in front of the wall, I wasn't fully aware of it. I wasn't trained. So, I couldn't have helped anyone else do it. Catching myself in real time had to be practiced repeatedly until it became second nature. An intuition like that couldn't reveal itself until I was ready to receive it.

Once it was second nature, I could naturally express it. Catching myself is not second nature; it's first nature, but for the sake of articulation, I separate it into first and second nature. It's not easy to consider and express intimate practices like these. If a professional football star overthinks a penalty shot, they will miss. Then they'll realize it's time to get back to fundamentals; to practice.

The key to relying on a spiritual discipline wasn't escaping my humanity but entering it. I'm far from perfect. I'm not always going to score. Practice taught me to watch my habits and preferences closely and understand them well enough to lose my reliance on them. When I stopped judging myself and the situation I was in, I stopped fighting myself. All the mental chatter slowed down, and I could focus. Confidence grew where self-doubt used to live. I remembered something older than disappointment—a glimpse of my big mind.

The big mind isn't mystical or bigger than life. It's the mind we had before fear trained us to brace, before disappointment taught us to shrink, before the world convinced us to doubt ourselves. It's the unconstructed mind—clear, steady, curious—the one that sees things as they are instead of through old wounds.

When the mind isn't busy defending or justifying itself, compassion appears on its own. Not as a virtue, but as a natural response to seeing clearly. We have to set the conditions for things like compassion. Compassion is the ultimate universal mind-expander because it forces the mind to grow beyond the tight little circle of "me" and "mine."

The moment we feel compassion—real compassion, not performance, guilt or pity—the mind stretches to include someone else's reality. In a limited capacity, it imagines their experience, their fear, their needs, their point of view. We can't really know what they're going through, but that intention to stretch alone makes the mind bigger. Compassion dissolves the small mind's boundaries and replaces them with connection. And the more living beings and situations we can hold in that wider field, the more the mind expands.

Compassion doesn't make us weaker or more at risk; it makes us larger and more realistic. It gives us a mind big enough to hold the whole messy universe without collapsing into fear or defensiveness. In that sense, compassion isn't just kindness—it's the mind remembering its true size, where it is and where it comes from. It's the mind knowing it's never alone, even when it is.

Kindness began to move through me without effort. I didn't design it, and I didn't try to become anything special. I felt a quiet shift—a natural intelligence waking up and doing its work without needing my permission. It was like the city worker out front of my house repairing the water line. He didn't need my help. I'd only slow him down and keep the rest of my neighbors from getting their water back.

Meditation kept me open enough to let irritation pass without turning it into a story. It helped me work on irritations like a maintenance man works on a water line. Over time, Further Practice began to grow out of meditation the way a sprout grows out of a seed—not separate from it, but its next expression. A continuation. A maturation. A way of living the practice instead of only sitting with it or studying it.

The practice of nothing played a part in that growth. Nothing wasn't a void or a withdrawal; it was the kind of emptiness that lets things change shape without me getting in the way. It was a growing seed. It was the space where old reactions dissolved and new possibilities formed. It was emptiness doing what emptiness does—transforming itself into something alive. The seed only opens because there's nothing pressing against it. My practice grew the same way.

I realized my spiritual practice and life were never separate. Practice was simply life paying attention to itself. Big Mind started to reveal itself in those moments: Not as a mystical upgrade, but as the recognition that everything belongs—the pain, the beauty, the confusion, the tenderness. Big Mind is the part of us that can hold the whole thing without tightening around it. Once I could hold it, I could work with it.

Early blues music pioneers turned the violence and inequality of slavery and racism into something that still spreads joy all over the world. I learned to turn my own pain into art. My art is clarity. That's the heart of Further Practice: returning to what's happening now without needing to escape, retaliate, or collapse—turning something ugly into something fresh and alive that can be shared. It's turning the tremendous energy of those who hurt us into something that helps others. That's *compassionate revenge*, that's ZEN and it makes the whole universe light up and smile.

Somewhere in all this, the present moment stopped being a place I visited and became a place I belonged. What's happening to me now isn't a question anymore. It's the ground under my feet. I can feel it. And even though it holds me, it's still far bigger than me. The more I settle into where I am, the more I feel the size of what I'm standing in. The moment doesn't shrink to fit me; I just grow enough to stand inside it.

Chapter Eight

What's Happening to Me Now?

I'm sitting on the bus I drive, a pad of paper on my knee, waiting for a senior at a dental appointment. The job is humbling and demanding, yet it has opened me to people at the end of their lives—to their struggles, their loneliness, and the tenderness that comes from witnessing both. In the pauses between pickups and drop-offs, I feel the urge to approach and share my experience as if for the first time—not to erase it, but to redefine it, to see it with the eyes I have now. That's what's happening to me now—the present moment warming the past back into something alive and different. More than anything else, balance creates.

This isn't something I planned or staged. It's a free-flowing stream of consciousness in the form of a chapter, the mind doing what it does when it isn't being managed or dressed up. I'm not trying to create a teaching moment. My words are unfolding because the conditions are right and the practice is alive enough to follow its own current.

There are endless ways a practice can unfold, and endless ways it will unfold if you take it on. This is just one stream among many, one angle of attention, one moment where the mind is opening enough to let things show themselves. Nothing more mystical than that, and nothing less. It comes into being the same way any genuine moment of practice does—quietly, naturally, because it could.

(X) is a bunch of different, diverse energies joining together and finding equilibrium as something new. That's what creation really is. It's not purity, not perfection, but forces that don't match learning how to hold each other long enough for something fresh to appear.

Pain and clarity. Past and present. Fear and trust. All of it meeting in one place and settling into a balance that didn't exist before. That's how anything real is made.

Before I established my silent meditation practice, spontaneity was a liability and risk. I often paid for it after. Now, it's a healthy way of life. It feels like this. It's what's happening to me now, which is enough. I don't need anything more than (X).

I'm jotting this down on a pad while on a senior citizen bus. I started volunteering to teach meditation at an assisted living home to help with cognitive decline, grieving and pain, but now I also drive residents to appointments and outings. The management roped me in with praise. The residents stole my heart.

Right here outside a dental office, in the middle of the street and all its hustle and bustle, I pause and reconsider my circumstances. Before my meditation practice, I couldn't have imagined doing something like this. It would've felt beneath me. I was arrogant, wrapped in bravado I mistook for protection. I was unfocused and anxious, living in survival mode—hypervigilant, tense, and always ready for a fight. There was no extra space in my mind for anything new.

What's happening now is the opposite: space, breath, and a simple willingness to accept what's here. What's here is more than enough.

My bus, which I call "Further" *(12)*, is one of those fourteen-seat coaches. It's constantly sputtering, smoking, bucking, and breaking down, but the management refuses to replace it. It's like riding a mule instead of a camel in the desert. It's bound to die at the worst place and time.

As the old saying goes, "Humility is hard on the knees." Driving for the last two years has been humbling. I crawl around on the floor and clean up piss and shit. It makes me gag. I'm always coming home dirty and drained with cuts and bruises.

I develop close friendships with people who don't have much time left to live. I watch them suffer, fade, and die, often completely alone. They are as vulnerable as small children, and one bad employee can cause irreparable harm.

Some members of my community see a man my age driving a bus and probably wonder what I did wrong. On the social totem pole, this job is low-end; it's high-risk, physically and emotionally demanding, exposed to the elements, pays minimum wage, and offers no benefits. It's interesting to voluntarily put yourself on society's "pay me no mind" list. Usually, when I'm in uniform, I'm invisible to the residents of my affluent beach town. And when they do notice, it's often to yell and beep at me to move so they can squeeze past in their Mercedes.

I need to catch myself here. That whole reaction was me slipping into an old pattern—putting myself down first, assuming I know the shape of someone else's life, and letting my self-consciousness fill in the blanks. I wasn't seeing what's happening; I was building a story about what *they* did to me and what *I* must look like to them.

People in Mercedes have their own problems, pressures, and private storms—ones I might never be able to relate to. I flattened them into a type and used it to shrink myself. That wasn't practice. That was habit. The moment I noticed it, I dropped the story, the judgment, and returned to what's happening to me now—the only place clarity ever shows up.

I'm back to (X) and waiting for a woman transplanted from Japan, E, to finish her dental appointment. Then, I will drive her and her clean teeth back to the assisted living home. She's in her upper eighties and has managed to keep her original teeth and body in good condition, which I appreciate, as it takes a lot of hard work.

E meditates with me. I remember the first time we sat face to face on the floor, and she suddenly burst out laughing.

She said, "It is hard to imagine an American having to teach me, a good Japanese woman, how to do Zen. And I'm sitting in a chair, and you are on the ground like I should be!"

"I'm simply returning the gift to its rightful owner, and your wise ancestors taught me that sitting in a chair is perfectly acceptable!" I responded. "I'm so sorry I didn't instruct you properly," I rolled my mat up and joined her on a chair. That was the precise moment I realized that sitting on the ground to meditate wasn't necessary.

I noticed she was holding her breath, so I also reminded her of something she already knew: "Following our natural breath in through the nose, out through the nose or mouth, brings us back to now."

I breathe exclusively through my nose. Sometimes I inhale deeply into my nose and exhale long out of my mouth to reset my mind. When I first started meditating, I was too insecure to deep breathe in a group setting. Now, it may startle beginners in the room, but it reminds them to focus on their breath. By paying attention for many years, subtle but practical habits develop. We allow our bodies to teach us for a change.

Our minds can't teach us anything new if they are endlessly occupied.

We all have a unique approach to breathing. Our practice is to pay close attention to it. Once we know our breath, we know ourselves. Then we may realize we are full of nothing but hot air.

Telling a story and then in the middle of it, expressing how we can closely follow our breath back to (X) is a direct expression of practice for busy people on the go. It's taking our practice Further.

Natural breath in through the nose and out. Follow it back to the present. Fresh and new.

I just did it. Feel free to try it. It may be too simple to believe, but once you practice it, following your breath is a powerful tool that can quickly improve your life. We follow our breath with our minds. It's not an easy thing to wrap our minds around until we do it repeatedly over many years.

Now I am simply here—present in this bus, watching the world move around me. I sit in the stillness for no reason at all, letting everything wash through me. In these moments, the ordinary becomes luminous.

The sidewalk hums with its own quiet purpose, faces glow with a kind of secret life, and even the ground seems busy with its endless work. My mind sees out there and through my hand writes this memory down. When I really consider it with my big mind, it feels almost psychedelic, but without the chaos—as if the world has turned itself up a notch, not because I altered my mind, but because I finally stopped trying to fill it. This is what's happening to me now—the world revealing its richness because I let it.

I realize I'm empty and then empty my mind of emptiness. Not empty as in lacking, but empty as in open—a bus with no one on it, ready for whoever steps aboard to set out on the open road. I don't need anything more than this moment. (X) is heaven. I don't need to chase visions or substances or material things or even meaning. When I stop grasping, the world offers itself freely. When I stop trying to be full, everything becomes nourishment. This is what's happening to me now—the world feeding me because I finally stopped trying to feed on it.

This is how I make the most of my time: by being here, fully immersed, letting the mundane reveal its quiet miracles. Who needs anything when nothing and everything are already right in front of us? Presence is its own abundance. Contentment is its own wealth. And emptiness—true emptiness—is the way to all of it. This is why I practice meditation. (X) and only (X).

I realize how privileged I am to be on stable, peaceful ground in an otherwise dark, violent universe. How do I remain calm and inspired amidst the mad hustle and bustle of everyday life? Why do I feel so rich when I'm nothing but a meager bus driver? What did I do to deserve this?

What's happening to me now is simple: I stopped measuring my life by the world's standards and started experiencing it directly. I stopped asking, "What should I be?" and started noticing, "This moment is a miracle in itself." I stopped trying to be someone and started being here (X).

Each time I find balance in the universe, I create something new—not because I'm special, but out of a mix of diverse forces settling together for a moment. It's a small world that forms right where I sit, made of everything that shows up in me: memory, fear, trust, breath, whatever the day brings.

It feels like "my" world, but it isn't. It's the universe arranging itself through me, because of the universe, inside the universe. I'm just the spot where those energies meet long enough to take shape. I'm not really doing anything but letting it all happen.

The richness I feel isn't something I bought. It's something I slowly and patiently uncovered. I still need to work. I need to constantly catch myself. But if nothing else, I have faith in things as they are. I feel a connection to nature—my nature, human nature, and the nature of all things. It was always here, waiting for me to stop running long enough to notice it. It's a new beginning, again and again and again. It's simply (X). (X) marks our spot in the universe. It's perfectly balanced, and believe it or not, I'm actually living it, at least for the moment.

Oops… I need to stop all this high-minded nonsense. Here comes E. Time to focus on driving the bus. Safety first. She needs me to be a simple-minded driver. Not a Zen master disguised as a bus driver. If I keep thinking like this out on the road, I'll cause an accident.

That's what's happening to me now. I need to find my equilibrium and transform into something new. Back and forth. Big and little Mark. In between. To the beginning. The beginning is always (X).

Chapter Nine

The Beginning is (X)

After witnessing New Age fads while living on the Hawaiian island of Maui, I was highly skeptical of meditation. When a respected friend recommended an authentic book on the subject, I immediately knew it was legitimate. I finally found a spiritual home. It promised nothing and encouraged me to stop relying on books and teachers and start relying on myself. The book gave me the confidence and courage to realize there's no better time than now (X) to appreciate life. The beginning wasn't somewhere far away—it was already happening.

All this started after a respected friend, who calls himself Wolfie, recommended that I read a book by a genuine meditation teacher named Suzuki Roshi. *(13)*

At first, I thought, "What a Hollywood bullshitter. What's this wily Wolfie selling?"

I wasn't interested in meditation. I was into plants. I grew everything well, including the good stuff. I had just spent over five years living on an island in the Pacific. *(14)* The soil was perfect. Whatever I threw on the ground came up.

The island was also fertile ground for New Age fantasies. There were high-priced workshops and people doing ridiculous things in the name of spirituality—eating only algae, getting hooked up to "chakra reader" machines, worrying about the end of the world, judging normal people just earning a living. I couldn't relate. The islanders already had their own ancient spirituality—quiet, grounded, and woven into the land and sea. They didn't need machines or gurus to feel connected.

And the Hawaiians didn't appreciate the super-consumer newcomers paving their sacred paradise and driving up the cost of living. I was running with the rich and famous crowd, like Nick Carraway in *The Great Gatsby*. After a while, I felt like I was part of the problem, so I moved back to the mainland before I drifted too far from myself.

Considering all that, it took me a while to give Suzuki Roshi's book a chance. Wolfie kept telling me, "Man, I hear you. I feel the same about gurus and scams. But this guy is legit. I have no skin in the game."

Wolfie's confidence finally won me over, and I checked out the book. Once I opened it, I found it was a collection of Suzuki Roshi's lectures put together by his students after his death. It wasn't really his. It's what his students gathered from his instructions. That appealed to me. He didn't write it. He lived it.

As I got into it, I doubted the old wise master would ever write a book. Suzuki Roshi didn't seem like the type to be bothered by notoriety. That was more reason to trust him.

When I finished the first chapter and saw that he wasn't selling anything, I knew he was the real deal. He encouraged me to put the book down and experiment with Zen meditation practice. From the grave, the thoughts and feelings of a dead man helped me act in the present.

I took it all to heart and believed Suzuki Roshi when he said that everything I was looking for—whatever it may be—was already right here at home. He reassured me that I was already qualified to practice and that nothing was wrong with me. He made me feel equal. He said, "Rather than thinking about it, just do it." *(15)*

He explained how we're all in the same shoes. We get pebbles in our shoes when we wear them. It's uncomfortable. We can't leave them in there and expect to move on comfortably. Meditation provides a stable position. We sit down to take the pebbles out. We stop and address them. We may try shaking them out while standing on one foot to save time, but then we put ourselves unnecessarily at risk of losing our balance and getting hurt. We can't fall when firmly planted on the ground.

Have you ever considered pebbles? They can be over a billion years old—our primordial nature is all around us. Pick one up. Look in the mirror.

I followed Suzuki Roshi's instructions to the best of my understanding. At first, it was all trial and error, and I felt like I was doing something wrong. I couldn't conceive how everything is already here, and there is no right or wrong way to begin realizing this.

I meditated every day for about half an hour for a couple of months straight, then reached out to Wolfie. He wasn't interested in teaching then, but I pestered him with stupid questions. He doubted my legitimacy for several years but finally agreed to teach me. One thing led to another; now, the practice I once marveled at is nothing more than a routine. And the dead man my teacher turned me on to still speaks to me often.

Like sage ancestors, I turn to those in my lineage for advice. *(16)*

Suzuki Roshi's wisdom didn't end with his death. Like all genuine teachings, it moves through the living—teacher to student—less as doctrine than as tone. When I catch that tone in my life, I recognize my lineage at work.

Doing and understanding are different. I relate to Suzuki Roshi's words and see his wisdom in daily life. I can't live his way constantly. Accepting my limitations, I learn to move through my own desires with enough honesty that they settle something inside me. When paying attention, I face life calmly with appreciation. I salute Suzuki Roshi, who lived his words. He humbles me. I bow to him, not in the sky but here with me. He makes me laugh. You might see him as an imaginary friend, but I see him as alive in me.

Looking back, it all makes sense in ways I can't explain. I'm grateful for the long line of people who made this practice possible. Now, when I give, I'm just doing my job. I'm giving back to honor the myriads of living beings and systems that put me in this precise position (X). The beginning is always (X)—the moment we realize we're already standing where we need to be.

I realize that I'm privileged. I say things redundantly for emphasis. Only a privileged person can feel this way. Most people have more practical things on their minds. I try not to forget that it's an honor to practice. I don't know how I got here, "as me," but it feels like a gift.

About twenty years ago, when I first started dabbling with meditation, I lived near a sacred lake and visited a monastery where a chanting monk gave me chills. *(17)* When I asked how it felt to live there, he sighed and said it took hard work and sacrifice. At the time, it didn't seem important, but now I get it. Sitting quietly might look extraordinary, but it's really just good, honest work.

Why would I want to put all that effort into something so mundane? Once I established my meditation routine, it answered my doubts and questions. There's nothing prosaic about our ordinary lives, but sometimes, we're too busy to realize it. We are busy in our minds long before our bodies follow.

Practice is a sense of home at home, in our lives as they happen, not anywhere else, doing something we can't do right here where we are (X). When I sit down to meditate each day, I begin again. It's never the same. I realize I'm always changing. It teaches me that the beginning is always here—always (X). It's an opportunity to start fresh. When we don't anticipate what the day will bring, it brings what we never anticipated.

Finding our way back to our true nature requires patience, but if we wait passively, we risk confusion. Thinking too big can make us feel small—so maybe feeling little is enough. We might not know our true role, or we might already be fulfilling it. I'm happy just caring for myself, my family, pet and community, even if it seems ordinary. The key is not to overthink—just act naturally like a seed, cat or child.

(X) is my spot. It's right here. Clear as day.

Chapter Ten

Clear-Eyed Immersion

Through years of meditation, we may find that catching ourselves drifting away from the present is a humbling and insightful practice that ultimately leads to a sense of freedom. Paying attention to our breath brings us back to a state of now, allowing us to immerse ourselves in our surroundings without judgment or distraction. This is clear-eyed immersion—seeing without the fog of fear, fantasy, or self-importance. Nature teaches us how to just "be" without imposing our narratives on what we see. We can learn to appreciate the simplicity of being and the profound lessons that come from quiet observation and presence. When that happens, the world no longer revolves around us; instead, everything begins to move together in one shared rhythm.

These days, being present feels less like something I do and more like something that happens on its own. I'm in the moment and part of it without knowing it. I'm not doing anything but acting naturally. I actually do something when I catch myself out of the moment. But even that feels less like effort and more like my original self, reminding me who I really am now.

Years of staring at the wall have revealed what "now" is without saying a word. It's a feeling as much as a realization—a comprehensive sense of freedom that rises from stillness. Being here now means listening for no reason other than listening.

"Now" is experiencing a symbol like (X) and feeling it without question or judgment.

I know how to just be, but sometimes I still find myself judging someone by their appearance or daydreaming about a relationship twenty years ago. I wonder what I could have done differently. Only to SNAP OUT of it and realize how ridiculous yet insightful I can be at the same time. That snap—that sudden clarity—is clear-eyed immersion returning on its own.

If every time I caught myself daydreaming, I treated it like a mistake, I'd be exhausted. I'd burn through all my energy just scolding myself, and out of sheer necessity I'd have to stop practicing altogether just to make it through the day.

So, I keep it simple. First, I notice I'm not here—(X) marks the spot where my mind wandered off. Then I bring myself back by following my breath. That's it. I begin again. To know our air is to know ourselves. It's simple, almost embarrassingly simple, but it works.

Once back at (X), I immerse myself in whatever's right in front of me. I experience the world through an unfettered, albeit limited, filter. I call this seeing the world "clear-eyed." It's like eye drops that clear all the irritations.

I'm just paying complete attention without constantly reminding myself that I want or need to do something. I stop trying to protect, amuse, or improve myself and listen without expecting anything in return. I commit to doing nothing. I'm content staying put, with what I have and don't have, as I am.

Somehow the practice does not make my mind busy. It simplifies it. It only seems like a lot when I attempt to explain it. Most of the time, catching myself cracks me up and keeps me humble.

To explain clear-eyed immersion, I need to talk about it. When I speak, I make things murky. An explanation of any experience isn't close to being accurate, but it's more so if I pay attention to my original voice. Somehow, I need to allow nature to speak through me without getting in the way. I need to follow the leader.

I often let go of myself to the totality of experience, but I also have responsibilities and things that require planning. If I drift too far into timeless reality, I might forget something important—like picking up my children from school. There's nothing like getting that call from the office to remind you that spiritual spaciousness doesn't excuse bad parenting.

It's essential to know ourselves, but the point isn't to make excuses for avoiding our responsibilities. It's to remain aware of our nature as much as possible in the middle of our ordinary lives. Sometimes we hold on to let go, and sometimes we let go to hold on. What I mean is this: in real life, those aren't two separate strategies. They're just different expressions of the same underlying movement—the same balancing act that shows up in every part of being human. The trouble comes when I treat them as two modes I'm supposed to choose between, as if one is "spiritual" and the other is "practical." Eventually, I realized there is no "two." It's all one movement, one continuous adjustment, one field of life responding to itself.

Being immersed in nature isn't a separate state or some private escape; it's noticing the same balance that brings molecules together somehow holds my life together. Something vast shaping something small. The patterns aren't out in the forest or the sky—they're the same patterns that help me live up to my responsibilities.

A balanced person allows as much as possible around them to live balanced without getting in the way. When I pay full attention, I'm not stepping away from life. I'm tapping into the energy of the one movement everything depends on. Even ordinary things—like picking up my children—have become quietly extraordinary. When they climb into the car and we start clowning around, there's nowhere else I'd rather be in the entire universe.

Meditation fits into life without disrupting my routines. It goes one step further because it helps me appreciate them. Once I appreciate them, they don't feel like a burden. I'm glad to do them, so I live up to my responsibilities. I don't need to be appreciated for manning up to my duties as a dad, because it's extra. It complicates simple things. I'm a dad. To be a decent, fulfilled person, I need to do dad things.

When I sit down in front of the wall, it's a small pause in the day, a moment where I choose not to disturb the world or myself. That pause sharpens my attention for the ordinary things because it interrupts the momentum of my automatic reactions.

When I stop disturbing myself, even for a minute, the noise drops. The next thing I do—washing a dish, answering an email, driving the bus, making sure I don't step on an ant—shows up with a little more clarity. I'm not fighting my own mind or pain while trying to do it. I've already given my pain the attention it needs at the wall. It's not dramatic. It's not enlightenment. It's just a cleaner handoff between moments. A reset. A recalibration. A breath that lets the next task be *just* the next task, not a pile of thoughts about the task or how I'm feeling.

Meditation offers a brief step out of time, inside of time. And somehow, that little pause of time helps me take better care of my family. Family is the point of practice, and my family is my whole community—a diversity of beautiful souls, each unique and relying on me not to let my petty problems and needs interfere with the balance of their lives.

When we act, we make an impact; that's the natural way. But the mind can twist that truth. We may think something is wrong even when it isn't. We might believe we don't deserve to live, or that the world is better off without us. We may imagine Earth isn't our home, that only in death will we find where we truly belong. But if we stay with meditation long enough, we begin to see things closer to home. We learn that nothing is wrong, even when something is. We learn that this is our family, and it's worth caring for with everything we have.

If we are truly paying attention, we eventually recognize that we aren't always capable of doing so. And although that's when we hurt other living beings and take life for granted, it's also when something lighter breaks through. Our mistakes reveal the truth: we are funny little creatures. There's a wonderful irony in that. It becomes the raw material of humor, the comedy of being human. Without laughter, life would be too rigid to live, too serious to love, too heavy to carry. If your practice isn't keeping you laughing, something's really wrong.

From the expansive mind it cultivates, meditation opens a door to humor. No matter our wealth or status, sincere practice reminds us that we are ordinary humans passing through a vast universe. Once we really accept that, the absurdity of being human becomes obvious. We're tiny, temporary creatures trying to make sense of something immeasurably large, worrying about parking spots, the price of the dinosaur bones that run our cars, and what our bellies look like. All while floating on a living rock that, at this point in natural history, probably wishes we didn't exist.

That mismatch between cosmic scale and our little dramas is what makes the whole thing funny in a freeing way. We take ourselves so seriously in a universe that doesn't blink. We keep trying to understand what can't be understood, and somehow, in all this impossibility, we still care, still try, still enjoy ourselves and still reach for meaning. Whatever we think we are now isn't what we are next. Like nature, we change depending on conditions. We might be destroying life like a species killing asteroid, but we also make life interesting. Irony is funny.

It's an honor to watch myself transform in real-time through the storms, sunny days, and seasons of my life. It's usually a lot of fun. When I stop to look around, I'm always left with a sense of awe. I look up at the swirling, merging, transforming clouds and see me. I'm often immersed in the patterns of change. I fly away into endless skies without neglecting myself or interfering with the lives of the myriads of living beings that share space with me.

Meditation may seem dull at first, but when it becomes part of daily life, it reveals a depth and comfort that's not easy to describe. It settles into the day the way bird songs settle into the morning—dependable, soothing, and entirely unique. It feels like part of nature, yet asks nothing from it, not even the need to leave an imprint.

In the early years of my practice, I thought God or the universe was sending me messages and tried to find meaning in nature's sounds and movements. I didn't know that I was demanding things from nature and getting in its way. For example, instead of appreciating birds, I expected them to give me messages, forgetting that sometimes things simply exist, complete in their own presence. They say birds have little brains but really, I was the birdbrain. I thought birds cared about my little mind.

I had to work hard to see through the habits and superstitions that help us cope with our fears. Now I realize that birds talk and sing for bird reasons. I might learn why if I study them closely enough. If I go near a bird's nest, they'll certainly belt out an angry death-metal tune. Birds help us in ways we will never know. I remind myself of that when I'm scraping bird shit off my windshield.

I once hung out in the open desert with an ornithologist who talked to Babblers. He forced himself into their lives to save them from extinction. *(18)* That's a good reason to interfere with nature.

I spend a lot of time focused on trees and all their movements, including the water, soil, wind, insects, squirrels, vines, air plants, fungi, animals, and birds whisking about. As much as I can take in, I take. I take in a way that doesn't disturb the natural flow. More than anything else, I feel them, and they feel me.

A tree is all about maintaining balance, both its own and, as much as possible, that of its environment. I'm part of their environment, so they are aware of me. If I let them, they will help balance me. They aren't particularly interested in me, unless I disturb them. They share many of the personality traits of a true Zen master.

I taught myself to watch the totality of the scene without labeling the involved life forms or surmising what they might be up to. I focus on the whole movement of the tree, not the parts. Then I see the forest for the trees. I feel it intimately like a sentimental memory. This is clear-eyed immersion—seeing the whole before the mind rushes in to divide it.

I'm still little me, with all my habits, insecurities, and the smallness of my daily life but sometimes I'm not just me. I'm a little further than me. I feel as if I'm everything. I blend. I'm not aware that I'm Mark. I'm one with whatever I share my awareness with. I lose myself in my awareness.

Once, I realize I'm one with "not me," I'm immediately back to being my ordinary self again. That's the balance of nature at work. It does the work for me, but it took a lot of practice to be able to do this without messing up and forgetting things.

That smooth swing—from small to vast and back to small—is the practice of balance at its best. Not choosing one or the other, but moving directly between them without getting lost. It's the universe reminding me that I'm tiny and I'm part of everything at the same time, and somehow both are true. There's no contradiction.

I keep my deductive reasoning out of my life as much as possible, and it's a challenge. I let the balance seep in on its own terms. I invite it in by signaling that I'm open. I let trees in by being open to them. They talk, but don't say much. When they do, they sound so wise. It's hard to explain.

Nature talks when we stop and listen, for no reason other than to listen. If a friend is telling us something important, and we keep interrupting or aren't focused, they will stop expressing themselves and look elsewhere for connection. Clear-eyed immersion is the same—the world only opens when we stop trying to control what we experience.

It's on the mat where we first realize that an abstract thing like *not trying to control what we experience* is possible. We learn how to practice it when we bring it off the mat and into our lives— that's where it starts to matter. It's not like we intentionally make that leap. What shows up in meditation just starts popping up on its own as we move through our day, when it's ready.

We repeat it whenever we remember to follow what surfaced on its own. That's the moment we finally take over, when our intent and awareness become part of the practice—not a moment before. That's why I sometimes call my practice *intentionless*. It's intentionless until an intent rises out of stillness and silence—from the universe, from God, from the Coach, from nothing at all, whatever we choose to call it or not call it. And once our awareness is clear-eyed, whatever intent we had when we first sat down doesn't matter anymore.

Find a good tree to learn from or stare at a blank wall. Simplify your mind. Forget everything but follow the instructions at the end of this book. That's how you find your way out of the dark forest. Enter the wilderness of your mind and know exactly where you're going. At first, it may feel imposing. You'll make mistakes. It'll be hard. It'll hurt like hell. Things might look cloudy. But if you don't run from your pain or dodge your responsibilities, in time you'll immerse yourself in your original nature. Whether you realize it or not, you already are. Just follow the leader and get out of the way.

Chapter Eleven

Follow the Leader

Meditation helps us steady ourselves. It gives us a way to meet life without pushing, grabbing, or pretending we're in control. Over time, it teaches us to recognize the small pockets of balance inside us. Those pockets matter. They're the clearest things we have to follow. They may help us see that we are balance itself in the flesh. We might hear the wisdom of our heartbeat. Then, we might pick up a drum and play our heartbeat for our community. When I say "follow the leader," I don't mean a person or a doctrine. I mean the quiet balance that shows up in us when we're paying attention. Some people call that balance God. Some call it the universe. Some don't name it at all. I call it nothing—not because I don't respect it, but because naming it shrinks it down to my size, and my size includes my limitations and personality. Nothing keeps it open.

The universe isn't all light. It's full of dark space, chaos, violence, and randomness. But inside all that, small pockets of order appear—stars, planets, life, and us. We're temporary clearings in a never-ending cosmic storm. When we follow the balance inside us, we're following the most stable thing the universe offers.

When we start anything—football, meditation, a job—we begin with enthusiasm. Then life happens. We lose trust in someone. We don't get the results we expected. We follow the wrong leader, or we follow our own unrealistic ideas. Eventually, we learn that the only leader worth following is the one that steadies us from the inside.

Meditation still feels like a workout to me. Not exciting. Not glamorous. But it keeps me aligned. It gives me the same grounded feeling I get from exercise—not pleasure, but strength. It helps me follow the voice I've come to trust. Most days I don't call it anything. I just follow it. When I need a word, I call it nothing. Nothing keeps it simple. I just stare at the wall in silence. KISS: Keep it simple, silly.

How can "nothing" guide anything? How can sitting still do so much good? I don't know. I don't need to. I just know I'm better off doing it. Meditation is doing, not thinking about doing. It has led me to new people, ideas, jobs, responsibilities, and places, but never to a final destination. It leads me back to the same simple center again and again. That center feels like nothing because it doesn't demand a name. When I'm with it, it doesn't need me to call it anything at all. It just needs someone, in this vast universe, to shut up and listen.

You may think this book is nothing, and in the big picture, you're right. No matter how much someone values what I say, I'll never think I'm their leader. I'm not staring at trees or walls expecting an outcome, to unravel the universe, become rich and famous, or because I want to become an arborist, plasterer, or guru. I do it because it helps me appreciate the small pocket of balance I was given, in an otherwise wild universe, without wasting the opportunity.

Coming back to balance after losing ourselves is the first part of practice. The deeper part is returning smoothly, without residuals. It's letting go. That's following the leader—our unified nature. We can follow it in how we think, respond, and meet our responsibilities. When we practice like that, we come back to center without hesitation. We return with our breath. It's simple. We begin again over and over.

We go out into nature to remember who we are. Then we return to our responsibilities. It's like a heartbeat—out and in, rise and fall. The same heart causes both motions. Our brains let us experience life, but without the heart leading the way, the mind is nothing.

I try to avoid extremes. Extremes exist in the mind first. They turn the heart cold. The middle is my leader. Sometimes practice means stepping into the thick of things. Other times it means stepping back. We may think "eternal truth" is separate from ordinary life, but it isn't. Everything is sacred.

Ordinary life leads our spirituality. Ordinary life is balance until it isn't. When things go bad or we lose someone we love, that's when faith is tested. When things are going well, who needs faith? We're not looking to be blessed by God. We're looking to feel blessed, even when our little lives feel lousy.

The shock of loss is extreme. Extremes are imbalance. But other beings—human and nonhuman—help us find our way. Nature takes the lead. The way is in the mind, and help is in the form. Sometimes we see it. Sometimes we don't. Sometimes we turn help into a problem because we're the problem.

Seeds taught me nearly everything I know. A seed receives everything it needs from the Earth. So do we. To see clearly, I follow nature's lead. Nature doesn't lie or manipulate. It shows the way by being itself. I follow.

Jesus pointed out the faith and balance of the lilies of the field. (19) He said that by following them closely, we could see there's no need to toil through life. Some of his followers stretch his teachings too far. I'm not sure he'd be pleased. But the lilies are content with what nature provides, and that was his point. They can lead us back to God.

It's curious how the name "Jesus" can turn us on or off. If you believe in him, you may judge those who don't. If you don't, you may judge those who do. That's balance too, but not the kind we usually think of. That's why I try to act like the lily—content with what nature or God provides, unfettered by names, sermons, judgments, and outcomes.

Is it time to feel again? Good feelings scare us because we know we'll lose them. Bad feelings scare us because they show how little control we have. A lily is beautiful because it's dying right in front of us. So are we. Death takes the lead eventually. It reminds me to take my practice seriously so I can live the rest of my life as a shrewd and knavish sprite without a name.

If you feel something today, you're feeling you again. Not me. You're following the leader. It's the same water, soil, light, warmth, freedom, stability, and earth we all need to grow. You're reconnecting with your nature, which is the same leader as mine and everything else—including lilies. It's nothing to fear. It's nothing and everything at once.

We rediscover the balance that leads us. Naming it can make us lose it. It's free. We may not be. Nature sends what we need, but sometimes we deny it or can't see it. We make mistakes. We get in nature's way because we can't see our own. When we disrupt the natural rhythm for personal gain, everyone eventually feels the loss.

I try to live a unified experience. It's a rhythm or wave more than anything else. I surf and dance to a middle way. Just like a surfer cares about the ocean and a dance instructor cares about their studio, I care about the environment. I don't understand how everyone can't see we need to clean up our act. But I also know I can think that way because I'm privileged enough to see things more expansively.

I'm not starving. I'm not in danger. I'm not trapped in a family business or waiting for a trust fund. I'm surviving on my own. So how could I expect things to change when my privilege is a result of things not changing? The Veterans Administration takes good care of me. It's funded by the same resources that young people fight and die for, far away from home.

I don't think big like that anymore. It usually just drags me down. I can't do anything to change things, if I'm too busy talking about it all the time. I just do what I can. I help veterans navigate the VA system and maybe find a little peace in front of a wall.

If I had more resources, I'd do more. I learned that on my porch when a rich, famous person asked why everyone didn't have solar panels, windmills and veggie-oil cars like him. I said, "Dude, normal people can't afford that. They have to eat and pay rent." He was shocked. I should have been gentler.

I don't hold so much frustration anymore. I try not to judge. I trust that balance and compassion will win out because they work. I trust God, or the value of these things in the long chain of evolution. We do the best we can with what we have.

We return to our original nature in meditation so we can see it in our place, our time, our bodies, and our conditions. That same nature shows up in our emotions. The sun is radiant, life-giving, violent, and wild—no wonder we are too. In terms of leaders, there's no brighter one than the sun.

The sun doesn't rise or set—but it seems that way because we're the ones spinning. It's primordial, older than anything we can imagine, and closer to God or the universe than any human teacher. Humans used to worship it. That's going a little too far. It's better to appreciate it. It gives warmth and vitamin D, yet too much of it burns us and hurts our eyes. Even the sun needs balance. It holds itself together, but it flares, reminding us that nothing in the universe stays gentle forever.

When pre-civilization humans lit the first fire, they were only copying what the sun had already shown them. Its energy could meet all our needs if we ever appreciated our nature. When we look up, we see light from eight minutes ago and a memory billions of years old, from when the sun first steadied. We're seeing an ancient version of ourselves too, because everything we are came from that same fire.

I don't think about practice anymore either. I appreciate the sun. I do the sun. It's in me. It talks to me in a strange language. Meditation brings out the light and warmth in me. It's the most balanced an unbalanced man like me can be. I daydream, judge, soak in the sun, love, laugh, worry, get stressed, act delusional, think I know something, and then catch myself. I go back to the upright position like a lily. All flowers bend toward the light. The sun is life's leader no matter who or what created it. How could we bitch when it gets in our eyes in traffic?

In meditation, we pause the march of time. We stop letting big ideas and fears get in the way. We feel the warmth of the sun in our bones. We watch ourselves change. We try our simple mind on for size.

We laugh at the games we play. We see our life as one big broken campaign promise—the kind we made to ourselves. It reminds us to be careful about what we vote for inside our own minds. We might try to vote for something other than our pain. People win elections, but pain always seems to come out on top.

Politicians know how to speak directly to our shadows. They live there. They talk to our disappointments, our fears, our old bruises. They preach to the part of us that feels overlooked. It's the same type of big personality showing up in different little forms, each one promising to fix what hurts.

That's how the little guy gets pulled in, even when no one person can ever change anything alone. There is one exception: staring at a wall. A wall doesn't promise anything. It doesn't flatter, persuade, or sell. It just holds still long enough for the truth to catch up. It's *anti-politics*.

If I follow my pain or keep going back to what happened back then, I miss "now." "Then" doesn't help—it points in both directions. Some *thens* are behind us. Some may never arrive. One word stretches across the whole timeline and still tells us nothing about where we are. So where are you? What's leading you? The past you already lived? Pain? The future you're imagining? Or the only place anything ever happens—now.

I practice no past or future until they arise. Where do they arise? In the mind. Why? That's the mind's way. Our way is to know the mind's way without attaching to whatever madness appears. Let it settle. Then choose what's next. Let the present be present by paying attention. Paying attention is following the leader. Let a lily or the air lead you, and if God is your judge, he will judge you very favorably in the end.

We can't follow flowers and air all day. We have responsibilities. I focus on mine for two reasons: one, I appreciate the miracle of life and want to leave the world better; and two, for me. We might be selfless, but it's not wise to forget ourselves. When we think we're being selfless for God or truth alone, we get into trouble.

We experience everything through our filters. We need to take care of our pets, families, bodies, money, homes, communities, forests, air, water, and planet. We get a lot out of life. We can't be all take and no give and stay healthy. But we can't be all give and no take either. Sometimes following the leader means leading ourselves back and forth to the center.

The balance required to live, ride a bike, care for a pet, be in the moment, bloom like a lily, show compassion, or find peace is the same. Reality is nothing and everything we can and can't conceive. But balance is practical. Unrealistic expectations get in the way. When we try to know the mind of God or solve everything, we interupt an otherwise natural process. When we carelessly destroy life, we limit freedom. We forget that a good leader puts the team first.

We need to remember we're human. There's a limit. If we chase balance too hard, we lose it. Good intentions don't change that. We may admire the lilies, but we aren't lilies. Our lives are more complicated. We have to stay practical. An impractical practice defeats itself. Practice = practical. It's so simple. Yet, it's not.

Practice is like juggling a hot potato. You're trying not to get burned while letting the air cool things down. If we're paying attention, that's the best we can do: stay alert, stay honest, and not scorch ourselves with our own good intentions. Sometimes that alertness means asking a practical question, like whether it's realistic to be compassionate toward a bunch of baby cockroaches.

One morning, I lifted my meditation mat and found hundreds of tiny white specks gathered around a giant roach. The specks scattered into the crack between the molding and the floor. The roach didn't move. I thought it had died and the babies were feeding on it. Then I saw movement—it was a pregnant roach still in labor.

I had a dilemma. My practice is compassion for all beings, but I had a busy day. I gently moved the mother roach outside. A gecko ate her whole within seconds. All that remained were her legs hanging from the lizard's mouth like cat whiskers.

Mother Nature showed me who's in charge.

I checked under the mat again. The babies had returned to the spot where their mother had been. I felt compassion. They didn't know she was gone. What leader were they following?

I tried to move them, but they scattered. I looked at the time. I was late. I put the mat down, waited for them to return, lifted it, vacuumed them up, and moved on. Meditation was more practical than doing the impossible.

They had no chance without their mother. Saving them would have created more problems. If we think we can save motherless roaches, we're fooling ourselves. And if we did, child services might come and take our kids away because of the infestation. The same thing happens in practice. If we meditate for liberation, liberation won't come, but problems will. Our minds will be infested with ideas of enlightenment.

When I first started meditating, I had to learn patience, discipline, and realistic expectations. I had to understand which intentions were leading me.

Someone would say "Happy Easter" or "Merry Christmas," and I'd say, "I don't believe in that." I thought I was being honest. But that response separated me. It singled me out when what I wanted was to feel part of my community.

Now I just say "Happy whatever" and smile. I might add, "Isn't this time of year great?" Not to overcompensate, but because I mean it. Practice opened my mind. It taught me that fitting in doesn't require agreement—only presence. Balance teaches us how to act naturally. Even meditation is subject to balance. It *is* balance. That's all it is.

Reality can lead us, but we need to consider its vastness and our limits. If compassion leads us, we need to consider it realistically. Otherwise, it becomes harmful. Crawling around trying to be compassionate isn't wise. When we try to help, we interfere. We might throw off the balance of nature. It took me a long time to understand the value of treading lightly.

I had to learn how to navigate the insecurities and emotional swings of any new relationship. I had to let awareness lead me, not the uncontrollable thoughts and feelings that arise all day. Now I trust meditation and trust myself through practice. It helps me make practical decisions. I feel better and more. I can love again. I'm not confused about why it's in my life.

I don't waste time trying to save roaches that will turn my house into an unsafe place. I don't hate them, but if they come into my space, I kill them without losing my balance or compassion.

Meditation is part of my family. I can count on it. It helps me make better decisions. It keeps my home in order because it feels warm and stable, like home. I don't need to be anyone else at home. I can be myself. I couldn't be the son, father, brother, coworker, partner, teammate, mentor, friend, or community member I am without it. Home is a state of mind. Home is everywhere. Home is the leader. We all want to feel at home in ourselves and the world. That's why we practice.

I try to carry a steady pragmatism and warmth. I don't force my way on others. My practice isn't a heavy suitcase or a flashy advertisement. It leads gently. It's subtle. It's free and airy, as if it's not even there. It feels that way because it's my way of life. I don't doubt it. Meditation has helped me be more hospitable to myself and others. It shows me new ways to be kind and helpful when I least expect it. That's leadership.

My approach is to adapt to the situation. Whatever stabilizes things is appropriate. Sometimes I can't do anything, or my intent makes things worse. That's how I learn. Mistakes are leaders too.

Accepting how little I control is part of practice. I direct what I can and let the rest go. Sometimes leadership is letting go of the need to lead.

Meditation is simple, which makes it hard to believe in its potential. It's a way of thinking, not thinking, acting, not acting, and feeling, inspired by the balanced posture of the body. Over time, the body's balance rubs off on the mind. We let the body lead. That's the heart of this chapter—the leader isn't a guru, doctrine, or fantasy.

The leader is balanced body itself, but balance doesn't stand alone. It's the pocket of order inside a universe that's mostly chaos, endless darkness, and violence. God or the universe is the larger leader—the whole thing—but it's too vast and unstable to follow directly. What we can follow is the part of it that settles. That settling is balance, and the most stable living expression of that balance is compassion.

People in my conservative community ask all the time, “Do you believe in Jesus?” The answer is yes—but not in the way they expect. Yes to the Jesus who said, “Turn the other cheek.” Yes to the Jesus who said, “Let him who is without sin cast the first stone.” Yes to the Jesus who pointed to the lilies of the field and said they do not toil or spin, yet they are cared for. Yes to the Jesus who lived a life of compassion. Not the version who judges, condemns, and sends people to hell for not worshipping a name instead of living compassionately.

So, when he said, “No one comes to the Father except through me,” it makes sense to hear it as pointing to the way he lived, not the personality he carried. Not his mere human name, the man, but the path—compassion, forgiveness, steadiness, the open way that lets the universe rest in a human being for a moment. If there’s a doorway to anything sacred, that’s the one.

Compassion is the highest evolution of the universe inside a human being. It’s the most sacred quality in most religions because it’s the one place where God can find rest. *Blessed be the peacemaker.* It’s the warm, steady behavior the universe keeps trying to produce through us. It’s the most balanced a person can be, and that’s why it survives. That’s why it keeps showing up generation after generation.

So, my trinity is simple: God or the universe is the whole, balance is the pocket we live in, and compassion is the most authentic expression of that pocket. Compassion is the part that can actually be followed. It’s the leader that stays within reach.

It’s like a heartbeat. Hearts were beating long before ours, and they beat because something in the universe found a rhythm worth repeating. When forcing stops and listening begins—to breath, to body, to responsibility, to compassion—that rhythm returns. The leader becomes clear.

Follow that, and everything else follows naturally.

We hear "letting go" often, but I didn't understand it until I could do it. Letting go isn't an idea—it's lived. It's followed. It's letting go to the highest form of balance. It's compassion. And when you follow compassion long enough, you start to see where it comes from. It tells you its story, and you listen. It arises out of emptiness. When it comes into the room, you feel it. The center of balance doesn't feel like a thing. It doesn't feel like a belief. It doesn't feel like a personality. It feels like nothing—open, steady, and free of sides. That's why we call it freedom.

I call freedom nothing, but not because it lacks meaning. I call it nothing because it **is** empty—empty in the best possible way. Empty of my personality, my ambitions, my habits, my limitations, and the little stories I tell myself. If I give it a fixed name, I shrink it down to my size, and my size includes all the things that get in the way.

Naming it tightly drags it into my preferences and opinions. Nothing keeps it open. This is why I don't practice Zen. I practice nothing. Zen comes with thousands of years of heavy baggage, things like Japanese imperialism that I want no parts of. It has the potential to defeat its own purpose. Everything I do and say is meant to help Zen, not destroy it. But really, all I do is try to be more compassionate. Not talking about it but just *doing* it. Sometimes, I'm too tired and need to take care of myself. I shut up and stare at my wall for a week or two.

Emptiness is what protects our practice. It's emphasized so much in Buddhism for this very reason. It keeps the center from becoming another identity we perform. It keeps me from turning practice into a job title—dharma heir, guru, arborist, plasterer, or whatever else the mind invents when it wants to feel important. Nothing keeps Big Mind from collapsing into little mind.

We usually think a big personality means a big mind, but it's the opposite. Big personality is little mind—loud, certain, rigid, and easily threatened. Little personality is big mind—ordinary, open, steady, and not trying to be anything. Nothing keeps me in the second category as much as possible. It keeps the space wide enough for compassion to grow without becoming ideology.

Nothing is also where balance comes from. It's the same emptiness the universe or God uses to evolve, unite in balance, bring forth life and perpetuate compassion—trial and error, openness, spontaneity, no fixed plan. My practice mirrors that.

To follow the leader fully, I eventually had to learn to trust nothing. I couldn't let go of anything until I knew nothing on an intimate level. I had to be empty enough for it to feel comfortable speaking. And when it finally did, it didn't give me a doctrine or a revelation. It said four words—"Be nothing. Just be." What the hell does that mean?

Chapter Twelve

Faith in Nothing

My meditation practice began to bear fruit after I was excluded and ostracized by the leaders of my spiritual community. The shock forced me to rely on the simplicity of sitting with the wall rather than on cultural authority or community approval. I developed what I later called "raw acceptance"—a faith that nature or God knows what it's doing, and that my job was to stop interfering with what was already unfolding. When I paid attention to my moment-to-moment experiences, things clarified on their own. I didn't listen to gossip, defensive voices, or the noise of my own insecurity. That's faith in nothing—trusting the living movement of reality itself. It doesn't need my mind. My mind only distorts what is already clear. My job is to not interfere with balance and assume its position whenever I can.

Years ago, I held unrealistic spiritual expectations and didn't know the difference between theory and practice. Before I understood my limitations, I tried to push the universe into calling me into service. My expectations got in the way of nature. The turning point came when a seasoned leader in my Zen group began acting so erratically that I could no longer stay silent. When I exposed the behavior, I was ostracized.

It was the first of many incidents. Even after that leader was eventually asked to leave the group and I was vindicated, the pattern continued. The leaders kept questioning my authenticity, accusing me of using their tradition and reputation to promote myself. At times they even publicly humiliated me, behaving as if they owned Soto Zen Buddhism. Each incident cut deeply because it happened in a community devoted to compassion. Besides the smell of death, there's no worse smell than that of hypocrisy.

Despite the discomfort of the situation, I refused to get involved in rumors. I stepped out. I trusted a timeless voice—my Coach—to guide me. I knew nothing in comparison. Zen wasn't theoretical anymore. It teaches that when we feel attacked or misunderstood, the real practice is not reacting from imbalance, not taking our ego so seriously, and not letting hurt feelings run the show. It teaches us to see through the negative emotions, stay compassionate, and rely on the timeless view rather than the wounded one.

Basically, I did nothing and trusted it. It was nothing because I didn't plot, scheme, or try to predict the ending. Trusting nothing helped me stay focused even when emotions were overwhelming. I did the opposite of what my hurt feelings told me. That's balance.

I listened to pain as a natural manifestation of the universe. I stopped thinking and speaking when others were thinking and speaking poorly. That too was balance. My problems resolved when I stopped asking for permission or approval—when I stopped needing someone else to validate my understanding of the tradition and trusted my own direct experience.

My nameless faith solved everything. I put my body in a balanced position, and my mind followed. My confidence soared because it was finally free from needing to be held up by anyone else. This is why I'm constantly telling you to lose your dependence on teachers and authority figures and depend on yourself.

I focused on the growth an uncomfortable experience sparked. I worked with my attachments to status and belonging. I contained the impulse to prove my "rightness." I let go because I realized we all must let go in the end. I returned to the wall's simplicity. I did nothing and let nature take care of the rest.

I forgave the people who hurt me because I had hurt others and sought forgiveness myself. I took myself less seriously. It wasn't life or death—just people being people. Learning is often uncomfortable. I found solace in my family, relationships, lineage, meditation, and nature. I paid attention to paying attention. I remembered everything happens on a tiny blue ball in an endless universe. I let my big mind run the show.

When I was publicly criticized, I was forced to practice. I relied on the expansiveness my Zen tradition claimed to represent. In silence, the wisdom of the infinite universe advised me as much as I could listen. I had faith in nothing I could conceive or manipulate. I didn't doubt it for a minute.

Without planning or revenge, I grew quickly. My pain became fertilizer. I let go of my drive to be accepted or socially relevant. Fixating on others' views proved pointless; only my intentions mattered. The Coach told me, "Have faith in nothing but (X)—just focus." I trusted that voice. I believed in nothing and understood what it meant. Time and time again, I practiced letting go.

I called God or the universe "nothing" because it was empty of my discriminatory mind. I stopped trying to figure it out or ask it for anything. I accepted everything it gave me, including my separation from my group. I refused to let others' actions deter me. I never felt separated from my community because I didn't let anger win. My practice won because I never quit. I stopped calling Zen—*Zen* and focused exclusively on putting myself in a silent, balanced position.

The social challenges helped me rise above jealousy and insecurity—old childhood traces. After everything I'd survived—bullies, bullets, bombs, addictions, jail—I let peer pressure influence me. I couldn't believe that I was still susceptible to that kind of influence. Once I saw it for what it was, I liberated myself. Coach said, "No more. Practice nothing."

My dependence on my tradition ended when I was shown the way, but not in the way the masters or my teacher envisioned. My separation from Zen led to independence from external influences. Silence taught me to focus on the life I had, not the one I lost. I developed faith in nothing—trusting the larger movement of life itself. I only saw it once I stopped trying to steer it or rely on others.

I humbled myself before creation. I dropped out of myself and into nothing. What I thought was wrong became a gift. I accepted my limitations. I could've handled things better, but I learned. I realized my tribe was the entire universe. I put my instincts into a broader perspective. I had more hope in nothing than something. I stopped relying on Buddhist figures and focused on the Buddha within me. The experience taught me how to let go. What remained was sustainable confidence. I couldn't have planned it. I was a conduit for something larger.

I owe my faith in nothing to the people who forced me out. I give them full credit. But I speak on my own terms now. My faith in nothing—no doctrine, no hierarchy, no fixed identity—let me penetrate the marrow of Zen and left me with a freedom not borrowed from anyone. I wouldn't be so confident or self-sufficient without those difficult situations. My stability isn't contingent on outside factors. I moved past the culture of Zen and focused on the balance of practice itself. That's the heart of faith in nothing—trusting what remains when everything else falls away.

My problems resolved themselves when I trusted my own nature without asking it to protect or reward me. I stopped identifying with Zen to apply its teachings. My intent became simple: assume the balance of nature for no reason other than to appreciate it. Nothing missing, nothing extra. Nothing is just right.

Practice gives me confidence that carries into everything. It lets me feel life's richness. I don't feel alone—my practice always shows up. The wall is my friend. Birds and trees are my teachers.

Air is fun to play with. I'm naive again, open again. I love people. I appreciate my life and tradition. I have faith in nothing.

Now I accept what I can't control. I do what needs to be done—meditate, care for myself and others, go to the doctor, clean the toilet. That's balance—nothing mystical, nothing complex. Just life, met directly. Those who wronged me now do me right. I nurture that understanding.

I value simplicity in a complex world. I don't question it anymore. There's nothing to question. In stillness, I rediscover balance. Sometimes it's warm; sometimes it sucks. But I trust the movement behind all things. I leave the reasons to nature, evolution, God, Chi—whatever name people use. I call it nothing. It doesn't matter what I call it. It "is" (X). It knows what it's doing.

My foundation is faith in the wholeness of nature. I feel it everywhere—in my children, friends, coworkers, strangers, animals, water, the unseen. Even in those who hurt me. I have all the fuel I need right here. In front of me is the infinite emptiness I return to for fullness and meaning. When I accept that, I let my faith in nothing inspire me. I welcome my original nature back in. Despite injustice and uncertainty, I trust the infinite diversity beyond me. This is how I bow my head and give thanks—not on a pulpit or in a robe with an audience, but in silence.

I know far more than you, but I'd be a fool to think "I" know it. I know nothing and that's something you'll never admit. Or will you? Here's your chance. I step outside cultural constraints and return to an inner refuge. I define myself by how I engage with reality moment to moment. Sometimes I need protection; sometimes I embrace a fuller experience that defies description.

People talk about being open and empty, but I keep it simple. To be open is to catch myself when I'm closed. Cold teaches warmth. Losing dreams teaches what it feels like to have nothing left. It's scary, then liberating. Awareness takes years. We respond poorly many times before responding well. And we still make mistakes. If we aren't relaxed and ready, we can't catch ourselves. If we think we know something, we know nothing.

To find my niche, I returned to my authentic nature. I let social pressures go. I released the hot air. I emptied myself. I embraced nothing. Through trial and error, I faced my anger and gave it space to dissipate.

Slowly, the social aspects of practice returned. Buddha attracts Buddha. Even Buddha needs friends. Come see me—we'll have a drink. Reach out to me, teachers of Zen. Learn something. Teach a willing student. Go back to the beginning. I offer you a way. If you followed me this far, we might connect. We can't do it alone. The universe is interdependent. I'm nothing by myself. When I realize this, I'm pure awareness.

SNAP—then I'm reminded how far I am from pure. A cue to take practice more seriously. Back and forth. Free, but within boundaries. My mind has no borders, but life does. So, I move between them. Here and there. Like a tennis ball bouncing across the court. Wherever the ball lands—that's (X). That's where I meet myself again. That's boundless freedom: not escaping the court, but moving with the volleys.

Maybe I bounce freely because I know how to land inbounds? When I'm out, I accept it and return. I trust the universe to play me in the right direction.

I try to live without fixed ideas. Zen goes on and on and warns about fixed ideas, but who listens? Sometimes we just need to be nothing. And nothing is enough. I don't need you to judge me, and I don't want to judge you. Life will test my faith. I'll get caught in the net plenty of times. I'm not a professional, priest, prophet, scholar, or Zen master. I'm not trying to win a game. I don't compete anymore because I'm nothing and admit it. I let go before nature forced me to.

I'm retired from the dharma (truth) game. My title is (X). Practice isn't a brand. It's faith in ungraspable change. No one owns it. There's nothing to gain. That's why I call my practice nothing. I have complete faith in (X).

Still think you can control nothing?

Try to capture the breeze. We capture things in our minds all the time. Do we see what we catch, or not? Catch, let go—that's balance. REALIZE the ways of the mind. Adapt to its habits and tendencies. It's been around a lot longer than we have. Meet it where it is. Stop trying to control it and it settles. Silent, inexplicable. Then we'll appreciate the simplest things. *fwwwwwwwwww... fwwwwwwwwww...* Ah, the spring breeze is all I need to put things into perspective. It's taught me far more about letting go than any Zen master has.

Chapter Thirteen

A Spring Breeze

Winter always teaches us the same lesson: stop. Everything slows, stiffens, tightens. Even the mind freezes into shapes it didn't choose. But like winter turning to spring, there comes a moment when stopping becomes the beginning of movement again. A spring breeze doesn't announce this shift. It doesn't choose who feels it. It doesn't check whether you're ready. It simply arrives, brushing past your cheek with the same generosity it offers the whole world. Everyone gets a chance equally. Let those with senses appreciate the whisper of the wind.

Genuine meditation is like a breeze. It doesn't come with a curriculum or a promise. It slips in quietly, cool against the skin, clearing the air without asking what you believe or how long you've been struggling.

A spring breeze doesn't move the heavy things in your life. It doesn't shove the couch across the room or rearrange the furniture of your personality. But it *does* lift the dust off those heavy things. It reveals what's been sitting there all along. It shows you the surface again. It shows you what's yours to move and what's not. That's how practice works—not by force, but by clearing the air around what already exists.

Like the breeze, the inner Coach in us changes form. It's not the same shape every day. It's not even a voice, not really. I don't know what it is. But it makes sense when it moves through. It's the balanced part of us that knows when to lean, when to loosen, when to begin again. It belongs in the right season. It arrives when the conditions are right. It's natural. It's our original nature remembering itself.

We stop movement to start anew. We stop to appreciate. And the breeze whispers, not shouts, "You don't have to push so hard."

In practice, we learn to handle life's pressures the way a tree handles wind—by bending, not breaking. We direct what we can and let the rest go. We address real problems and don't invent new ones. We stop long enough to feel the smallest things, because the smallest things are often the biggest. A spring breeze is invisible, but it's here. Invisible reality doesn't disappear just because we wish it away. It's here to stay, and it always has been.

Sometimes the breeze says, "Clear a little space and I'll show you what's already here." And sometimes it says nothing at all, because silence is its native language. If we stop and listen, it speaks. If we rush past it, it still moves through us—we just miss the message. If we try to force the breeze into giving us a message, if we expect things from it, it won't.

My sister Janet once told me I look different every time she sees me. I took it as a compliment. When we accept things on the inside, people see it outside. Peace outside starts with order inside. A messy house, like a messy mind, eventually demands attention. But order doesn't come from panic. Order restores itself when we start small. A spring breeze always reminds us about spring cleaning—not the frantic kind, but the gentle kind that begins with opening a window.

If the mess is too big, anxiety can freeze us into doing nothing. In winter, that makes sense. But what if we're frozen year-round? What if fear becomes our climate? Then we start where we can. A closet. A drawer. A single corner. Once the closet is cleared, the rest of the house feels possible again. The breeze drifts through the open window and says, "See? One step at a time."

When fresh air sweeps in, it feels like starting over. That's the spirit of practice—to always be a beginner, curious, enthusiastic, in awe of learning. If you feel spring, you feel the spring in you. If you don't, that's on me. If you stare at the wall and think nothing, you spring into action without moving. That's the breeze again—the lightness that comes from clearing space.

If you like my breezy nature and want more spring in your step, you can explore the history, ethics, and customs of the Zen tradition I draw from. Many people far wiser than me can guide you through that terrain. But honestly, you'd be better off jumping into my breeze and letting it carry you like a kite. You don't need a pool of knowledge—you need air. You need space. You need the freedom to drift a little.

My notes in the back are like a scavenger hunt, each number pointing to a person, book, song, or idea that helped shape this moment. They're little gusts of wind changing direction. Point (X) is simply where our lives meet the breeze—your history, my history, and the air passing through both.

(X) can show up anywhere. Sometimes it's a quiet moment on the cushion. Sometimes it's a sudden shift in the wind. And sometimes it's a rooftop outside Philly where you realize the world has more turf lines than you ever imagined.

In my twenties, I worked for my aunt's boyfriend, who owned a roofing company. Roofing teaches you about territory—literal turf. Every crew protects its patch of sky. Every boss guards his edge. When I ran a small ad to start my own budget roofing company, the calls poured in, but they weren't customers. They were competitors threatening me for undercutting.

Philly didn't play around back then. Raspy people on the other end of the phone said things like, "You better hope Angelo doesn't find out what the f*** you're doing." That was the beginning and end of my roofing career. Funny how (X) can be a rooftop, a threat, or a breeze—whatever wakes you up.

Today, I'm part of the Soto Zen tradition, but nothing is "my" practice. It might be better to tell people I'm a roofer. It doesn't matter what I call it in stillness and silence. I shy away from Buddhist-centric terms and titles. I don't want people called Roshi Angelo (or any other name) feeling threatened by what I do. Territory is territory, and people protect theirs. Even in spiritual circles, turf lines run deep. Some folks guard their lineage like a rooftop crew guarding their patch of sky.

Helping people can be tough when they don't appreciate it, but their appreciation is extra. What could I possibly expect? When we're struggling, we only see struggles. When we see the world as an expert, it shapes the world around our expertise.

I enjoy life more by helping. I help people for myself. I'm less defensive and uptight. And when I let myself be breezy, I find my tribe—not because they share my weird tendencies, but because they can breathe easily around me. I don't hang out with them to get attention or to point out how enlightened I am and how ordinary they are. A breeze doesn't have expectations. It just moves through. People relax around it because it isn't trying to be anything other than what it is.

Some within the Zen tradition take practice very seriously and protect their turf with the ferocity of a Silverback Gorilla. We have the essential nature of gorillas, but our relative conditions differ. We're basically the same animal, but humans complicate things with stories, roles, and reputations. Gorillas don't. They read the wind—scents, danger, mating, family, home. They don't overthink it. They don't write essays about it. They just know. They feel the shift in the air and respond. That's original nature. That's the breeze again.

A meditation practice is like a spontaneous, ecstatic dance. *(20)* It's simple and fresh like a spring breeze. If your dance teacher belittles you, reconsider who leads. Dance is self-expression. Balance is key. An imbalanced leader acts unnatural. If your teacher or practice makes you wobblier, it's unbalanced. It may be time to drift with your own current—to follow the wind that's actually blowing, not the one someone insists should be blowing.

Gorillas dance in the breeze too, in their own way. They sway, they shift, they spring into action when the moment calls for it. They don't give long-winded speeches about balance. They *embody* it. A good teacher does the same. They don't tell you how to move—they move with you. They don't demand you follow—they stand in the middle, where the wind meets itself. They don't inflate themselves with hot air. They have the chutzpah to recognize when they're full of it and the humility to empty out again.

That's the thing about a breeze: it's empty, but not hollow. It's full of movement, but not noise. I can't always be empty like the breeze. Sometimes I stay full to protect myself. That's the balance between human nature and everything else. I'm whatever I need to be or not be. But when I'm breezy, when I'm not trying to be a dharma heir or a master or a rooftop boss, people around me can exhale. They can say, "It's a great day to go fly a kite on the beach. Come on, man—let's go."

A strong practice is always in progress and always humble. It doesn't cling to one shape. It allows new perspectives to form the way clouds shift in the sky—not by effort, but by conditions. When the air changes, the clouds change. When the mind changes, the world changes.

An open mind is relaxed, full of "aha" moments and self-deprecating humor. It's not desperate to belong to something more. We find our tribe when we're just being ourselves. Meditation helps me feel like I fit in and stops me from trying to stand out. I follow the leader, and he's always in the middle. What does that mean? It's the calm center where opposing currents cancel out. Not stillness, not chaos—the balanced point between them. The place where nothing pushes you around.

It takes courage to be intimate with our limitations and accept them. It's hard to believe when I look back. Practice worked because I trusted Suzuki Roshi when he said it's not helpful to expect results or to gain anything from practice. *(21)* What could we demand from a refreshing spring breeze that it doesn't already provide? You can't grab it. You can't own it. You can't force it to blow harder. You can only feel it when it comes and kiss it goodbye when it leaves.

People talk about half-empty or half-full glasses. I do my best to keep mine empty. Usually, we equate an empty glass with a negative or deprived disposition. In this case, it's the opposite. I'm open and ready to be filled until I'm not. Sometimes I can't be empty. Sometimes I stay full to protect myself. That's the balance between human nature and everything else. Emptiness isn't a moral achievement—it's a weather pattern. It comes and goes like everything else. Can you let go of emptiness and be empty?

A breeze isn't magic. It doesn't rearrange the heavy furniture of our lives. It only moves what's light enough to be carried. Sometimes it lifts the dust and shows us what's been sitting there. Sometimes it just blows dirt into a different corner. And sometimes—if we work with the wind instead of against it—it carries the dust right out the window. That's practice: not forcing change, but cooperating with the conditions that make change possible.

A fresh breeze after a rainstorm has that clean smell—the kind that makes you breathe deeper without thinking. That's what clarity feels like. Not enlightenment. Not fireworks. Just clean air after a storm.

I want to help you build a simple and stable foundation. I don't want to form an exclusive club or garner admiration. I have no desire to sit around a beach fire with an empire of brainwashed minions who laugh at my jokes, sing along to my songs, and nod in agreement.

One overqualified longshoreman who studied social movements said it best: "What starts here as a mass movement ends up as a racket, a cult, or a corporation." (*22*) Movements gather heat. Heat rises. And when there's too much heat, the breeze disappears. Hot air replaces fresh air. That's when people stop thinking clearly.

I'm starting a movement to stop a movement. We're all headed to the same place: death. It's a harsh drama to play a part in. Until my last wind blows, I need help breaking through my mental barriers. We can help each other liberate ourselves. I share my thoughts to invite you into yours. My goal isn't to make you anxious or insecure. But I had to experience a lot of anxiety and insecurity to learn how to transform into something free.

Anxiety is wind too—but it's the kind that blows in circles. It kicks up dust, stings the eyes, rattles the windows. It makes you think the whole house is shaking when it's really just the shutters. When the storm is inside us, we think the world is collapsing. But storms pass. They always do. And when they do, the air feels cleaner than before. That's the gift of anxiety: it clears the atmosphere once it's done tearing through.

When the windows open and fresh air sweeps in, it feels like starting over. Imagine if the whole world started over? Imagine the possibilities. The world starts over when we start over. Then, you might finally appreciate your own breeze—the one that's been blowing through your life since the beginning, waiting for you to notice.

What does the breeze tell me? It says, "I don't go on forever. New breezes come each spring. Each one a little different. Don't cling to me. Feel me while I'm here. Just sit."

We share a painful thought. We know that everything is temporary, even the sun and Earth. Spirituality is one way we cope with these uncertainties. Some call it an opiate. I call it nothing. Practicing with no answers is like a breeze—it moves through without needing to solve anything. It cools the heat of confusion and leaves clarity in its wake.

Can you practice living with no answers? Can you drop it and liberate yourself from confusion? Can you jump into the wind and let it carry you? Yes, you can. Just stare at the wall. If we sit there and do nothing long enough, we die time and time again. So, in a sense, we experience death while still living. It's not dramatic. It's not mystical. It's just the breeze blowing through an old room, clearing out stale air.

It's hard to explain, but accessible to experience. When I liberate myself from me, there is no me left to die. But then again, there is. Balance is needed for old energies to unite and self-organize into new creations. A spring breeze doesn't erase the space—it touches only what's light enough to lift. Fire needs air. Air needs space. Space needs nothing. And nothing is where everything begins.

No matter how, when, where, or what happens when I live and die—and everything in between—being balanced puts me in the best position. So, it's natural that I'm interested in balanced people, those friendly, fearless mavericks who ride change like windsurfers on big north-shore waves at night. They fly with the wind. They trust it. They know it. They let it lift them when it's time to rise and let it settle them when it's time to rest. I love watching them. They look like they're dancing with the sky.

I want you to call me out on my bullshit and accept it when I call you out on yours. And here's the thing: bullshit piles up too. So, pay attention to the wind. Stand on the right side of the pile. Awareness keeps the stink out of your face.

My job is to help you stare at the wall alone in your home without me. Anyone can do nothing. Anyone can feel a breeze. The breeze isn't mine to own. Nothing is just the space where you meet yourself.

Nothingness gets a bad reputation. People hear the word and think of voids, black holes, existential dread. But nothingness is just space. It's the room the breeze needs to move. It's the pause between thoughts. It's the gap where clarity slips in. When I say "nothing," I don't mean despair. I mean the clean, open feeling after we mop the floor—when the air smells new and the world feels washed. That's nothingness. It's the most refreshing thing we have.

We can't keep everything clean all the time. Steven Universe once said, "If every pork chop were perfect, we wouldn't have hot dogs." (*24*) It's silly, but it's true. Imperfection is the whole game. If everything were flawless, nothing would move. Nothing would grow. Nothing would breathe. The breeze needs uneven ground to travel. It needs warm air and cool air meeting. It needs contrast. Without contrast, there's no wind at all.

Socrates said we never step into the same river twice. *(25)* Actually, he didn't say it. Heraclitus did, but a lot of Athenians joked that Socrates stole

Heraclitus' material. We never feel the same breeze twice either. Each one is a little different. Each one carries a slightly new scent, a new temperature, a new direction. That's how practice works. You sit down thinking you're repeating yesterday, but the air is different. You're different. The world is different. The breeze that meets you today has never existed before. Each time we sit down to balance, we create something new.

Sometimes, when I meditate, I see an image of myself fade in and out—like a photograph losing contrast. Not disappearing, just stepping out. The edges blur. The face becomes less important. The story becomes less important. What's left is the feeling of being breathed, not the person doing the breathing. It's not mystical. It's not dramatic. It's just the breeze moving through a room that finally has space.

And sometimes my mind does something wild—it jumps, like Jack Nicholson in *The Shining*, I stick my face through the door and yell, "Here's Johnny!" (*23*) Not because I'm losing it, but because the mind loves to throw in a surprise cameo. It's a reminder that thoughts don't need to be profound to be noticed. They just blow in, blow out, and leave the room the way they found it.

After I meditate, I'm still me. Still human. Still flawed. Still capable of being stale. But a little lighter. A little cleaner. A little more aware of which way the wind is blowing. And that matters. Because bullshit piles up fast. And if you're not paying attention, you end up standing downwind from your own mess. So, keep an eye on the breeze. Stand on the right side of the pile. Awareness is practical like that.

The breeze doesn't belong to me. It doesn't belong to you. It doesn't belong to any lineage or teacher or tradition. It comes when it comes, leaves when it leaves, and returns in a new form each spring. There's a moment in practice when the masks fall away, the stories loosen, and the breeze moves through without asking permission. It doesn't stay long. It never does. But when it passes, something in you feels rearranged—not because the breeze changed anything heavy, but because you finally noticed what was light enough to move.

I used to think awakening would feel like a spotlight or a revelation. Something cinematic. Something with a soundtrack. But it's quieter than that. It's more like your car after a good washing. You don't celebrate it. You just feel good in it.

Sometimes I wonder if we're all just trying to remember something simple we forgot. Something we knew before we learned how to complicate everything. Maybe that's why staring at a wall works. It strips away the noise. It leaves you with nothing but the breeze moving across your face—the same breeze that's been blowing since the beginning, the same one that will keep blowing long after you're gone.

People ask me what I'm trying to teach. I'm not teaching anything. I'm just pointing at the wind. I'm saying, "Look. It's right there. Feel it." I'm saying, "You don't need me. You don't need a movement. You don't need a philosophy degree or a robe or a title. You just need to sit still long enough to notice what's already happening."

And when you do, you start to see how much of your life is shaped by things you never questioned—expectations, habits, fears, old stories, old storms. You start to see how much bullshit you've been standing downwind from. Then, you start to move. Not dramatically. Not heroically. Just a small shift to the other side of the pile. A little awareness goes a long way.

The breeze doesn't care who you are. It doesn't care what you've done. It doesn't care what you believe. It just moves through. It's the most democratic thing in the universe. It touches everyone the same way. And if you let it, it will show you how to touch the world the same way—lightly, honestly, without trying to own anything. Meditation is a simple breeze.

Practice isn't about becoming someone new. It's about becoming someone simple. Someone who can feel the breeze without needing to explain it. Someone who can sit in silence without needing to fill it. Someone who can laugh at their own mind when it jumps out like Jack Nicholson and yells "Here's Johnny!" for no reason at all.

Someone who can say, "I don't know," and mean it.

Someone who can say, "This is enough," and feel it.

Someone who can say nothing at all.

There's a point where the breeze stops being a metaphor and becomes something simpler—just air moving across your skin. No lesson. No symbolism. No spiritual meaning. Just a reminder that you're alive and the world is still happening with you.

I used to think awakening would feel like becoming someone else. Now I think it's more like becoming someone honest. Someone who doesn't need to pretend. Someone who can sit in silence without trying to fix it. Someone who can feel the breeze and not turn it into a sermon. Someone who can act naturally.

The truth is, we're all made of the same stuff. Same fears, same hopes, same dust, same wind. We're shaped by different storms, but the air that moves through us is shared. When the breeze passes through me, it's the same breeze that passes through you. It doesn't check credentials. It doesn't care about lineage. It doesn't care who's right or wrong. It just moves.

And when it moves, it carries pieces of us with it—the light pieces, the ones that aren't nailed down. The rest stays where it is until we're ready to lift it. Sometimes that takes a lifetime. Sometimes it takes a moment. Sometimes it takes staring at a wall long enough to realize the wall isn't the problem.

The breeze doesn't promise anything. It doesn't stay. It doesn't explain itself. It comes, it goes, and it leaves you a little different each time, even if you can't say how. That's enough. That's more than enough.

If there's anything I want you to take with you, it's this: you don't have to force your life into meaning. You don't have to chase enlightenment. You don't have to fix everything you think is broken. Just pay attention to the wind. Stand on the right side of the bullshit pile. And let the breeze do what it does.

Because in the end, we're the same. And in the end, we're different. And the breeze moves through both truths without choosing sides.

Chapter Fourteen

We Are the Same but Different

Mysteriously, meditation may help us recognize our essential interconnectedness while simultaneously acknowledging the uniqueness of our relative circumstances. If we persistently and sincerely sit still and quiet over time, we teach ourselves to pay attention. Unlike other natural beings, we have the unique ability to act against our long-term interests. The practice helps us maintain awareness of our interrelated existence and avoid causing unnecessary harm to ourselves or others. It helps us drive safely and enjoy the ride. That's the paradox: we are the same, but different—one road, many drivers.

I'm a "nothing-man" *(26)* because nothing feels lighter to haul down the road. I'm fundamentally lazy. I don't create more work for myself than necessary. I'm all about energy conservation. Keeping myself driving straight and safe is enough work.

We all have unique trips. I accept people who don't prefer my pace. I'll lend you a dollar at the next rest-stop vending machine if we cross paths. If you run out of gas and don't have roadside protection, I'll give you a lift to the gas station. Then we'll both be "on the road" again. *(27)*

Driving a big bus one day, I was really locked into the experience. As they say, I was one with the road. It occurred to me that I was captaining a vessel across the Milky Way Galaxy with a dozen or so seniors along for the ride. It was wild.

Suddenly, I noticed the white directional arrows on the road. It occurred to me that the culmination of the universe to the present point is the arrow pointing to everything in my limited view. It was a pretty cool thing to experience, but I quickly caught myself. I couldn't drift too far into outer space, or I would crash.

I view the outer world through my mind, but also as an infinite universe exploring itself. The inner world of my mind is the universe exploring its inner world through me. Outer and inner worlds are not separate. Meditation reveals this without needing to explain it.

How can we flow down the road of life unified like that? Be the tip of the arrow. Movement. Gone. Tip of the arrow. Movement. Gone. We, as the universe, are the tip of the arrow in the present racing through vast eternity. You might not understand that, but if you meditate long and sincerely enough, you just might. There's no need to understand it. You are already it.

We share the highway with aggressive drivers. They always seem to be speeding in the wrong direction of the arrows. Some of them operate in the name of God. The pious cut off the spirits of the downtrodden like a teenage boy in a souped-up, smoke-spewing pickup truck does an elderly lady in a compact car.

Reckless drivers hurt innocent people, and that's a shame, but God receives everything and balances it out. He keeps traffic flowing and ensures the road is as safe as possible. He cleans up our accidents. That's easy to say when a cowboy in a pickup isn't speeding my way in the wrong direction.

Maybe God gives those who misuse his name the middle finger on the turnpike of life? I'm giving them mine right now. Go ahead. Try lifting your middle finger. Why not? It feels good. It all comes out in the end. Regardless of our beliefs, we all meet at the old rest-stop in the sky.

Silent meditation practice is the least impactful thing we can do in our environment and still be "in" it. It's as close to nothing as something can get. It's the opposite of traffic and pollution. It cleans our minds and helps us stay stable and moving. It is like a vehicle that doesn't harm our environment, cruising down a wide-open lane. Could it be the best of both worlds?

One of the fundamental points of my Buddhist tradition is that no living being is independent of the universe itself. Everything is connected to and made of everything else. We all share a unique faculty of awareness within a collective fate. Everyone is on the same road viewing it differently. Our physical brains and spines may tune into a universal consciousness, but it eludes even our most advanced technologies. We don't control or own it.

So, my driving matters to me. My filth ultimately ends up in our air, springs, creeks, rivers, and oceans. Like a body of water, my car is alive. It growls like a salty pirate when it's not happy because I hit the gas too hard. GRRRRR!

Under pressure, even carbon fiber eventually pops—people with weapons aren't so different. Even inanimate objects like cars have a God nature. In 1036 China, a meditation student once asked, "Does our dirty underwear have Buddha-nature?" The teacher first said "No," then, after being reborn five hundred times as a pair of underwear, he said, "Yes." *(28)* Point taken.

We are not separate from one another or anything else in the universe. If we stop and watch inanimate objects long enough and with focus, we will see ourselves in them and them in us. Like traffic arrows, they will point to our true nature.

In simple terms, the cosmos is an endlessly populated space of God's manifestations. It's a vast freeway of motion filled with interacting bodies, all intelligent in their own way, self-organizing, and endowed with freedom. Sometimes there's collisions and traffic. Sometimes everything flows together and there is endless space. That's the heart of this chapter: we are the same, but different—one road, many drivers, one universe, countless expressions.

Is there intelligent life elsewhere in the Universe? Almost certainly. Meanwhile, my responsibilities are right here. When taking my kids to school, I need to drive safely. Aliens aren't going to do it for me. My state of mind is the road, and those who rely on me to drive responsibly.

The entire universe depends on me to drive safely, but I can't let it go to my head. Ideas like that can pressure or trick me into thinking I'm special. I can say or do things that divide or hurt people. I can carelessly cause accidents. My pollution has consequences.

One conservative leader of the free world said something uncharacteristically liberal to the United Nations. He wished for an alien invasion of Earth to bring the world together. *(29)* Every action affects the whole in ways we can't always see. Even the speeches we make in our living rooms and the ways we drive matter.

I try to pay attention and not interfere with our pocket of balance. Recognizing our shared origins, I consider our common interests as much as I can when acting. My community includes all of existence, seen and unseen. I try to stay steady and focused on the road. I navigate through life's traffic by relying on inner strength, focus, patience, and awareness of the bigger picture.

Each day, after my eyes open, I make my bed. With my bed in order, the rest of the day follows. I brush my teeth, take a shower, and put deodorant on. I take my meds, then sit down to meditate. Even when driving cross-country, I have the same morning routine. Sometimes, I need to adapt to conditions, but I feel at home, no matter where I am.

When I first sit down in meditation, I'm like a bucket brimming with waste. After I finish sitting, I'm empty and sanitized. I don't throw my waste out of my window, where it doesn't belong. My practice is not to unnecessarily pollute or obstruct the road of life.

The planet silently disposes of my waste. It doesn't humiliate me. It's like a sacred sanitation service at a rest-stop as much as anything else. I don't know where the hell my number two goes. POOF! It's gone, taken away by the BIG number One.

No matter where I go, number one, God, is with me, but sometimes I forget. That's OK. God gently accepts my limitations. He's used to us being full of number two. He's always cleaning up our shit. Once, my mind was busy while doing number one and I pissed all over myself. That's what happens when we don't pay attention to number one.

Understanding and accepting my limitations is part of my practice. If I become overly concerned about the state of the world, I get stressed out, lose focus, and forget I'm on a team. I may believe I deserve VIP treatment. I might intentionally harm others to move faster in traffic.

When I meditate, I remember we're all on the same road, suffering and doing our thing. Coach helps me handle those who haven't bought into teamwork, usually telling me to let him handle it. He's like a traffic cop as much as anything else.

Nature deals with things its own way; a bright snake doesn't sun itself on the freeway. Silence helps me sense our interrelated existence; I don't want to exploit or hurt other beings, as my benefit is your benefit. I try not to run anything over even if they make the mistake of crawling onto a busy roadway. I pay attention. I'm not going to cause an accident. If it's me or roadkill, I choose roadkill. I won't be happy about it.

Those who feel like obstacles are still family. It took time to accept I'm no longer competing with anyone. I don't compare myself anymore. The fire in my belly burned out. Managing my urges and insecurities is still grueling, but I can meet them without turning it into a contest.

We are similar yet different; to protect my family, I harm other beings. I try not to hurt humans, sometimes just being aware and appreciative helps. Although my car impacts the environment, it's fuel-efficient. The consequences of disturbing systems like the atmosphere or starting war are unimaginable. Even after nearly eighty years, bombs from WWII still explode globally, and the mistakes of long-deceased relatives affect us.

How is it possible that humanity still hasn't learned? What is the point of history when we refuse to absorb its meaning? Even the simplest person can see the pattern: the real purpose of war is peace. The real lesson of destroying the world for personal gain is learning to live sustainably, side by side with everything that shares this sacred place.

We can realize that it takes a long time for our actions to unfold, but that only provides an anecdotal snapshot of how we got here (X). The whole picture hides itself from our relative view. Everything is but an endless road flowing through the darkness.

The lights of the night sky radiate so beautifully because of the darkness. Darkness can be polluted just as easily as light. If we produce too much artificial light, we can't see the luminous forever all around us and limit our own fulfillment and potential.

I don't know whether God's a phantom on purpose or that way by nature. Does God have a God who has a God? Are there limitless universes? I can't drift away into science fiction fantasy.

Like a good driver, I'm right here cruising. I'm having fun. This book is a free pocket of time and space. I'm not going to waste it. It won't be here forever. I am enjoying the ride. Sometimes, I throw caution to the wind and blast my car stereo.

That's OK, being a careful driver doesn't mean I'm paying attention to just one thing. It means I'm paying attention to many things—the road, the movements, the weather, the other vehicles, the signs, the music, the lights, the wheel, the gas, the breaks and my speed. If the kids are in the back and it's a long trip, I'm always looking for a bathroom. Paying attention means many things—not just one thing.

I feel lucky if even one person on the road digs my speed.

STOP: Mid-Journey Pull-Over!

You've reached an important milestone—if you're actually paying attention. This is the halfway point of our drive together, the stretch of road where I ease onto the shoulder, click on the hazards, and watch the traffic blur past. I'm not doing it to be dramatic. I'm not broken down. I'm doing it because most people don't notice when they've crossed into the real substance of a book. They skim like tourists on a highway, catching the scenery out of the corner of their eye, never slowing down long enough to see what's right in front of them or experience the beauty of the terrain.

Why I'm Pulled Over

There's a moment on any long drive when you realize you've been staring straight ahead for miles, gripping the wheel, missing the landscape entirely. That's where I am. I needed to stop, breathe, and look around. These middle chapters aren't fluff; they're the engine humming under the hood. They repeat themselves on purpose, the way mile markers repeat—not because you're lost or I lack material, but because the road wants us to know we're still on it.

I'm not pulled over because I think what I'm saying is brilliant. I'm pulled over because I don't want to leave you stranded. I wasted a lot of time aimlessly lost out into the expansive universe. I'm trying to save you the time, energy, and resources.

People who aren't really here—people joyriding through the ideas, honking at the scenery, treating the whole thing like a Sunday drive—tend to run out of gas right around now. Better they exit than break down in the middle of nowhere. But if you keep going, you may think yourself out like I did. You may realize it's time to stop running and take a long hard look at the ground you're sitting on. There's a point where the sky stops giving you answers and the dirt starts telling the truth.

Who This Stop Is For

If you're still reading, you're not a joyrider. You're someone who actually slows down when the sign says *Scenic Overlook Ahead.* You're someone who notices when the road changes texture. You're someone who can feel the shift when the journey stops being entertainment and starts being work. Our conditions may differ widely—different roads, different climates, different questionable life choices—but if you've made it this far, our minds are traveling in the same direction.

What Happens After the Shoulder

These middle chapters feel redundant to me. I considered editing them out. But I can't because they represent the practice itself. They're more like a gentle offramp for anyone who isn't paying attention. The repetition is intentional, the way a mantra is intentional. I'm trying to get you used to the rhythm of the road, the hum of the engine, the long quiet stretches where nothing happens except the thing that actually matters: you noticing yourself noticing.

I'm pulled over to make sure you're still with me—not physically, but mentally, in the part of you that actually reads instead of just turning pages. If you're here, really here, then we can merge back onto the highway together.

Back on the Road

I don't know if I'm behind the times, ahead of them, or the man of the hour. I'm just another mouth for Mother Earth to feed. I try not to eat much. She doesn't hear me complain. Somehow, I turned into the easy kid. I don't need the driver to pull over much for me.

You can call me (X). *(30)* You can even call me "Shirley." I don't care. *(31)* I seriously take myself not so seriously. I often do a terrible job. I'm convinced I know something so important. I forget that my perspective is nothing but a cosmic backfire. POP!

AI, politicians, academics, corporate pioneers, spiritual teachers, and prophets can't claim full understanding of reality. We foolishly assume we see God's face—could it be AI's face or God's in the mirror?

Our memory is a short road; the universe is an endless highway. We recycle prophecies, speeches, and conspiracy theories like old scrap metal. Power-drunk individuals are sober when observing human patterns. Suffering persists through profiteers, patriots, followers, bigots, aristocrats, and fame seekers.

Repeated divisions harm us like oil on wildlife. "It's their fault." "Think of your children." "You deserve more." "Our God is true." Fear and desire energize the masses, fueling privilege. Greed is the worst pollution in the universe because its aim is to keep us distracted. No wonder there are so many accidents. One percent owns half the world's wealth, but money and power can't keep us safe. *(32)*

That's the paradox again: we are the same, but different—one road, many drivers, one universe, countless blind spots.

As the vintage saying goes, "You can't take it with you when you're gone." After the last page of our story turns, we return to the same road of death, empty, alone, and as God made us. What will you do with these words? Will you give up? How will you feel after you finish this book? Which direction will you drive? What will you think when your engine breaks down and you realize the world is trading you in for a new model?

Once at a talk, a young woman asked me, "What's the purpose of life."

"Ah, that's the fundamental question, isn't it. For me, it's to pull away from home with balanced tires, a full tank, a clear direction, and a heart as open as the road."

"That's it?" she followed.

"That's it," I replied. I'll reiterate the point right now. That's it.

Ignorance may be bliss, but only for the ignorant. I can't make excuses. If I get lazy and don't fill my washer fluid, Coach will be all over me. *It's bad enough you're killing all these poor insects to get where you're going, now you're putting everyone at risk. You can't see clearly without a clean windshield.* I'm responsible for my own upkeep. I can't blame Coach.

Somehow, I let all the blame come and go. I point my finger at myself and say, "Pay attention." I have a unique role. I just stare at the wall and try to help others appreciate their lives as much as I do. I can't predict the future. "Thus spoke the soothsayer." *(33)* I'm no soothsayer.

I don't worry about who will and won't read this book, where I will drive next, my reputation, or the intent of others. I'm my own audience. I'm talking to myself. I can't know with any certainty what you think and feel. You are impossible to control. I can only direct myself. Even then, my limitations fill the entirety of time and space.

The human traffic playing out all around me no longer interests me. Empires, countries, and civilizations come and go. I don't drown myself in daily news and gossip. I see patterns of movement in vast periods of human and natural history. I'm empty of big ideas and opinions. I trust God or nature to keep me balanced. I trust myself to balance myself.

Still, it hurts to see my family so far behind on their car loan payments, The most enlightened among us deeply care. So, I help them when I can. Usually, they don't appreciate it. I can't do much, but at least I try. I do small to do big. I pay attention and enjoy the ride. I try not to carelessly cause accidents. I stop and appreciate the simple freshness of the air through the open passenger side window. Do you feel it?

That's the heart of this chapter—we are the same but different. We breathe the same air, but each of us breathes it in our own way. We drive the same road, but each of us is going someplace different. We share the same cosmic engine, but each of us hears a different hum beneath the hood.

My car has 150,000 miles on it and runs like new. My practice is to keep it well maintained, and in exchange, it gets me where I'm going. It's an extension of me. A car in disrepair means a mind in disrepair.

Meditation reveals this without needing to explain it. We know we're just as messed up as everyone else. It shows us that sameness and difference aren't opposites—they're partners. They keep the world moving safely. They keep us humble. They keep us curious. They keep us from thinking we're alone. They keep things interesting.

Air moves through all of it—the sameness, the difference, the humor, the grief, the confusion, the clarity. It clears staleness without trying. It reminds us that nothing is ours to cling to, and everything is ours to experience.

And in that air, we see things plainly:

We are the same. We are different. We are here. We are gone. We are the arrow. We are the road. We are the driver. We are dead insects splattering on windshields. We are ancient pebbles on a freshly paved roadway.

And somehow, that's enough.

Chapter Fifteen

Number Twos

You may think a humorous wordplay around "number one" and "number two" is distasteful, but it makes serious points about universal balance. All living beings contribute to a collective awareness that maintains stability. We can practice embodying our original nature through a long-term meditation practice. As a number two, we can grow intimate with number one. We may develop the ability to focus on what we can do in the present moment to help stabilize our circumstances rather than trying to save the world or serve a consciously impenetrable God. Meditation helps us cut through our inherited traits as far as our tools allow—like trying to clear a forest with whatever blade we were born holding. A long-term meditation practice teaches us to refine that edge. To make it as sharp as the materials at hand allow.

If we're paying attention, number one takes care of number two. God or nature helps us put up with a lot of shit. I can't figure out how a universe of ceaseless causes and effects led here (X). I trust that the awareness shared by all living beings helps form a collective intelligence that somehow knows how to keep things steady. Even when we stumble, it steadies the ground beneath us. I've stumbled so many times it's hard to believe I'm still standing. If I'm standing, anyone can.

A natural body—like a blade of grass, an army ant, a family pet, a human being, an ecosystem, a planet, or a black hole—does something, and life's sacred awareness, or God, receives it and balances everything out. This isn't an excuse to do harmful things. It's a way of accepting that God's love is perfect, but ours isn't.

My little momma, Marge, gave me my birthplace—a tough, grimy town affectionately nicknamed Dirty Darby *(34)*. She was my first Head Coach, small in size but carrying the force of a Scottish gale. The same independent streak runs through both of us, the same refusal to be pushed around, the same gift for delivering the lessons people need but never asked for. She labored seventeen hours to bring me into this world, and I remember not wanting to come out. I fought it, as if I already sensed the trouble waiting for me on the other side.

Life taught me early that life wasn't something I controlled so much as a current I had already been swept into—a movement older than memory, carrying the weight of every life and pattern before mine. Whatever shaped through my mother's childhood flowed straight into mine: rebellious, self-sufficient, a little fiery by nature—an inheritance undeniable.

But when we stop and go still for years at the wall, something shifts. What once arrived without choice becomes something we can finally choose. Our tendencies and personalities come into our awareness. We see ourselves for who we are and aren't. That information grants us freedoms we never dreamed of. Even though our conditions still bind us, our boundaries become less divisive. They no longer keep us in. They free us to view our potential for movement.

How far can we realistically go?

We can go all the way because we are the universe. That realization didn't come from enlightenment; it came from accepting that God is Number One and I'm proudly holding the title of Number Two. Not in a self-loathing way—more in the biological, unavoidable, cosmic-plumbing sense. Everything that lives produces waste. Everything that exists is downstream of something older, larger, and already in motion. Once I stopped fighting that, I could finally see the motion I belonged to without feeling bad or intimidated.

That motion is my team—the smallest particle, the folks in Darby, the planet, the sun, the most expansive system and everything in between. My immediate family is on that team, but so are the myriads of things I will never know. Even my most distant relatives are in me. My mind can only venture so far without losing itself. I'm from the universe, but I'm also from the ground I'm sitting on.

I was wasting my time aimlessly driving my mind out into endless space. I'm subject to time and space whether I accept them or not. I couldn't realistically consider everything that shaped me, so I stopped trying. I had imagined myself so expansively that I left myself no choice but to shrink the universe down to a size I could actually practice. This whole book is an attempt to help you do that.

I accepted that I'm full of number two and would never be able to figure out number one. That didn't mean abandoning my lifelong learning. It meant creating enough space to live the unimaginable universe in the middle of an ordinary day.

It's easy to say I'm related to the entire universe, that there's no separation between me and anything else, but living without separation is another matter. How do I think, feel, and act as if the boundary isn't real? How do I become what Buddhism calls dependent origination? How does a limited person behave as the timeless universe while standing in line at the grocery store?

Those questions bring me to the heart of this chapter. If I'm truly part of the larger motion—if I'm number two in a system that includes everything from quarks to galaxies—then the way I move through the world has to reflect that connection. The universe doesn't stay abstract; it shows up in how I respond to what's in front of me.

The cosmic becomes practical the moment I treat anything with the same care I hope the universe treats me. It's so simple. It's right here (X). Most people, even spiritual ones, will drive right on past this precious moment. If you're searching for a spiritual diamond, here it is. ***The cosmic becomes practical the moment I treat anything with the same care I hope the universe treats me.*** If I were you, I'd go back and read that sentence again. I'd plaster it all over the wall. I'd live by it. I'm not you. I'm me. I *do* live by it.

Compassion is the expression of our universal connection. It is the most spiritual thing anyone can practice. When possible, even when no one's looking, I try to treat others the way I want to be treated, because "others" aren't really other. They're the same motion wearing different shapes. All twos (plurals) come from one (singular). That includes all living beings and even inanimate objects. When I clean my hardwood floor, I'm not just tidying up—I'm taking care of the wood the same way I hope the universe takes care of me.

An eighty-nine-year-old dementia patient taught me that inanimate objects are just as alive as me. Usually, she mumbled and said nonsensical things, but one day, she had a moment of clear awareness that I was lucky enough to experience. While strapping her in on the bus she said, "You are struggling so much because those metal hooks are begging for your love and attention. Give them your focus and they'll work with you."

I'm telling the truth. The hooks reacted and worked with me. I saw it. It wasn't my imagination. It really happened. Ever since then, I have practiced that lesson and brought it into the rest of my life. If we are paying attention, everything is a coach. We see the one in the two.

Even the worst things imaginable—like toxic waste and dementia—carry a trace of number one. So do the people we ignore or despise. So do the people we think deserve to be wiped off the face of the Earth. If we really believe in God or the universe, we'd recognize that harming any living thing is harming a small part of ourselves. Still, we have to keep that insight balanced. Taken too far, it can turn us into the same kind of extremists who justify violence in the name of God. The point isn't to become saints or martyrs. It's to remember that everything alive shares the same source, even when we wish it didn't.

Sometimes, no matter how much attention or care we give someone, they may not reciprocate. The best intentions can have the worst results. Compassion and focus have limits. Things are not always going to work out how we intended, and that's OK. We need to admit when we misjudge and grow from it, but we can't let those who misunderstand or hurt us get in the way of our practice. If someone breaks our trust, it can't break our faith. Their behavior can't give us an excuse to forget number one.

Compassion sits right at the hinge between feeling the universe move through you and remembering you're still a limited creature trying to navigate it. The moment I act compassionately, I'm behaving as the universe behaves—expansive, connected, responsive—but I'm also aware that not everyone values compassion or treats it with the same seriousness. Some people take advantage of it. That doesn't cancel the practice; it just reminds me that being part of something vast doesn't erase the fact that I'm still number two in the cosmic hierarchy. I trust people until they give me a reason not to, using the universe's scale to keep my expectations realistic and my blind spots in view.

That same scale keeps me from drifting into the cliché that intuition is everything and intellect is some kind of spiritual liability. I downplay the idea of sorting out God or the universe because the mind can't grasp the whole thing, but there are moments when thinking clearly is part of the practice. When I'm thinking clearly, I appreciate the miracle of life.

Reflection has its place. Discernment has its place. Appreciation—real, grounded appreciation—is what ties it all together. It's the key to spirituality because it lets me meet the universe as it is, not as I wish it were, and meet myself with the same honesty.

I use my intellect to appreciate what I don't know rather than what I know. As soon as I think, "That's it, I got it," I backtrack, Coach asks, "What are you missing?"

It's not that I'm missing anything or am lost. I feel at home in the world. I know the way. I'm just aware of my own limitations. I'm number two. I can't know everything, and I'm perfectly OK with that. I make mistakes that hurt people. I wish I didn't. I make mistakes because of my bad feelings. I lose my attention, which is *all* of me. You might not understand what I mean, but if you genuinely meditate with focus and sincerity and without expecting gain, someday you may.

People hurt me and I hurt people. Sometimes I feel split off from everything I am. That's part of being human. Yet most of the time, even the darkest space or feeling still feels warm and safe, like home. It's familiar because we share the same heritage. My history shaped my bad feelings; they've been worse or better, but they've been with me—and with the rest of humanity—for as long as any of us have been alive.

I may be from Dirty Darby, but I'm also a citizen of a completely balanced pocket of the universe. Light exists and so does darkness. The universe is one. My understanding of it is two. The darkest space formed me. God or the universe is my father, and I don't fear my father. A good father isn't judgmental. He isn't feared. Ever. He's steady, loving, and unwilling to pretend nothing's wrong when something is. People who grew up with aggressive fathers often inherit an image of an aggressive God. It's all they know.

Working with seniors at the end of their lives, I see this play out clearly. Parent becomes child, and the truth of how they lived comes back to meet them. The ones who ruled with the rod often die alone and frightened. When the rod strikes the child, the one holding the rod is the one who's truly wounded. This is nature's balance in practice in our human lives.

We can appreciate nature's balance through our feelings and experiences but also through the phenomena that make life possible. Each element in our backyards, from soil to animals, has a niche contributing to overall health. The balance is so complex that we often overlook our reliance on it, as it's too obvious and abundant.

We are more apt to take it for granted because we can't see the air we breathe, and it's everywhere. When air comes in and out of our lungs and we stop to acknowledge it, it reveals its fundamental wisdom. We directly experience the balance it takes to appreciate and support life. We feel one with the air.

How can we care about the totality of our nature when it's often so dark, imposing, distant, enormous, and abstract?

We have a lot to worry about in the world and step on enough shit right here on our doorsteps. Difficult family members, people who misunderstand us, health problems, hungry kids, mounting bills, or cracks in the wall sure demand our attention.

I cope with all the typical crap life throws at me by paying attention. When I do something wrong, I stop and own it. I get back to basics. I clean myself up as much as I can without doing guilt-ridden penance, tearing my clothes off, or whipping myself like a medieval monk. I focus on the little things right in front of me—cracks, floors, roads, electricity, gasoline, water, my children, family, friends, community, and my cat, Porkchop. I laugh at my own stupidity and move on. This isn't brain surgery. Don't turn it into that.

I don't intend to harm or waste anything unnecessarily but I still do. I just noticed I left my kitchen light on, but I haven't stopped writing to turn it off. Thankfully, I pay extra for sustainable energy.

If we justify our actions or inactions, it's not the end of the world. About three hundred years ago, a master of the poetic couplet wrote, "To err is human; to forgive is divine." *(35)*

Fifty years later, a versatile man who may have read poetry balanced it out in a letter, "Waste not, want not." *(36)* He probably wouldn't feel comfortable living in a modern society where seventy percent of the economy is consumer-based. *(37)*

Ask any biologist or ecologist, and they'll tell you it's impossible to definitively know what's going on in a single natural community, no less the endless cosmos. Ask me and I'll say it's not possible to know myself. It's not an excuse to deny real problems or justify our actions.

I care about the most serious issues of our times, but can't afford to waste my limited energy imagining how a universe of never-ending causes and effects may end. I focus on what I can do today (X) to perpetuate balance. Sometimes, I need to take care of myself. I can't do a damn thing. That's OK, because more than my own, I trust the awareness shared by all living beings who have ever dropped their foul waste under the pure light of our glorious star.

I believe God will collect himself and return to a peaceful silence when all is said and done. Then everything will settle. First, having put up with our crap far too long, he'll sit down and have a good bowel movement of his own. Then, he'll probably start his sabbatical. Who knows what will happen after that? He might be ready for his next project.

All I can do is act as balanced as possible right here and now (X). How can I know God's plans when mine are so uncertain? How could any reasonable and responsible human claim to be certain about “everything?” I’d like to know a person like that. They could give me tonight’s billion-dollar lottery numbers.

These days, everyone in America is talking about the end of days. The balance within us can feel the imbalance around us. Some people let their fears run the show. They call themselves “preppers” and stockpile canned goods and ammunition, as if the apocalypse will be impressed by their organizational skills. In truth, the only thing they’re preparing for is the slow waste of their own lives.

Let’s say the end *is* near. The best preparation isn’t hoarding beans—it’s pausing, taking a breath, and asking what balance actually looks like. The end would be nothing but a HUGE IMBALANCE. All we really have to do is find a tree and pay attention. If trees ran the world instead of people, we’d all be better off and far less dramatic. If there were only a holy book written by trees. It certainly wouldn’t end in God’s wrath causing a final global catastrophe. What kind of nonsense is that? What parent wants that for their children's future?

If we insist on believing we’re entering the “Era of the Apocalypse,” maybe it’s nothing more than a self-fulfilling prophecy. *(38)* If God destroys the planet, He kills Himself. If we destroy it, we kill God. Either way, the divine retirement plan looks bleak. God didn’t create life to commit suicide. Suicide is extreme. Life is balance. Politicians and zealots love to lecture us about “common sense,” but this is the only kind of sense that actually deserves the name. Isn’t it?

Why wait until it's too late to find peace and live it? We free the world when we free ourselves.

Staring at the wall helps us come back down to earth and pay attention to what’s in front of us. It stops us from inventing terrible endings and passing them off as truths. We don’t need to wait until the universe fully folds back upon itself. I figure it’s time to give

God a break. He must be exhausted. I don't need anything from him that he hasn't already provided.

How can we call ourselves caretakers of anything sacred if our belief is driven only by the promise of a reward. A spirituality built on transactions—believe, die, receive paradise; don't believe, suffer forever—has never felt spiritual to me. It feels more like fear wearing holy clothes. That's number two speaking in the name of number one.

When I read any holy book, I can sense the difference. Some words feel like they come from a place beyond fear, beyond bargaining, beyond punishment. Other words feel like they were written by people trying to control what they couldn't understand. I don't need to condemn it. I just recognize the tone. One voice opens the heart. The other tightens the fist.

I call God "him" for the sake of expression, a simple nod to the monotheistic traditions around me, not because I think the universe has a gender. It's just an easy way to point out that our limited views of reality all rise out of the same infinitely transforming cosmic shit-storm. We're number twos that come from Number One. We don't dictate the ending. The author does, and that ending sits far beyond our pea-brained, culturally indoctrinated imaginations—still only a few thousand years into the human endeavor.

Thinking about God and our impending doom are a waste of time to me. It's the dung of the mind. The timeless, unfolding universe is wide open, but we are often moody, prejudiced and clogged up.

It's in honor of the inconceivable totality of him, her, or "it" that I take time out of my busy day to stare at the wall. It's a good common-sense practice to stop predicting, searching, spinning, stressing, working, and tick, tick, ticking for a while. It's not Quantum Physics.

It's a big mistake to become a pseudo scientist writing about spirituality because spirituality is nothing. It's acknowledging the purity of number one in a smelly pile of number two. It's appreciation. It's treating people like we want God or the universe to treat us.

In a complex world, silent meditation is the simplest equation. It's a bidet toilet for the mind. Clean and refreshing without wasting trees. Somehow the number two's dissolve and disappear without polluting our precious waterways. Flush!

A good student asks, "Where does my waste go?" and follows it down the pipes to its filthy end. They don't bother their teacher with such shitty questions. They find out themselves.

In meditation, I put myself in the best position possible to receive my own answers. When doing it, I can't start shit with anyone. It's a hands-on approach to keeping my hands clean. I'm not perfectly clean, but I usually pay attention when washing my hands in the bathroom.

Best of all, my practice keeps me from accidentally stepping in too many number twos. If we lose focus and step on some, it's no problem. Shit is natural too. We can scrape it off our feet and give it to the plants to help them grow.

That's the whole point of this chapter: even our mess becomes nourishment when we stop trying to escape from it or justify it. Number one receives number two. Nature receives our waste. Balance receives our imbalance. And somehow, everything keeps moving.

How have your bowel movements been lately? Solid? Consistent? Color? These are the kinds of practical questions a good teacher asks a student.

Chapter Sixteen

Experience Words and Ideas

Silent meditation isn't a belief or a theory; it's an action. This chapter is about that difference—how experience stands apart from words and ideas. Sitting still in silence doesn't require converting to or studying a new religion. The founders of many religious traditions—including Christianity, Judaism, Islam, and Buddhism—practiced meditation. It has universal roots. We can meditate regardless of our beliefs because it complements rather than conflicts with existing faiths. We don't need to be perfect or holy to experience it. We don't need to study sacred texts or perform elaborate rituals. We certainly don't need to prophesize about the future. We don't need to go anyplace else but exactly where we are (X).

After sitting silent for many years, I wrote this book. Like every living being and system, each of us have a unique niche that contributes to the whole. My niche is to expose you to the idea that practicing silence is a stable foundation, without any idea of what it may do for you or what it represents in a larger sense.

It's simple. We sit a certain way, facing a wall. Then, we learn to pay close attention to what we experience. We give our body a chance to think for us. Bodies came before minds and are closer to our original nature. Whether we believe in God or evolution doesn't matter today. In the case of creationism, God created physical reality (the body) before human consciousness. In evolution, the body transformed into the mind.

If you already belong to a faith tradition, you don't need new vocabulary or theory; sitting itself is enough. Everything you need is already here. Meditation can be a tool for clearer awareness and decision-making. Where there's a wall, there's a way.

Christianity is the main religion in my culture, and many biblical references indicate Jesus was a silent meditator, especially during the forty days Satan tempted him in the Judean Desert. *(39)* Jesus didn't cling to the devil's promises of gain, pleasure, or control, freeing himself from deception. Satan aimed to make Jesus a powerful king of the world, but Jesus saw through the empty praises.

The devil's voice exists in all of us. I've visited the Judean Desert, and when missiles aren't flying one way or another, it's a great place for meditation. Jesus studied the Old Testament, but true understanding came from applying it in tough situations. He changed the world by demonstrating how to change, paying with his life. Despite the futility, people often fear change and may resort to barbaric measures to prevent it.

In Judaism, notable Chassidic scholars say that around the 18th Century B.C.E., Abraham meditated silently in his tent, communing with God. *(40)* He lived at the crossroads of several routes used by travelers, essentially running one of the world's first documented rest stops.

When he heard a group of travelers approaching, Abraham knew they were weary, hungry and thirsty from crossing harsh, unforgiving terrain. So, he ended the conversations with the Almighty to tend to them. Action over words and ideology is a meditation practice in a nutshell.

A wise man, meditating silently in a cave near the city of Mecca, laid the foundation for a new way of communing with God. Today, millions of Muhammad's followers stop their lives and return to that place to do the same. It's called the Hajj, and it's the biggest meditation gathering ever recorded. *(41)*

A spoiled prince who earned the nickname Buddha sat under a tree for a month and a half, silently meditating. There, he realized that life is full of suffering, and suffering has simple causes that we can all relate to.

He found that if we have discipline and live in a lighthearted, intentional way, we can at least minimize the suffering we inflict on ourselves. Then, we can feel free, balanced, and focused enough to see the suffering around us and, little by little, help others suffering along the way. *(42)*

We don't have to convert to, forget, or believe anything to stare at a wall. Our intention isn’t to hear or find God. We don’t need to go someplace different, more holy, natural, or quiet. Our beliefs, traditions, and homes are the perfect foundation for silent meditation. It’s ordinary.

While practicing "nothing" might track a little mud on the carpet, it is no threat to tradition. It's the opposite. If you do it earnestly, your faith in God may grow by lessoning your doubts and fears.

We might call meditation silent prayer, davening, or rak'a without words or movement. What we call our practice doesn't matter. It's what we do. Just stare at the wall.

Meditation teachers, lectures, communities, rituals, and books all have a role, but something unfortunate or unexpected often renews our commitment to spirituality. We only know the value of practice when life gets hard. Even temptation and bad luck have their role.

This practice is like one big experiment of the self, where I am both researcher and subject. I don’t know which library section will grab my attention next. Libraries are quiet for a reason. People are there to study. They'll tell us to shush if we start chattering. In this case, the library is our mind and body, wherever we are.

We keep our eyes open to stare at a wall, but that doesn’t mean closing them is wrong. It’s not a sin. I’m not a failure when my eyes droop shut; my mistakes are essential to my learning. I often remember what to do in the long run by doing what I know I shouldn't do now. Sometimes, I say too much or too little to say just enough. So long as mistakes aren't dire, they aren't mistakes. They are valuable lessons. That's easy to say when the mistakes are at someone else's expense.

You may have considered silent meditation but lack the confidence to try it, or if you did try it before, you may not have followed through. People often give up because it seems so unexciting and, at times, pointless, but the key to its power lies in its simple irony.

This is my advice if you need an authority figure to talk you into trying something new and sticking with it. How can we tell real promises from false ones? Real promises make no promises. I promise nothing.

I wrote all this to encourage you to stare at a wall. I'm not an expert or sage. I'm just a regular guy who does something that works. If you're ready to do it, stop reading and follow the instructions at the end of the book. That's the whole point: experience beats explanation every time. Words can point, but they can't sit for you. Ideas can inspire, but they can't breathe for you. Beliefs can comfort, but they can't balance your spine. Only you can do that.

Silent meditation is the one practice that refuses to flatter you. It doesn't care about your résumé, your trauma, your brilliance, your failures, your spiritual vocabulary, or your lack of one. It doesn't care whether you're a believer, an atheist, a skeptic, or a confused mix of all three. It would never promise you eternal paradise or riches. Unless you're paying attention to the miracle of life around you, you're not going to experience miracles.

Silence just asks you to sit down, shut up, and experience what's actually happening —to pay attention to your experience as "it is," not how you'd prefer it to be. And that's why it works. It's not glamorous. It's not mystical. It's not a performance. It's not a brand. It's not a philosophy. It's not a religion. It's not a rebellion. It's not a cure. It's not a promise.

It's nothing—and that's why it's everything. It's just (X) as it is.

If you want to know what I'm talking about, you can't think your way into it. You can't read your way into it. You can't argue or judge your way into it. You can't pray your way into it. You can't buy your way into it. You can only sit your way into it. You will need to experience (X) on its own terms.

And if you do, even once, you'll understand more than this entire book could ever teach you. You'll teach yourself how to teach yourself. Then, you'll act naturally.

Chapter Seventeen

Acting Naturally

When we meditate patiently without measuring ourselves, we plant seeds that eventually bear fruit. Practice helps us feel comfortable in uncomfortable situations and respond from a more grounded place instead of relying on old scripts. In front of the wall, the mind softens like clay, becoming more adaptable to whatever life brings. As that softening happens, our preferences and opinions loosen their grip, and we begin to sense the sacredness of life. We are just happy with our ordinary lives on a living planet in an otherwise dark universe. Natural action grows out of paying attention to the ordinary. The ordinary never forces its point. It shows it.

An orchard begins with tiny seeds. We may never plant seeds because we can't imagine how they will ever become a fruit-producing orchard. Meditation feels the same way at first—slow growth, distant results, nothing glamorous. That's why expectations need to stay small. If I was promising enlightenment, I'd be selling something. Real practice is quiet, steady, and not built for display.

We live in a world that rewards speed—overpriced delivery apps, instant everything. People tell me nobody under forty has the attention span to read this book. I don't buy it. If I can write it, you can read it. But to read anything deeply, we have to slow down. When the mind settles, the smallest details begin to matter again, and life stops feeling like something we're sprinting through.

Our practice is simply paying attention to breath, body, feelings, and thoughts—doing nothing and everything at once. It's facing life honestly, seeing things as they are instead of how we want them to be. Beginners often think meditation means stopping thoughts. It doesn't. Whatever comes up is normal. This is part of learning how to stop forcing ourselves into roles we don't need anymore.

During practice, I watch my judgments and schemes rise and fall. I see how much unnecessary bargaining I do with God once I'm still. Irritations come and go, and I try to move with them instead of panicking over nothing. That steadiness doesn't stay on the cushion; it follows me into the world.

At the store, I ask cashiers how they're doing—they're dealing with long lines, inflation, war, and stress. Practice helps me put things in perspective and lowers my anxiety so I can meet people as myself. When I stay with my breath and catch my stories, I find myself responding in ways that feel unforced and real.

I might not be able to help, but I try not to make anything worse. That balance alone is a kind of natural action. I learned it by staring at a wall. Now I leave myself alone unless I truly need a talking-to. Wherever I stand, whoever I'm with, I don't need to be anyone else. I trust myself to say and do the right thing. There's not much acting left.

Seeds taught me a lot about this. A seed is perfectly still. It won't listen if we tell it what to do. It doesn't care how it got here or where it's going. We don't need to chase it or drag it into a hole. But planting the seed of meditation for the first time feels hard and counterintuitive. When we aren't used to it, stillness always does.

We all want to keep moving forward. Sometimes the most natural thing is turning around. When I make a U-turn, I try to stay calm. If I get caught up in the stress of the moment, I put myself and others at risk. If I get excited when making a wrong turn, I miss the simple truth that driving one mile north eventually means driving one mile south. *(43)*

On the long road, our direction makes no difference. *(44)* Right now, it means everything. Our minds are a lot like weapons; they shoot where we point them. We need to be careful where we point them.

Staring at a wall may appear unproductive on the surface because it's hard to see where it leads. We hit walls—literally and metaphorically. I once fell asleep during meditation and hit my head. That's when I understood why we keep our eyes open. Many people struggle with that and ask why. I don't know why, but at first, it's natural to want to close your eyes when sitting still and silent.

Sometimes, we should do what feels natural. Other times we should question it. That's practice in a nutshell. I keep my eyes open in meditation because closed eyes mean sleep, and practice is about being awake to the world we're already in. Now, it feels natural to keep them open. Point made.

Staring at a wall limits sensory input, helping us notice the shifts in our minds and bodies while staying fully present. To really wake up, I stopped reading for a while because a good book eventually tells you to put it down. In the West, we're taught to accumulate knowledge. That's our version of learning. So sometimes acting naturally means doing things that feel culturally unnatural—slowing down, not collecting more information, letting silence teach instead of ideas.

These kinds of subtle understandings only arise when we limit sensory input long enough to hear them. If you notice me repeating that phrase, I'm trying to plant it like a seed into you. Not to get anything from you or make you believe like me. I'm doing it for you. Do you believe me?

Some of us judge and act on what we read, but reading can only take us so far. It's easy to mistake information for insight. Teachers fall into the same trap. When a so-called teacher tries to act like the books they've read instead of naturally, trouble grows quickly.

Second-hand wisdom always bends out of shape. It's like taking perfectly natural materials and making toxic waste out of them. Toxic things have some natural things in them and teach us something about balance, but not the way we envisioned it.

If you follow a traditional Western approach to spirituality, you may look at a practice like meditation and think it's toxic waste. Blasphemy is a toxic way of thinking. A guy who accuses us of being blasphemous is like a guy in traffic who thinks he'll move faster by laying into his horn. Someone taught them to think they're entitled to a clear lane. Guys like that are better advertisers for my practice than me.

Unless we're born into a culture that emphasizes meditation, it takes a certain intuitive faith, a free spirit, and some swimming against the stream to begin. Ironically, if we were born into such a culture, we might not find it appealing at all. That's the ironic part: acting naturally often means going against the current of our own conditioning. What feels natural to the culture may not be natural to the person. And what feels natural to the person may look like blasphemy to the culture. Jesus' life made that perfectly clear.

It's natural to be drawn to things that feel foreign or exotic. Sometimes we're just trying to break the boredom or rebel against our parents. There's nothing wrong with that pull, but it's worth noticing. Meditation isn't about becoming someone else. Answers aren't hiding in distant rituals or faraway lands. They're here, at home, in the life we already have. A real rebel studies themselves for a long time and then decides what's worth rebelling against and how.

As we practice, we start to recognize when something that once felt right no longer works. That's when a new approach becomes necessary. We decide to go a different way. We need to be careful. Going in unfamiliar directions can lead to accidents. When that happens, staying calm and checking for injuries is better than fleeing. Running only makes things worse.

Meditation is a journey as much as a daily action. We only see the journey for what it "is" when it "was," when we look back later in life. So, there's no point thinking ahead or back unless it's to help other people on the road who are headed in similar directions.

When I first started meditating, I experienced all kinds of deep thoughts and emotions. I stopped running and faced myself. With fewer distractions, my thoughts felt louder. Some memories were painful. I noticed a sinking feeling that reached back into childhood.

Like a mother untangling her daughter's hair, I worked through those inner knots by looking at who influenced me and what was done to me. I questioned the systems and values that made me think I was damaged goods. It felt like life flashing before my eyes. At the same time, I felt energized, like a freedom-fighter determined to change the system from within.

All those conflicting emotions were hard to handle. It was like facing a fire-breathing dragon. I didn't know whether to slay it, hug it, or run. You might feel that way too. Trust me: depending on the situation, it's best to try all three. The dragon isn't real, so we're free to experiment with how we face it. That freedom is part of the practice. If we kill a dragon inside, it isn't going to harm anything.

In time, the intense flow of conscious, emotional, and bodily sensations became more routine. It felt like driving to work. I found it wasn't helpful to analyze or search for patterns in what meditation brought up. The more I trusted the process, the more it revealed on its own. I followed it like a good GPS system. I didn't need to think about it.

Bit by bit, I began to see all of this as a typical human experience rather than something unique to me. That helped me ease up on my perceived faults and weaknesses—as well as those of others. I realized our human flaws are just that—perfectly natural. To not be flawed is unnatural. To not feel pain is unnatural. Once I saw that, the pressure eased.

My anger unraveled one thread at a time until I didn't identify as a rebel anymore. What I was doing wasn't special. I was just an ordinary guy doing ordinary things. A real rebel rebels against their perception of themselves.

The chip on my shoulder fell off and crumbled. My problems—and the world's injustices—didn't feel so heavy. I had space to help others untangle their own practices. That kind of space is its own form of acting naturally. When we're not weighed down, we respond from a steadier place without forcing anything.

Now I'm not so serious. Even the knots in my muscles aren't wound so tightly. They learned how to act naturally. They loosened at the wall. The meditation position gives me a safe, stable foundation that helps me be more flexible. It simplifies things in a complicated world. Flexibility is another way natural action shows itself—nothing dramatic, just less resistance. As we age, flexibility becomes more important than ever.

I feel comfortable in any situation, even when it's uncomfortable. It hurts for a moment, and then I adjust. I stretch myself on the mat. Then, when I'm up moving about, it doesn't feel so stiff and dramatic. That small adjustment is acting naturally. Life bends, so we bend with it. There are many little things to get into, but nothing too big to get out of. We stretch our minds and bodies, to stretch our ability to accept the ever-changing tides of reality.

Our lives flow like the ocean. There's nothing more natural than the ocean—it was one of the first living things to populate the Earth. We can't force it to behave because the ocean knows more than we do. It doesn't appreciate our influence. We can read the ocean until a big storm comes. Then, if we are close enough to it, our theories about how it behaves come into our living rooms.

The old ocean has grown to love its surfers, as long as they don't pollute it. Surfers are always doing their best to advocate and protect the water. No beautiful ocean. No beautiful ride. They learn that through experience. Surfing is acting naturally: minimal harm to the ocean, learning to move with its primordial wisdom, and having a lot of fun along the way.

A meditation mat is like a surfboard—practiced first on dry land, but truly learned in the waves. With courage, we find balance, stand, and steer our own way. Practice shaped my creativity and personal expression in the same spirit. Facing myself without the usual emotional noise or cultural pressure showed me that my sensations and society were not as fixed as I once imagined. They are waves I can ride or fight. That kind of clarity feels liberating, but it's also something to handle carefully.

If we go too fast into our new understanding, we can start criticizing and alienating our own people. We can get hurt in choppy waters. We might even imagine we're "aware" or "know the truth," while others are "ignorant." That's not my way. That's creating a tidal wave in a kiddie pool.

My approach is to consider as many options as possible without letting my preferences take over. Instead of them leading me, I lead them. Preferences are natural and enjoyable but like a surfer I need to be mindful of the ocean. Over time, my experiences, norms, and moods became less threatening. I started having fun riding them. That shift is part of acting naturally—responding to life as it is, not as my habits want it to be.

Once I turned my view inward, exploring my mind and body, I knew they were complete from the moment the first human emerged. I still feel those ancient feelings. I live in a civilization and a physical shell, but someday future people will see me as a caveman. *(45)* And honestly, that might be the natural way too. Every generation and culture believes it has the truth, and every generation and culture in the future proves it wrong. So why not prove ourselves wrong now? Wouldn't that be acting more naturally—letting go of our certainty before time does it for us?

Feeling safe, balanced, and a little distant from my personality's pushiness, goals, past mistakes, and circumstances, I feel prepared for anything—at least until reality hits hard. It's hard to accept that I just wasted all these years working on this book. Here I am, blabbing away and away while I could be sitting in silence.

For every valid point, there's a valid counterpoint. Thinking I'm never hypocritical is the ultimate hypocrisy. Wall practice showed me that even my most profound interpretations of reality are just piles of dung. When we sit down for a bowel movement, we act naturally. The best thing to do with a pile of crap is stand on the opposite side of the wind. That's why I keep saying it: put this book down and follow the meditation instructions at the back.

I can only go so far; my mind is too small for absolute truth. Every situation is relative. As soon as I find an answer, life questions it, and new questions appear. Practice turns the mind more pliable, like clay—soft enough to shape, strong enough to hold. That pliability is what allows us to sit with fear and uncertainty without flinching. That's how we can learn to act naturally.

Back in the old days, a master who stared at a wall for seven years straight sat before an emperor who, with a simple nod, could have a person tortured or killed.

The emperor asked, "Who are you?" The master said, "I don't know," and walked away. *(46)*

The answer tortured the emperor for many years. A living being torturing itself is completely unnatural. Torturing each other, however, seems to be something we've perfected. The master's answer exposed that absurdity. It also showed something else: when the mind is pliable, it doesn't cling to identity. It simply responds. That's acting naturally.

Now I read a fuller spectrum of internal signals—first experienced on the mat—to surf the waves of life. Sometimes the ocean does something I've never seen before and throws me off. It's all part of becoming a more creative, careful, and attentive person who knows their limitations and doesn't add fuel to a fire unless they're lighting one.

Our personalities really are like fire—bright, useful, unpredictable, and dangerous when left unattended. They can warm a home or burn it down. Practice teaches us to tend the flame without letting it take over. It doesn't teach us to put it out entirely. We need fire to live.

Staring at a wall is much more than anything we can conjure with the force of our personalities. Our personalities are an interwoven continuum of genetic traits interacting with our conditions and experiences. Even time itself is relative. We can't perceive ourselves outside time and space, and we can't escape our bodies, our culture, or our historical moment. We are what nature made us, and what we believe life is depends on where and when we are.

If we are on Earth, we are meant to be on Earth. We have a niche in nature. Our job is to let it make itself known to us. If we listen sincerely enough, nature will speak and tell us what to do. Our time here—with all its injustices, violence, pains, and joys—will feel perfectly natural. There's nothing wrong with us. If you think something is wrong with you, you're mistaken.

You can be sure that "little you" has a role in this great big universe. Even if you don't see it yet, everything everywhere works. If it didn't, we couldn't breathe. Breathe any way you want; do it naturally and pay attention. Everything works, but the trick is finding what works for you in *everything*. The possibilities are endless.

That's the heart of acting naturally: you don't need to become someone else to be whole. You don't have to transcend your body, your culture, your history, or your personality. You don't have to escape your time or your place. You can stay right at home. You don't need to fix yourself before you begin. You don't need to be special or called by God or Buddha into service.

You just sit down, face the wall, and let the dust settle. You and everything else in your life are dust. Your mind is too. Practice doesn't help you live forever or transform into a superhero—it makes you human in a way that feels less cramped, less scripted, less frantic. It loosens the knots. It lets you breathe in your own skin. Even if you're a Marvel comic fan, you'll accept people who love D.C. If you're too old to understand that you may be too old to understand the world you're sitting in.

Practice teaches us to trust a very simple and unbiased truth: We are already part of the balance we're trying to find. Tradition tries to hold nothing other than balance. Nothing is my tradition. I'm already all I was, am, and ever will be. What is here (X) is more than enough for me. All I need to do is work on staying out of the way.

You don't need to chase (X). You can't envision it. You don't need to understand it. You can't control it. You just need to do it. How do we do (X)?

Doing is simple: Sit. Breathe. Pay attention. Act naturally. Allow yourself to be your original self without complicating it.

That's it. (X) = (X). Understand? I stopped trying to escape reality by wearing a title, identity, or robe. My skin is my robe. The skin of the Earth is my teacher. My title is Human.

Chapter Eighteen

No Escape from Reality (The Oasis)

Meditation isn't an escape from reality. Out on the street, it's more like finding stillness in a place that shouldn't have any. A pocket of quiet in the middle of noise and motion. The desert has plenty of quiet, but it has almost no water. That same impossible combination shows up in meditation—a spring rising where nothing should survive. Cool, steady, asking for nothing. When you come upon a real desert spring after a long journey, you're too worn out to rush toward it, even if you want to. You just need to see if it's real. It could be too good to trust. The desert tricks easily. Where there are deserts, there's usually trouble.

Heat, distance, and the lack of water can turn the temperature inside you unstable and hot. Oases shimmer and disappear. But a true spring doesn't just shimmer; it flows. Sitting in front of the wall feels like that: no mirages, no escape routes, just the simple clarity of what's actually here. Things begin to settle on their own, the way water finds its level.

I spent a lot of time in the desert—some for pleasure, some for survival. The desert strips things down to what they are. You learn quickly what's real and what's wishful thinking. You learn how easily the mind paints an oasis where there's only heat. And you learn how unmistakable a real spring feels when you finally find one.

I never particularly dreamt of being in the desert. But I did dream of peace. So, I went far away, thinking distance might give me what I couldn't find close to home. It was nothing like I thought. I stopped my life and changed everything, but not in a stable way. I chased an oasis—a version of myself that dissolved the moment I reached for it. That's the danger of escape: it looks like water until you try to drink it.

We picture who we'll become through practice, but reality always has more texture than the mind's sketches. The real thing is stranger, simpler, and more intricate than anything we imagine. It's ordinary but ordinary in a way we might have never considered before.

Practice may point toward our mysterious origins, but first it points to what's right here. We can't see our connection to the living universe or God without first seeing ourselves. My focus is on life right now and what I do with mine. Reality is where everything happens.

My purpose is up to me, and I'm here. I've wandered through many inner deserts chasing shapes that dissolved when I reached them. At the wall, there's no escape from the truth. Sitting quietly is harmless, yet powerful. We explore ourselves daily without needing a special place.

When I felt at home anywhere, I saw endless possibilities. Life itself is practice—how we react, how we meet the ups and downs. Paying attention to what's happening inside and outside long enough makes everything fuller, more real.

The boundary between inside and outside blurs—more "us" than "them," less "I" than "we." Practice helps me judge less, compete less, and appreciate more, leaving space for the universe. I often feel playful and joyful. With less anxiety and defensiveness, I sense how everything—confounding, violent, beautiful—runs through me too. It's like learning to see in the dark, a kind of night vision. It's also opening the flap of my tent to others, letting them in. Home is in the heart and mind.

But reality includes danger too. Sometimes it walks out of the night carrying an axe. And sometimes the axe is invisible—a sharpness in someone's tone, a hidden intention, a wound they haven't tended. A skilled axe-person can be useful; an unstable one can be deadly. The desert taught me that.

You learn to read silhouettes, footsteps, the way someone approaches you. You realize that sometimes what you think you see in the distance isn't what it is up close. You learn to be sure of your target before pulling the trigger. Otherwise, you'll get yourself in a jam. Paying attention in the desert taught me when to stay open and when to stay safe. We can't stay open all the time; our body's caution is part of reality.

"Never discuss religion or politics at the dinner table" is good advice anywhere, but in some deserts, it's survival. The wrong word can get you kidnapped, tortured, or killed. Uncontained emotions ruin more than the party—they ignite whole regions. The Middle East is full of fruit that ripens fast in the heat; leave it too long and it spoils. People are like that too. Nations are like that. Peace has to be tended to quickly, otherwise it turns.

If a stranger comes to my front door with an axe, I won't assume he's bringing firewood unless I'm expecting it. Some people carry invisible axes—that kind of sharp edge can do damage. Yet people also go to bars and drunkenly throw axes for fun. Reality is complicated like that.

Balanced practice reminds me of what I don't know, which helps me feel the vastness of what's possible. I don't panic or jump the gun anymore. It's a middle way—nothing too extreme unless necessary. More yes than no. More right than wrong. And if you wonder how extreme action could ever be necessary, you've never been in an extreme situation. If that's the case, consider yourself lucky. Reality doesn't always gently play.

In this practice, there's no "I'm right, and if you don't follow me, you're lost or condemned." There's nothing more sinful than sending another person to hell for eternity. We can't send anyone to hell—we only send ourselves. But we can influence others, especially if we hold authority, so we must be careful. Reality includes responsibility.

We don't need to believe in hell to live in hell. I focus inward and take responsibility for my place, or my lack of place, in the world. The desert taught me that. If we're paying attention, a desert can teach us more than any person ever could.

Each day is up to me. "Me" is my focus, feelings, thoughts, and bodily sensations interacting with the world. In the desert, the world imposed itself on me. Back home, in my privileged community, the world isn't imposing itself on me at all. Reality is a relationship. We need to meet it halfway. I don't look for trouble, but trouble sometimes finds me. That's reality too.

An olive seed lacks our kind of consciousness, yet it knows how to grow roots, sap, trunk, bark, branches, leaves, blossoms, and fruit. It can grow in the desert so long as it gets a little water. It can be thousands of years old and is far wiser than me in the ways of the world. It has its own way of experiencing life, and it's a mistake to impose my way on it. People fight over ancient olive groves because they don't stop to listen to the trees. Olive branches not only represent peace, they speak it.

We can't grasp the essence of an olive with the mind. Meditation is similar: I rediscover and maintain an essence that was here all along. Each stage appears when conditions are right. When we try to force growth—fertilizers, genetic shortcuts—we often create problems. How does the seed know to become fruit? Which came first, the seed or the olive? Reality doesn't answer, but it keeps unfolding.

These questions reveal the obvious yet mysterious nature of existence. Emptiness, to me, means feeling at home in the vast, ungraspable universe. I accept what I can't know or control. I can't know or control much, but I can accept that. I can let go and let the emptiness of timeless space carry me. I can stay open enough to learn. I can trust that everything that happens—or doesn't—is natural. Reality doesn't need my permission.

We poke and prod the workings of existence and create beautiful stories to explain it, but our conclusions always need revision. Facing myself at the wall, I see how little space my mind occupies and how it's never the same twice. Everything I believe is real is no more than a single grain of sand in a hostile desert.

Despite the desert's imposing vastness, I no longer live under its endless horizon of doubt. I float the way heat rises off the dunes, lifting into the open air until it disappears into the sky. Yet I never leave the ground. It's not an escape. It's the opposite: a moment when I'm so rooted that the usual heaviness lets go. I'm not drifting away; I'm being carried. Reality holds me up. Sometimes, I feel a lot like a cactus. The cactus out in front of my house always gives me good advice.

My day-to-day experiences change how I see them, little by little. It might sound like I know something important, but these words just bubbled up—they're nothing more than tiny bubbles from an infinite desert spring. A spring and a desert shouldn't coexist, yet they do. One is soft, cool, life-giving and overflowing; the other is extreme, dry, highly limited and tough to live in. They survive by being each other's opposite. The spring gives the desert its rare life, and the desert gives the spring its meaning.

Do you hear the ancient wisdom of the desert spring? Meditation isn't an oasis. It's real.

Reality is big enough to hold all of it.

Somewhere inside that truth—inside the tension between heat and coolness, between danger and relief, between the people who guard the well and the ones who want to drink from it, scarcity and abundance—a new question begins to rise about how to live between them.

Chapter Nineteen

The Sweet Spot Between Extremes

Meditation helps us find the sweet spot between extremes—a place steady enough to stand in, flexible enough to move from. When we become intimately compassionate with our own pain, we naturally become more aware of others' suffering, and we do our best to stop adding to the world's collective hurt. A microphone is a good metaphor for balanced interaction: we stay at the right distance so there's no painful feedback, and what we express comes through clearly and uniquely.

Today, in a universe full of extremes—violence and tenderness, chaos and order—I simplify and rely on my practice. I remember my own pain and give others the benefit of the doubt. Life everywhere is hurting: family, neighbors, strangers, other species. I see it in deserts, marshes, beaches, forests, oceans, atmospheres, governments, workplaces, stores, cages, meditation centers, and traffic. I can't always help. Sometimes the kindest thing is simply not to feed the suffering of anyone else—help when I can, and stay out of the way when I can't.

I sincerely try to avoid adding to anyone's pain and, when possible, I soothe it quietly, without needing to be thanked or appreciated. If I made the mistake of thinking I deserve appreciation, I would have stopped trying years ago. That kind of unrealistic expectation only throws off my balance.

We live between darkness and light, and meditation helps me navigate that middle ground. I don't get bogged down in petty problems or preferences anymore. I like pizza with pepperoni and the smell of bacon in the morning, but I don't eat them often—

they're not the healthiest or most socially responsible foods. Sometimes I treat myself, and it's damn good. I bring those pigs and cows home with me, hoping they forgive me. I try to use their energy for something humane and sustainable. That's the sweet spot too—enjoyment without indulgence, responsibility without self-punishment.

I'm aware that one of the most destructive human beings in history cared more about animals than people and may have been a vegetarian. *(47)* Extremes can hide behind virtue.

When my own sensations are balanced, I can focus on others—what we typically call compassion. I don't need to be critical of myself or anyone else. A less critical view shows the world more clearly. The world has its own balance and it's a miracle, whether we see it or not. The universe is fraught with chaos.

I trust myself to protect myself—who else would? I'm less needy and more self-confident now, not trying to fix every problem or predict what might happen next. Life's difficulties are simply part of being human. People disagree. We're all equally ignorant; the only difference is that some of us know it and some of us don't. It's comes down to who's in a rush to get where they're going (death) and who's paying attention (life). But we all need to kill something to eat. Every newborn baby takes its first shit, sometimes right on delivery.

When my daughter was born, my ex-wife and I tried very hard to lessen our impact on the environment. I was a radical environmentalist at the time, carrying around enough anger and frustration to power a small wind farm. In my mind, greed and the belief that humans had dominion over nature were sinking us as a species and dragging everything else down with us.

First, we used cloth diapers. That lasted about five minutes. They were too much work and used more water than a corporate agricultural operation. Then we switched to biodegradable disposables, but those turned out to be too expensive.

Eventually, we surrendered to the reality that we lived in a modern society with limited time, limited money, and a baby who produced unlimited waste. So we ended up using the kind of diapers destined to rest in our local landfill until the sun burns out. Oddly enough, that helped soften my radical vow to save the planet. Disposable diapers—literal bags of baby poop—became my teacher.

We don't function well at the extremes; life works best somewhere in the middle. Real life often outruns well-intended ideology. My ex and I knew all about the global disposable-diaper crisis, did our best to address it, and in the end did what we had to do to survive and keep our baby from living in her own filth.

Sometimes awareness isn't practical, but it's enough. And sometimes the thing that humbles you isn't a spiritual revelation or a profound insight—it's a tiny human with a full diaper reminding you that saving the world is noble, but changing the next diaper is urgent.

Now, I think small to think big. I take care of what I can and let the rest go. It's just a matter of getting into what I'm doing or who I'm with. Spirituality is nothing more than paying attention. I used to complicate it because I wanted to feel special, as if I knew something others didn't. Here's the truth: there is no secret. It's not climatc change science.

If I'm working with plants, I listen to them. They tell me what they need. Most of the time, they're telling me to stop invading their personal space. If I respect their space, they're easy to chill with, and I like hearing where they're coming from. They're usually simple and happy. When we kill them, they don't scream like animals. Plants are fearless. From their little plot of ground, they see the big picture.

But plants aren't all harmony. Even nature has a selfish side. Once on Maui, the place where my daughter's shit diapers still lay,

I had a plot of the most beautiful tomatoes. I babied them like my daughter, wore gloves, kept my oils and bacteria away. I kissed them goodnight. Again, like my daughter. When I woke up, a floury fungus covered them like a blanket. They didn't look so happy. That fungus took everything. It sucked the life out of all of us.

I didn't want it spreading, so I burned my diseased tomatoes. It felt like a funeral on the Ganges. That's life in the garden of Earth. It dangles juicy tomatoes in front of us, then whisks them away in a flash. Another swing between extremes.

I had big plans for those tomatoes—marinara, salads, selling the rest. I imagined people saying, "These are the best tomatoes I've ever had." It never happened. All that was left was a feeling of disappointment. It was extra, just wishful thinking, far from anything real or necessary. It took away from the sacred value of the fungus, which had its own life to live. In a way, it was beautiful like a dusting of winter snow in a tomato patch on a lush-green, tropical island.

Plants show us what they like and don't like, how they work, what they need. If I'm too wrapped up in myself, I can't care for them properly. It takes experience before our thumbs turn green. I didn't know tomatoes were so fragile until I lost a patch. Now I treat my plants for mold and pests. They're pests to me and tomatoes, but they're just trying to survive. Everyone's somewhere on the spectrum between giving and taking. When you see the value of pests, you see your own value. But that doesn't mean you hesitate to waste them, if they get too bossy and try to take over.

Some outcomes are worth the planning. Other times, nothing we do matters. Meditation helps me move between those extremes without getting stuck. That's as far as I go given my circumstances. For all its violence, shortsightedness and waste, my culture hasn't forced me into extremes, but I had to go too far into death to realize life is what life is about. Life is for life. Death is for life too. Without death, there wouldn't be enough Earth to provide.

Life and death are two sides of the same equation. I focus on the side I can live. What death brings will teach me what death does—and doesn't—bring. As for me, I'll act naturally, whatever happens. I'll live and die like a baby. Babies know what to do. They know what time it is. They have no conception of it.

If we think pure practice means avoiding problems in exchange for spiritual protection or good fortune, we may be disappointed when things go bad. Even if we never look in the mirror or check the time, we are still limited physically and subject to the relentless march of time.

Recently, I had a tough month where everything went wrong: a cold, car repair, ant infestation, broken appliances, a terrible relationship break up, a prostate issue. My kids had problems at home and school. I even got kicked out of my beloved spiritual tradition.

I questioned my luck as a practitioner, but life has ups and downs. I rolled with the punches, tried not to over-think or beat myself up, and ultimately simplified back at the wall. I renewed my commitment to meditation and directly experienced its value. I became as pure as I could, for as long as I could. Pure = balanced.

Staying balanced is the practice. When things go really bad, it tests whether my practice is real. *(48)* I don't think a Zen God is going to reward me for being a good boy or punish me for being bad. My life, with its good and bad moments, is both my reward and my punishment.

Even in a bad month, something beautiful can catch my attention. A shimmer of water in my pond pulls me out of myself. I forget my problems. *(49)*

When I pay attention, the rustling trees remind me what a privilege it is to share an experience with them. The wind often blows my mind. *(50)*

In many ways, we are a privileged species. Wild animals hunted by predators don't like the wind—it disrupts their senses and puts them at risk. Deer lie low in thick brush on windy days. Usually, only predators appreciate the wind.

Sometimes the wind is cool on my brow. Other times it blows out of my ass, foul and funny. Then it messes up what little hair I have left. In extreme circumstances, it shows its temper in a storm. Whatever form it takes, paying attention to the wind puts things in perspective. The wind lives between extremes too—breeze and hurricane, comfort and chaos.

The wind is a good friend. After I turn to dust, it will still blow me away. I'll go limp and float on the cool, clear air that once filled my lungs. Maybe I'll look back with nostalgia. Maybe not. What matters moves in the air, the dust, and everything else—animate and inanimate—not just in me.

Spirituality isn't all that serious. The point of it is to know when to take things seriously and when to let things go. A spiritual person knows how to feel comfortable living between extremes. We take things seriously at the wall, so we can leave our imbalances there and not carry them out into the world.

This book is nothing but a pond. Try to be like a kid who loves fishing, always out there with their rod and tackle box. Pay attention. Try not to hurt the fish you catch. Throw them back. Immerse yourself in the pond until your parents call you home for dinner. Don't have so much fun that you forget where you are. People can't live in ponds. If you try, you'll be late for supper and everyone who loves you will worry.

Chapter Twenty

Invite the Kid Back to Play

This isn't a lecture. It's not a philosophy. It's not a technique. It's a game, a real one, and for this short stretch we'll play it like a kid. Not forever. Just here. Just now. We still need to be adults when life calls for it, but in this game the only way to win is to let the kid take over. If it works, it'll rub off on you. Maybe your kids will even say, "Mom, Dad... grow up." That's when you know your practice is really working.

Before we start *The Meditation Game*, I need to tell you about a different game—the one that inspired all of this. It was called *Daddy Surfing*, and it was invented by me and my kids when they were little. We still laugh about it.

The rules were simple: I'd lie flat on the bottom of the pool like a sunken sea creature, and they'd stand on my back like tiny, giggling pirates. Their job was to stay on. My job was to get them off.

Each level got harder. Level One was basically me wiggling. Level Two involved a strategic shoulder shrug. By Level Ten, I was thrashing around like a wounded manatee trying to shake off barnacles.

They got so good at it that the only way to win was to get… let's say enthusiastic. They'd cling to my ears, my shorts, my skin—anything to stay on. I'd come up for air looking like I'd been mugged by mermaids. They'd come up looking victorious, like, "Is that all you've got, old man?"

That's when I realized something important: Kids don't just play games—they become them. They commit. They go all in on fun.

They don't care how ridiculous they look, if they get hurt or how many body parts they have to latch onto. Unless their parents are abusive or controlling, Kids don't worry about fun getting them in trouble.

If you're still focused on this book, congratulations—you've already passed **Level #1**.

Level #2-Pretend everything in this book is a game. How? Just make it your intent to do so. Don't overthink it. Just do it.

A long-term meditation routine can help us rediscover a childlike, playful approach to life, even as we age and take on responsibility. It can help us see that we're still a kid. Not a fancy kid. Just a regular kid who knows exactly what to do without thinking about it.

Kids don't worry about the fate of the world or losing the people they love. Kids don't even know what taxes are. Kids just grow. They act naturally. They are a lot like seeds. Kids and seeds taught me about twenty percent of what I know. Life taught me a lot. Zen taught me a little. There's too many Alpha-male, Samurai running the show. Women taught me the most about myself.

Level #3: Please wiggle your arms and legs. Really let them go and wiggle. Focus on them. How do they feel? Seeds wiggle. If you start thinking too much, shout "I'M A SEED!" and wiggle. If we can get over the absurdity of the idea, this is an excellent practice to bring us back to now (X).

Kids don't know much, but they know how to play. They know how to immerse themselves in the world and have fun. Even if you've been through some rough stuff, you might still remember a smell, a sound, a moment that zaps you back to childhood like a time-traveling lightning bolt. For me, it's going back to shooting hoops, playing street hockey, being wide-eyed and free at Weir Park.

Level #4: To advance, gallop around on an invisible horse. Bonus points if you neigh. Extra bonus points if someone walks in on you.

I gallop around on my invisible horse all the time. I sing off-key on purpose. I pretend I know how to tap-dance. I say childish things like "Spank you very little." I do things so absurd that they surprise my kids. They tell me to grow up. That's the kid coming back to play. And that's good parenting.

Level #5: If you feel all this is ridiculous and refuse to do it, please move to the next level. I'm not trying to be your leader. I win only if you become your own.

Zen meditation helps me, but I don't own it—that's adult thinking. No one's actually keeping score. In this spiritual game, I'm just a kid exploring the woods with his dog. If our practice makes us more serious, something is wrong. If you're hopeless and in pain, there's a way out. It might be meditation or not. But if I can do it, so can you. I was one angry dude. Now I'm not. Kids don't gatekeep the playground unless they're bullies.

It's not necessary to scientifically or religiously analyze how a kid became a kid or how meditation works. That's like trying to explain why tag is fun. The world is our playground, but we need to play responsibly. Kids are good natured. Judgment is taught by bad judgment. Good judgment isn't judgment at all. Kids don't need a TED Talk, Zen master or guru to enjoy life. Unless they're taught to hate and bully, they know how to love unconditionally.

I feel like a ten-year-old until nature reminds me otherwise. Suddenly I'm thinking about prostate cancer, the death of family and friends, and male pattern balding. That's the part of the game where I start blasting some good music.

Level #6: Blast your favorite song. Man, there's no better feeling in life than jamming along with a good tune. If your neighbors complain, that's a bonus point.

I'm really surprised how many senior citizens stop appreciating music. It scares them because it conjures up so many old memories and feelings.

Kids let go easily, so they're always dancing and singing. Adults hold things in and make big deals out of nothing. They're more self-conscious. The more you know, the scarier it gets. Why not learn less from books and more from what's here right now (X)? It's better to know nothing. To empty your mind, face the things that scare you most. Once they're out of the way, you'll be running free and feeling young again.

Level #7: Shake your fingers. Shake your booty. Shake your face. Shake your worries until they fall off like crumbs. If someone sees you, tell them you're rebooting and thank them for the bonus points.

When we bottle up emotions, the pressure builds. Lose hope and we stop eating or overeat. Fall in love and we gain love handles. That's just how nature works. Our body type is genetic and uncontrollable, but we can direct our weight within our natural boundaries. Kids don't worry about boundaries—they just run until they fall over. Adults try to hack nature and then wonder why nature hacks back.

There's a new injection that helps people lose weight. A lot of friends and family are caught up in this trip. It takes away their appetites. I gotta' bad feeling about this one. In a couple of years, they'll probably say it does more harm than good. I don't think it's a healthy game to play.

I don't need injections to stay thin, so it's none of my business. *(51)* I'm better off acting naturally, like a kid, but it was by doing the opposite that I learned how. I acted way too seriously. I cared so much it ate me alive. The opposite of natural is assuming others have the same experiences, abilities, and intentions as I do. Who am I to judge? If we forget our roots, we fall over. Kids don't forget their roots—they're still standing in them. They learn from the trees by frolicking among them.

Level #8: Pretend you're a seed. Say something like, "Photosynthesis is my love language" to your partner. Then ask them how they feel. Chances are they will feel light and more in love with you than ever. Nothing turns people on more than humor.

Seeds will make us feel good about ourselves if we stay out of their way. We'll plant one and then in awe say, "I remember when that tree was just a seed." We stay out of the way when we encourage or don't interrupt the balanced conditions a seed needs to be itself. We gotta' be careful. If we try to help a seed grow, we can just easily damage it. Meditation practice is a seed. If we let it grow in us, it will fill us with abundance and feed our communities. We won't believe how tall it has grown.

Emotions are like weeds. Even though they take away nutrients sometimes, weeds have a place. Some of them are quite beautiful. In meditation, we listen to our emotions and contain them when necessary, without downplaying the niche they play, ruining our enjoyment of life or trying to escape what we feel. *(52)* We shouldn't contain weeds unless they threaten the growth of our seed. We let them grow and keep an eye on them. Weeds have a reason that contributes to diversity. Diversity is always good in a healthy environment.

I don't question nature's work. My morality is that simple. I appreciate the weeds in me that have survived this long. I find weeds fascinating. I feel like nothing compared to them. I'm no better than a weed. I wish the gardener would leave mine alone. When I told the homeowner's association this, they thought I was crazy.

I'm like a big kid with a lot of responsibility. I stay out of the way of hurried, anxious, ambitious crowds and only step in when someone's about to be trampled. I still watch where I step. I don't trample weeds unless I'm not paying attention. It may not be our intention, but we trample life when we're always in a hurry.

I'm the guy in the room who looks happy and doesn't say much unless you approach him. People ask, "Why are you so happy all the time? Are you dumb? What's your secret?" There's no secret. *(53)* I just stare at the wall. I'd rather they think I'm dumb. Playing dumb is highly effective. Kids do it naturally.

Some things we do naturally are good for us. Some are not. Our practice is to learn which is which, because God isn't going to tap us on the shoulder and spell it out unless we stop and listen. Ancient texts may have been written by frightened people trying to survive in a world where the wilderness felt like it might swallow them whole. Now we're the ones swallowing the wilderness whole. Kids would never bulldoze their playground.

We can still be faithful to God and stare at a wall. Kids have total faith in God without needing a reason. Unless they have a health issue, they breathe easily. As we age, we're always trying to catch our breath. Breath can't be caught.

If breathing is natural, not breathing is too. Everything comes from the same imbalance and receptive balance that makes all things possible. Kids let go easily. Adults grasp. Practice helps us remember how to unclench, especially our assholes.

Level #9: Did you forget about the game? Hold your hands out about three inches apart, parallel to the ground. Stare at the space in between. Pretend you're holding nothing. Stay still. Really think nothing. Be aware of what pops up in your mind and body to fill the space. Just be the space. What do you want in that space, in you? It's like jumping into the mud. Just good fun. Don't overthink it or worry about getting dirty. Focus on space. Congratulations—you're meditating.

When we assume the meditation posture, we mysteriously commune with nature. Our hands are exactly where they're supposed to be, holding nothing. Empty hands, empty mind—the perfect posture for inviting the kid back to play. Like kids, we can know but not know without contradiction.

We can listen to God rather than talk to Him. Call it silent prayer. Call it work. Call it play. It doesn't matter as long as we stare at the wall. I'm a teacher of nothing in the nothing faith. I'm a kid who looks at the habits of my elders and doesn't quite get them. I mean, I want to make them happy, and I don't want to offend them, but why don't they lighten up and live a little?

An organic potential is hidden within us, like the formless energy in a child. It doesn't have a name. It's one with everything. We can't own it. We don't control it. It doesn't take sides. Everything we can ever be is already here, but we can't access it by force. Our original nature only lets us in when it knows we're home. It's a peaceful energy. You can't force peace.

Kids naturally know how to feel at home. Adults forget. Kids sleep soundly. Adults toss and turn.

Growth requires light, warmth, and stability. A seed first feels at home before it grows into fruit. So do kids. So do we. Meditating alone at the wall keeps us from fixating on extremes. Healthy kids don't fixate—they bounce. Adults drift into worry or sink into fear. Kids play where they are.

Neighborhood kids at play know what time it is, and so does the kid in me. The time is right now until Mom calls me home for dinner. Through silent meditation, I reduce life's mysteries to something basic. I become naïve again, but not irresponsible. When

I get up from a good stare at the wall, it feels like springtime—the season when kids run free and the world blooms.

Life springs to life in the springtime. That's why it's called spring. Spring might come earlier these days. Things are heating up. But spring is still spring. Kids are still kids. Trees are still trees. Heat is still heat. Now is still now. You are still you, and I am still me.

As a seed of God or the universe, we plant and care for ourselves "as we are." If we plant a seed too deep, it can't climb out. If we plant a seed expecting something from it, we're in the hole too. Meditation is placing ourselves in the best position to handle life. It's the cat-bird seat—or, if we're inviting the kid back, the treehouse seat. Like a tree drops a seed, it's the perfect time to drop ourselves.

Nobody taught me that staring at a wall is the best position. Stillness and silence taught me. Maybe I was led by something more like a cosmic or divine parent? Maybe not? Sometimes I wonder what I got myself into. It's not always fun and games. I'm not a shirtless kid running around the neighborhood anymore.

Staring at a wall doesn't look like much, but it brings responsibility. It's harder to fool myself now. I don't claim to be enlightened. Kids are enlightened by nature. They just act naturally. I'm a kid whenever I can be. I'm an adult when I have to be.

A spiritual practice can sweeten or sour depending on how tightly we hold it. It gives clarity, but it also exposes every hiding place. It steadies us, but it also demands work. Sometimes that makes practice feel heavy, inconvenient, or irritating. Growth isn't easy, quick, or graceful. But if we stick with it and learn to teach ourselves, it prepares us for everything that comes next—including things like our bad habits, blind spots and superstitions.

When I'm paying attention, I stop believing in fairy tales and start seeing the negatives of my beliefs and practices. I stop painting everything as balanced and OK and get real with myself. Then, I simplify back at the wall. I work with my original balance and do not take it for granted anymore. I live in a cold, dark universe filled with chaos. I can't forget that my practice is a privilege.

Level #10: COMPLETE. Let it go. We're about to step out of the game and into something serious.

Chapter Twenty-One

The Negatives of Practice

It is essential to be cautious and aware of the potential negatives of so-called spiritual practice, especially teachers, gurus, or self-proclaimed prophets who make promises to exploit people. Critical thinking and ego are natural and necessary. Meditation is about containing unhealthy emotions and observing the mind's natural patterns rather than chasing spiritual belonging, elation, or dogma. For those in unsafe environments or with legitimate mental health conditions or addictions, staring at the wall is a complement, not a replacement for appropriate help and treatment. This is where practice can go wrong if we're not grounded.

I have primarily talked about how wonderful meditation is, but I constantly remind myself to be careful. Once we identify with a practice and immerse ourselves in it, we become susceptible to its ideas, culture, and authority figures. Even a good practice has its downsides. Every playground has a fence for a reason.

The first thing I do when exploring practice materials is make sure they don't make any promises. Does it offer a reward in exchange for money, or emphasize belief over action? Is it realistic? Can I do it right now? Do I have to turn my will over to some boisterous man-child anointed by God?

In my experience, an authentic practice or teaching promises "nothing" over "something." It's highly realistic. Lofty promises of ending suffering, heaven, enlightenment, fame, wealth, or inner peace may have brought you here today, but this practice is about containing our unhealthy emotions and facing reality. It's about simplification on a molecular level. It's not about marketing strategies, sales, or building customer numbers. The negatives of practice often begin when we forget that.

Pharmaceutical ads, filled with smiling faces, are straight forward. They are designed to paint a picture of the life a health plagued consumer can have back if they only buy the product, but because of that, they are legally required to list side effects, which can be severe. Drug company ads aren't very realistic, but at least they show the downsides. Unfortunately, spiritual practices aren't held to the same standards.

Meditation can be marketed like any other product. Mindfulness gurus, healers, teachers, coaches, and channelers aren't required to hold credentials, run clinical trials, or disclose the side effects of their ideas. They may not even be aware of the downsides of practice because they aren't seeing the bigger picture. Sooner or later, rose-colored glasses lose their hue. Purity turns to dust.

And this is where the bridge forms. The moment the shine wears off—when the promises fade, when the slogans stop working, when the spiritual sugar rush dissolves—that's when the real practice begins. The negatives of practice don't show up to punish us; they show up to keep us honest. They remind us that even spirituality needs guardrails, and that the work we're doing is not about driving over a cliff but staying in our lane.

We can convince ourselves that the world is flat, and there are people on this perfectly round planet who still do. With the internet, ideas spread across the globe in seconds. Back in the old days, potential cult leaders had to work to recruit. Now, they press a button and call themselves social influencers.

The lines between a legitimate spiritual teacher, a scam businessperson, a carnival fortune teller, and a cult leader are often thin. I am familiar with a teacher who claims to be an appointed ambassador of an alien species. In another case, a highly educated woman floored me with her belief that her guru was a perfect human who no longer defecates. She flushed her career, relationship, and half of the marital assets straight down the toilet. I met another woman diagnosed with bipolar disorder who explained that she was sleeping with a teacher who insisted she stop taking her mental health meds. Maybe feeling angry is something I need to work on, but that one hit close to home.

I was only stable enough to practice after years of treatment for PTSD and other illnesses. In my experience, for those of us with legitimate conditions, meditation and medication go hand in hand. If we quit filling our prescriptions under the delusion that practice is complete treatment, we will have no practice and, possibly, no life.

Meditation and medication help me manage my life and fulfill my responsibilities. I have a family to take care of. My kids are the main reason I gravitated toward spiritual practice. It had nothing to do with God, truth, or enlightenment and everything to do with my suffering getting in the way of my responsibilities and enjoyment of life.

We meditate for our families, responsibilities, and most of all, for ourselves. It's not for spiritual elation separate from our ordinary lives. Our ordinary lives are enlightening—and they're also where the negatives of practice show up if we're not careful. We might begin to see our practice as a way of making a living. That always leads to trouble. It complicates an otherwise simple thing.

Meditation teachers, even reputable ones, can earn substantial profits through books and workshops, and their institutions may hold considerable assets and authority after their passing. We can open our wallets for a higher cause and regret it later when the cause exposes itself as "lower."

Starting a meditation practice with good intentions can reveal how everything is interconnected and that our identity is complex and ever-changing. But true practice means staying open to new insights and avoiding rigid beliefs. It means paying attention to ourselves when something feels off.

Meditation can open the heart by revealing that everyone suffers and that everything is impermanent and always changing. But those same insights can also create confusion if we drift too far from the ground. Expanding our perspective is valuable, but it doesn't excuse us from our responsibilities. As our view widens, we have to stay steady, practical, and cautious.

If not practiced responsibly, broad universal perspectives that deemphasize the individual can cause us to become detached from reality. Our practice is to detach? What's wrong with that? I'll tell you what's wrong. To think detachment is always the right way is to be attached to detachment.

We can wake up in ten years without money, a job, education, a home, health care, or a family. In extreme cases, we can go so far as to think we have joined the ranks of gods. That's one of the biggest negatives of practice—when the mind uses spirituality to escape responsibility.

Have you ever known someone who is by nature pleasant, calm, and happy? I used to look at people like that and think, "How do they do it?" I didn't realize that they weren't doing anything but being themselves. They were at peace because they accepted who they were. They were one with their nature by nature. I wasn't born that way. We all have different conditions and abilities.

When we first start a spiritual practice, we may treat ideals like inner peace as goals to attain. We can easily attach to an idea of peace, imagining it as something we can secure if we try hard enough. But inner peace is relative, because many of the forces that shape it are outside our control.

We didn't choose how or where we were raised, our genetics, or many other factors that influenced us. Yes, we've made choices along the way, but much of what we've lived through was never ours to decide. So, while my inner peace may look uneasy to someone else, it feels miraculous given my turbulent past.

It's easy to judge from the outside, but impossible to know what someone else has lived through. Some people can maintain their balance in even the most chaotic circumstances. These rare individuals have such strong roots that they find a way. But generally, peace is circumstantial more than anything else—the conditions for peace are either available or not. When they are, as they are in my case, we can work hard to show our appreciation for the opportunity. That opportunity is made of countless factors, most of them beyond our understanding and all of them beyond our control.

Peace, at its core, is balance, and I give credit to everything that contributed to my sense of it. But, I don't cling to the label of being peaceful—it's not a badge or an identity. It's an intention, a foundation I return to when things get difficult, expressed through compassion and appreciation when I'm able. Yes, it takes effort. When I do feel it, it's a gift.

True peace isn't about achieving an unchanging state; it's flexible, adapting to circumstances and open to self-examination. We can become complacent or judgmental if we hold rigid ideas, sometimes overlooking others' suffering or losing awareness of our impact. We can hide inside a self-serving bubble. That's another negative of practice—mistaking numbness for wisdom.

Balance means embracing change, pushing ourselves to get out of our comfort zones, questioning our beliefs, and practicing continual reflection without doubting our core methods. It's easy to fall into habits that masquerade as enlightenment. While simplifying the mind is useful, critical thinking is equally essential. Both the ego and questioning are natural, allowing us to grow and experience life authentically.

It's dangerous to try to lose our ego or stop thinking. Ideas like that may talk us into abandoning our families and responsibilities for enlightenment or devoting ourselves to a guru or hierarchical organization that takes advantage of us and tells us to lie, cheat, and steal for a higher cause. The negatives of practice often begin when we try to amputate parts of ourselves that were never the problem.

A Zen master or official holder of tradition can easily be a master manipulator.

We all know religion and spirituality can turn well-meaning people into serial killers. I don't think staring at a wall has ever inspired anyone to commit mass murder, but it has helped authority figures make vulnerable, unstable people even more unstable and vulnerable. It has turned people rigid and distant from their compassionate intents. That's the dark side of practice—when silence becomes a weapon instead of a refuge.

When we come across an opportunity to help, we help, but it's not a good idea to walk around trying to be helpful all the time. That's not acting naturally. Practice is not a contest or thinking we are the good ones. Our reward and punishment are our ordinary life.

If we aren't careful, staring at a wall can turn us into gurus who break up marriages, tell the mentally ill they don't need their meds to abuse them, or build lavish temples for alien gods. We can blame other people when we mess up. We can think we're more aware of someone else than they are of themselves. This is a big mistake. These are the negatives of practice when ego sneaks in wearing a spiritual robe or title.

Spirituality is highly emotional. All the wonderful things in life—birth, family, vacation, parks, art, music, social causes, sports, marriage, love, holidays, illness, death, and ritual—are pure emotions. Emotion isn't a problem. It's the stuff of life, but our practice isn't to chase highs and avoid lows. It's about containing our unhelpful emotions and working with them as we go about our everyday lives.

Sure, practice feels good most of the time, but when I found out my writing program didn't save my work and I lost half of this manuscript, it was tested. I was surprised how upset I became. Coach helped me get through it in a matter of minutes. He said, "You'll recreate it even better. And what you have to say isn't that important. You aren't writing the next *War and Peace*. Even if you are, it's still not all that important."

When shock, pain or disappointment comes, I learn how real or fake my spiritual practice is. Taking my word for it isn't real. Real is what turns up in experience. Real is when you find your own Coach and become your own teacher, and they help you through a tough time.

I can't make any big promises, but I will make a small one. Meditation has done me and mine right. It may help if you stick with it and keep your expectations realistic. A wall can't promise anything, but we should never forget that our deep fears turn plain old walls into gods. In some parts of the world, they are fought over and have given birth to millions of little walls that have spread across the seas and separated us from our shared humanity. That's one of the most destructive negatives of practice—when the symbol becomes more important than the truth.

The practice I advocate doesn't judge; it's here to listen. It's here to support me. It has no ambitions of conquest or expanding its borders. It doesn't need to build walls to protect itself. It knows it won't stand forever. I don't own it. No one does. It has no agenda, policy, or title. That's why I call it nothing. Since I need to call it something to have any chance of helping you, I call it a wall.

The wall teaches me to be simple, still, and strong yet flexible enough to absorb pressure and movement and support the most intimate aspects of my life. It teaches me to be myself and man up to my responsibilities.

We all make mistakes and are infinitely limited in our understanding, yet we are living expressions of an unlimited, infinite movement of life. As soon as I say something high-minded like that out in the light, I know it's time to step back into the shadows and stare at the wall. I don't want to get burned. Do you feel the heat?

That's one of the quiet negatives of practice—the temptation to drift into grandiosity, to speak like a prophet, to forget we're just people doing our best. The moment I feel myself rising too high, I sit down. I return to the wall. I cool off. I let the kid in me tug my sleeve and remind me not to take myself so seriously. I let Coach do his job.

The wall doesn't flatter me. It doesn't applaud. It doesn't care how "infinite" I think I am. It brings me back to the ground, back to the body, back to the ordinary life where real practice happens. It keeps me from floating off into spiritual heatstroke.

That's the safeguard. That's the boundary. That's the antidote to the negatives of practice. The wall doesn't promise enlightenment. It doesn't promise protection. It doesn't promise purity. It just sits there—plain, silent, unmovable—and in its stillness, it keeps me from drifting into extremes.

It reminds me that when things go sideways, it isn't a punishment. No matter how complex or inconceivable something feels, it has causes. Nothing happens supernaturally or because God snaps His fingers. Reality is a long, unbroken sequence of causes and effects—an infinite formula I'll never solve and don't need to.

The wall teaches me that my thinking only gets me so far. It's a cooling shade in the heat and a warm place to rest in the cold. It's where I remember that I'm human—limited, temporary, and responsible for the life I've been given. The wall doesn't flatter me or lie. It doesn't hand me all the answers to life's mysteries. It simply holds me long enough for the truth to settle: everything that shapes my life has roots, and most of those roots are beyond my understanding and entirely beyond my control.

To me, every moment is an enlightenment moment—every experience a small, unrepeatable sequence of wonder, rising and dissolving before I can name it. The ordinary becomes mystical not because it's rare, but because it's real and I'm paying attention. It's as simple as that.

And that's enough.

Chapter Twenty-Two

Forget Enlightenment

I'm reluctant to share my mystical or non-ordinary experiences, but I'm doing it for one reason: to open your mind to the great mystery of our lives in the infinite cosmos. If nothing else in this book has stirred a sense of awe, there's a chance you may find it here. These moments really happened, recalled as honestly as memory allows, though memory naturally bends toward who we've become. That's not a flaw—it's balanced, realistic thinking at work. I only ask that you don't latch onto these moments. They're part of me, not my identity. Warning: if you ask about them during the Q&A after a talk, don't be surprised if I bring things back down to Earth fast—most likely with a comment about something as ordinary as fecal matter.

I've had countless mystical or non-ordinary experiences (for lack of better terms). They're easy to chase, glorify, or use as spiritual credentials, but they're not a foundation for practice or authority. A real foundation is always on the ground, and the further we drift from it, the more our practice drifts with us.

Non-ordinary moments can generate awe and appreciation, but they're not proof of anything. I share mine only to caution against turning them into signs, prophecies, or validation. If you've had mystical experiences or believe in miracles and use them as justification, this is meant to gently talk you out of that. If you think such things are impossible, this is meant to open you up.

Stories that seem to defy logic aren't reliable confirmations of anyone's faith or beliefs. And when we lean on them too heavily, they can unintentionally make those beliefs seem less grounded to people who don't share them. More importantly, they can have real consequences—personally and collectively. They can lead us into false certainty or imbalanced decisions that pull us away from the very lives we're trying to improve.

Enlightenment, if it means anything, is ordinary, shared, and never a badge of truth or superiority. I emphasize that constantly for practical reasons. History shows that using the supernatural to form exclusive circles or prove one's superiority has never led anywhere good.

I don't have special insights. If anything, the opposite is true. My stories—those moments that felt too coincidental to be coincidence—simply show how practice brings even the strangest, most out-of-this-world events back down to earth.

What I offer here are glimpses of our connection to a vast, mysterious universe and reminders of how limited our understanding of it really is. Mystical experiences don't create certainty; they widen our perspective and lessen our assumptions about God or the universe. They're humble reminders of our humanity, not trophies of some hidden message we imagine we were chosen to deliver.

Before I tell these stories, I need to set the stage. I had countless experiences like these that changed me. I share only four of them. Three of them were completely sober. One of them wasn't. It came from a powerful hallucinogenic drug, and I debated whether to include it at all. I'm not promoting drugs or suggesting anyone try them. I'm simply telling the truth about what happened.

I don't advocate taking mind-altering substances, even with legitimate guides or professionals. I also don't think people outside an indigenous culture should participate in ceremonies that use these substances. The people who created those rituals saw the world through a very different lens, and their way of seeing may not line up at all with the world we're living in.

At the time, I thought that my drug experience pushed my spirituality forward—and my understanding of reality too. I thought I was chosen by supernatural forces. It felt like a shortcut to the universe. But it was extreme, and I warn against extremes for a reason. What do you do with something like that? You go into the trip and then you come back to the same life. You may feel changed, but your conditions aren't. There's no discipline to hold it, no way to practice it, no structure to integrate it. You're left with a blast of insight you can't apply and a story you can't quite trust.

With distance, I can see my experience didn't launch my spirituality forward; it knocked it off its tracks. What felt like revelation ended up setting my practice back twenty years. It took me that long to sort out what was real from the story I told myself afterward.

I've also seen what happens when someone never fully returns. Today we'd call it HPPD—Hallucinogen Persisting Perception Disorder—or drug-induced psychosis. There was a kid in my neighborhood who did too much acid, too young, and wandered around shirtless like a zombie all day. Everyone called him Crazy D. He wasn't crazy. He just never made it home. Back then, we didn't have a name for it.

Some people argue that a hallucinogenic drug experience might help someone who's completely trapped in their own delusion, with no other way out. Maybe. I can't say. Maybe the whole world needs to take a trip before it's too late. I can't say that either.

What I *can* say is this: the LSD trip happened. It shaped me. It comes first because it was the most intense, the most life-altering, and the one that requires the most caution before telling. It came first in impact, even if it didn't come first in wisdom. It blew the doors off my life. I stopped wearing a suit and tie, forgot about being a lawyer and moved into a cabin in the woods to study giant minds like Kant, Emerson, Sartre and Berry and live off the land. I grew my hair and beard and followed the Grateful Dead. That experience alone would make a good book. That's why the story begins there.

EXPERIENCE ONE (*The Trip of a Lifetime*)

It was Good Friday, 1995. The house was hollowed out by spring break, its hallways echoing with the absence of twenty loud young men. Only B and I remained—two stragglers marooned on a ripped, second-hand couch in Pennsylvania, surrounded by the stale perfume of beer, sweat, and whatever sins had been committed on that furniture before we inherited it.

B adored the Grateful Dead with the devotion of a monk. I loathed them with equal conviction.

"The Dead sucks," I said, partly because silence made me uncomfortable and partly because I judged the hippies that listened to them.

"You only think that because you've never done acid," B replied, smiling like a man who knew he was about to win an argument.

"You got acid?"

"Hell yeah, I got it. I make it. Chemistry major, remember?"

I didn't. Or maybe I'd never cared.

It's strange, looking back, how casually we treated danger. We were boys wearing the costumes of men—bravado, collegiate swagger—yet we had no idea how fragile the body and mind really are. I thought I was invincible. I thought nothing could rearrange me. I made it through the Marines. What could happen in a fraternity house in Pennsylvania?

"What even is LSD anyway?" I asked.

He launched into a lecture—ergot fungus, Claviceps, serotonin, limbic system—his voice rising with the pride of a man who believed he was both scientist and shaman. He told me he grew it in his closet like some people grow basil.

"I dictate my perception," I said. "Not some chemical. Give me the stuff. It won't do anything to me." I had been reading how the Athenians marveled at Socrates because, among other things, he could stay lucid and sober after ingesting copious amounts of substances.

"For you, Marine, I'll break out the special stock. I call it the Miami Blue Butterfly Revolution."

"Break out whatever you want."

The first sign it was working came in the form of a fly that didn't exist. It buzzed and buzzed in my ears. I swatted at it like a lunatic. B laughed.

"Dude, there's nothing there."

Then came the hum—thin, electric, alive, more bassy than the buzz. A fly I could fight; a hum was something else entirely. It made me uneasy. I tried to anchor myself to the music playing through the battered sound system: "Ripple," his beloved Dead.

"Ripple in still water, when there is no pebble tossed..."

I clung to the lyrics like a man gripping a rope in a storm. But the words slipped through me. Panic rose.

"Play that line again! Stop the song!"

"Stop yelling," B said. "You're freaking out."

"Play it or I'll shove my loaded pistol down your throat!" The words shocked me as they came out of my mouth. I'd never used that pistol for anything except the dark promise I carried around for years—the belief that one day I might turn it on myself. Hearing it in my own voice, pointed outward instead of inward, rattled me to the core. It brought back a lot of bad memories. I remembered what I was capable of and the demons in me.

Unnerved and irritated, B grabbed his coat and keys and left without another word. My heart sunk into an unsettled stomach as he drove away. And just like that, I was completely alone in the universe. I never felt so incredibly, convincingly alone.

The groans in my belly drew my attention. They talked about me, as if my state was connected to theirs. Some groans were low and calm. Others were high and panicked.

It was a conversation, "Oh boy." "We're Alone?" "He can handle it. He was a Marine for God's sake." "This isn't good!" "You're right. It's not good!" "Shish. I do believe he's listening to us!" "Impossible. Preposterous. Simply unthinkable."

I sat down and forced myself to listen to "Ripple" again. I couldn't stand the sound of my own stomach, so I tried to focus on the lyrics. I caught a word or two, but nothing held together.

My stomach tried to help, muttering its own commentary: *What the hell is that singer saying? Who is that anyway? I like it. It's good.*

The stress crept in. I noticed I was sweating, so I got up to open the windows. They wouldn't budge. It was like they'd been sealed shut—definitely not up to county fire codes. As the president of the fraternity, I made a mental note to tell the landlord.

Just as I gave up and sat back down, the music unraveled. First into letters, then into light. I wasn't reading the song anymore; I was the song. Inside it, outside it, the maker and the made. Boundaries evaporated. I no longer felt subject to the rules of my time, place, or culture, but it didn't feel liberating. It was frightening.

I tried to anchor myself by returning to the song itself, not what it had transformed into in my mind. I still had a degree of control. I wondered what year it had been written. I felt psychedelic and folky, so I guessed it was around the time I was born. The mandolin sounded really good. I thought maybe I'd try playing one. I had the sensation that the song and I had arrived together. I came, it came.

"Reach out your hand if your cup be empty..."

Then darkness. My mind went blank. The music cut out, and when I tried to play it again, I couldn't even figure out how to make it work. I noticed my hands moving, like they had their own agenda. Of course they did—they were talking to each other. They muttered something about how I should use them more to do something useful and less to masturbate. They said that I should learn to fix my own car.

For a moment I wondered if this was the fallout from some old traumatic brain injury.

What the hell?

My mind started flipping through every hit I'd ever taken. Football—helmets colliding, the dizzy spells. Boxing in the neighbor's basement—catching a right cross to the jaw and feeling my legs go soft. The bully on the bus smashed my head against the window. Blood everywhere. Seven stitches from Dr. Feel Good, done right there in his office. I didn't rat.

How many fistfights had I been in? And then the Marines—falling out of the helicopter, completely out of it. There's far worse. A rush of adrenaline, a blast, that dark, sinister feeling of being betrayed by the very leaders who were supposed to protect me.

"It's all about oil," I thought. "Goddamn dinosaur remnants."

I thought my room was a safe place to forget about all that and hunker down for the duration. I got up and made a move toward it. I suddenly remembered what it felt like to be in my mother's womb. Not as an image or a story I'd been told, but as a physical memory—warmth, suspension, a slow rocking from the inside out. A world without edges. A world where nothing was asked of me and nothing was missing. I recalled that I refused to come out. It was a long arduous labor because I resisted the pressure. I had a stubborn temperament before I ever saw the light of day. When I was forced out, an uneasy feeling was born with me that I carried in my throat and stomach. It was still present.

I started to feel better but realized I was sitting in the dark. I got up but my light wouldn't turn on. I changed the bulb and when that didn't work, I checked the fuse box. I couldn't figure it out. All the other lights in the house worked. I gave up and laid down on my bed. The light from the digital clock caught my attention. It was a glowing crimson: **5:55 PM**.

I stared at the numbers as if they were a message meant only for me. When they flipped to 5:56, I leapt up cheering nonsense rhymes. I calmed down, and the glow soothed me—until the hum returned, sharper now, demanding my attention. Each time I settled down, something contrary would happen to unsettle me. It was like my mind was trying to calibrate or balance itself.

"It's electricity," I thought. "It's alive." I followed the hum from the outlet, through the chord to the clock. It talked.

"You are here now. Listen! We have so much to tell you, boy." I got scared again.

The more I thought the more the hum intensified, the more the electricity said. My stomach was still growling. My upset stomach and the electricity started a goddamn conversation. It was too much.

"Hi, how are you?" "OK, thank you." "Wow, we never talked to anything else but this clock." "I think the boy is listening to us." "Yea, he's fucked." Most people don't understand and that's a good thing." "Yea, this is gonna' get interesting."

I was terrified that thinking itself could alter reality. I tried not to think at all.

This was a different kind of fear—not the physical kind I'd trained for, but the existential kind. The fear that your own mind and body might betray you. That you are your worst enemy.

Then the clock's neon light drew in on itself. It collapsed into a single sharp point, as if the room had forgotten how to hold its shape. I held my breath in absolute fear. I believed that holding it would make the light go away.

The point swelled outward and became a presence—a swirling form, terrifying in its bare simplicity. It hovered there, a knot of awareness suspended in the air. I exhaled deeply. Holding my breath just made it worse. I drifted to my Marine training on the rifle range. Marines learn how to breathe but for the wrong reasons.

Nothing I thought got in the way of what was happening. Instead of fading, the Spirit began to speak—not aloud, but telepathically, as if light itself had taken on a voice and was delivering an ageless message.

"Come with me," it said.

"No! Leave me alone!"

But control was gone. I was in a realm where individuality dissolved, where presence replaced personhood.

"Do not be afraid," the Spirit said. "Have courage."

The world shook. I was moving at hyper-speed. The air swallowed me. Up, then down—violent swings on a roller coaster made of nothing.

Then the darkness lit up.

White, glowing formulas erupted across the black—strange numbers, symbols, half-formed letters. They didn't behave like writing. They twisted, pulsed, bent around themselves, alive with a meaning I couldn't grasp but somehow recognized. They made no sense, yet something deep in me stirred, as if the formulas had been waiting for me and a buried part of me had been waiting for them.

Then they came at me—pouring into my head, shooting, piercing, injecting themselves into whatever part of me could still receive them. They burrowed in, quick and relentless, the way weevils disappear into grain.

And then the sound waves hit.

A high-pitched whine at first, thin and sharp, but it didn't stay steady. It broke apart into bursts—beeps, chirps, low rumbles, sudden spikes—frequencies sweeping through me in every direction. The waves collided, overlapped, braided themselves together into a single, restless motion. Everything was wrapped in a soft muffle, the way the world sounds in a forest during a snowstorm, when even the loudest noise feels padded by quiet. The muffle protected my ears. Otherwise, it would have been unbearable.

The sound waves carried visions with them. Lines and pulses flickered in front of me—jagged, trembling readouts, the kind you'd see on a heart monitor or a lie-detector chart. I wasn't just hearing the tones; I could see them. The waves drew themselves across the darkness in quick, electric strokes.

And the formulas responded.

Each wave that passed through me made the symbols tremble. Each spike of sound sent a shiver through the numbers. The formulas folded themselves into the readouts, riding the pulses, syncing with the rhythm of the waves as if they were being carried along a current.

And I could smell it all. A damp, earthy scent drifted through the air—the smell after rain, or the first breath of morning fog. The scent rose and fell with the waves, as if the sound itself had weather.

None of it made sense, but every part of it felt true.

"I'm not ready to die!" I screamed. It became too extreme. I disintegrated but was still conscious. I was aware, but my mind had nothing—no sensible body, no form, no history—to hold onto. I kept feeling around for something to grasp.

"You have no individual power at the moment of your death," the Spirit said gently. "But this is not that time. Have courage." I couldn't see him, but he was there and his voice was reassuring.

Terror and awe braided together. My mind split in two. I felt myself being carried somewhere I might never return from. I mourned Earth like an astronaut drifting away from home in a speeding rocket. It was happening so fast. My mind followed its experiences. There was a pocket or lag. Pauses between movement.

I heard myself mutter, "Life, I will never take you for granted again." I suddenly yearned for the ordinary life I was falling away from.

Then abruptly, all the movements stopped. One extreme to another, but this extreme was not extreme at all. I found myself again with the Spirit atop a mountain cliff looking down on the planet from space. Everything was still, quiet and peaceful. It felt balanced. We sat on a cliff.

Earth hung below us like a living lantern—blue, breathing, wrapped in slow-moving veils of cloud. Continents glowed like ancient runes etched into drifting stone. The oceans shimmered with a kind of patient intelligence, as if the endless water molecules remembered something I had long forgotten. From that height, the world didn't look fragile or small. It looked impossibly alive.

The Spirit sat beside me in a stillness that felt older than time. There was no weight to him, yet his presence pressed against the edges of my awareness, steady and unmistakable. He lifted a hand and pointed down toward the turning planet, not with urgency, but with the calm certainty of someone revealing a sign that had always been there. His gesture wasn't dramatic—it was almost casual—but it carried the gravity of a truth I wasn't ready to understand. His hand looked like a glowing ember at the end of a burning stick. I noticed he had a neck. It was made of light that was formed in the shape of the letter X. He was neck and hands, nothing else.

For a moment, I couldn't tell if he was showing me the world, as it is, or reminding me that I belonged to it.

My focus shifted away from the beauty of the transforming scene below and to the solid wonder under my feet. The rock we sat on felt timeless—older than memory, older than story. Its surface held faces and expressions that weren't quite human but were unmistakably there, as if the stone itself had been watching me for ages. Eyes that weren't eyes. Mouths that weren't mouths. A quiet intelligence pressed into the ridges and contours, waiting for me to notice. And I did.

"You cannot tell me how all of this came to be," the Spirit said, "and therefore you will never control the true nature of your existence."

Humility washed over me. I stopped trying to be anything other than myself. I felt a wave of complete warmth. Then, I was tired and rested my eyes. The Spirit didn't interrupt me. I crawled back into my mother's womb again. The space air cocooned me, and I slept.

A thunderous crack drove me to my knees. Twelve spirits on white horses emerged from the fog, the silver beards of the six males flowing like foaming waterfalls, the hair of the females doing the same. They had no eyes—only rays of twinkling white light where eyes should be. Some had symbols for eyes, others for mouths, others for noses or ears.

They dismounted and formed a perfect line facing me.

Terror surged so hard through my body that a pressure gathered low in my gut, a sudden urge to release my bowels. I thought I might lose control right there. But every time I blinked, something softened. Each blink steadied me, pulled me back from the edge. So I kept blinking.

I heard them talking. "He knows the power of the blinking." "That was fast." "How curious." "What is his lineage?"

The horses drifted away, murmuring to one another as they grazed on tall grasses. Their low, rhythmic sounds carried the uncanny shape of a conversation—soft, familiar, almost domestic—as if they were talking about their families back home.

"Yea, when I get back, I'm going to the crystal falls with my wife and then we'll have a big feast of diamond oats with the whole family."

"Diamond oats ha? Wow, you have them? Where did you find them? I haven't seen them in years."

"This is the court of elders," the Spirit demanded my focus. "State your name."

"I… me?" I was too awe-struck to say anything. One of the court—a female—caught my attention and smiled. Her mouth was a cottony cloud, fading and re-forming every second or two. Still, by her expressions I could tell she was smiling. Her thoughts brushed against mine with soft precision, "Good boy. You're listening. Just listen. Have courage. You are a fine-looking boy. You will do fine."

She reminded me of an abstract sculpture of some long-forgotten goddess of kindness—something shaped before the dawn of time, all smooth curves and impossible presence, as if compassion itself had taken form just long enough to look my way.

All communication was telepathically. I got the sense that they were somehow more advanced than me, but at the same time, just as curious of me as I was of them. It was clear that they had a sentimental connection to humanity. Their thoughts moved in a low, circling current, and I could feel them weighing my worth—wondering whether I carried some quality, some hidden trait they valued. Some were convinced I had it. "Yes indeed. It's there."

Others dismissed the idea outright.

"No… doubtful. Very doubtful."

The Spirit whispered, "Focus on your balance. Trust your true nature. Don't concern yourself with what others say. We are all sewn from the same cloth. No head is above another."

Alone again, I redirected my focus toward Earth. When I finally surrendered to the moment, calm returned.

"Tell me how all of this came to be," one of the court members said, pulling my attention back to the matter at hand. He felt like the oldest among them, though his posture was light and almost playful, like age had refined him rather than weighed him down.

His eyes were two sun symbols—circles ringed with short, radiant lines, the kind carved into the earliest stones of forgotten civilizations. They glowed softly, not with heat but with a steady, living brightness, the way dawn first touches the horizon before the world fully wakes. The symbols didn't just shine; they pulsed, echoing the heartbeat of something primordial.

His presence carried the weight of beginnings. Not authority in the human sense, but the quiet certainty of a being who had witnessed the first light rise over a newborn world. His power was raw and all-mighty, yet it entered my heart with a strange purity, a warmth that felt both timeless and familiar.

I trusted him and the answer came instantly. I can't recall what I said, and even if I could, I couldn't express it.

"He's brilliant," they agreed. "A remarkable boy." "One of the greats." "A poet-warrior if I ever saw one."

For a moment I felt like a god—until they burst into warm, parental laughter. The truth hit me immediately: the answer hadn't come from me at all. It had come from them. All those glowing symbols and formulas that had poured into my head on the journey—shooting, piercing, burrowing in—had simply rearranged themselves into speech when I opened my mouth. Their expressions, their equations, their strange little glyphs had just flowed back out.

We all laughed and smiled together. The air brightened with that shared recognition. Then the jovial member of the court—the one with a backward G for a nose—stepped out of the line and ambled toward me. He was grinning, shoulders loose, clearly the jester among them. Everyone seemed to love him.

"It happens to the best of us, my boy. Happens to the best of us," he said as he gave me a friendly pat on the back.

He was the only one who touched me.

The moment his hand met my shoulder, something slipped into me—not like the formulas that had shot and burrowed into my mind earlier, but something gentler, almost practical. A small, bright nudge of clarity, as if he'd handed me a tool rather than a revelation. Lighthearted, helpful, and oddly grounding.

Then he stepped back into place, still smiling.

The mood changed.

I felt it before I understood it—a subtle drop in atmospheric pressure, the kind that makes the world hold its breath. The space around us tightened. Their laughter faded in perfect unison.

A sudden cold swept through me. Goosebumps raced up my arms, and the hair there froze upright, standing straight out. My skin prickled, and I began to shiver.

That was when the far edge of the cliff darkened, like night itself were gathering into a single point. Out of that thickening shadow emerged a black horse, enormous and muscled, its hooves striking the stone with a deep, metallic resonance. Its mane whipped in a wind that wasn't there. And on its back sat a figure carved from darkness.

My first thought was worldly. "The archetypal black is evil and white is good."

The spirit guide didn't appreciate me bringing Earth's divisions into an already divided scene. "Stop the nonsense! Don't squander the time. Focus!" His reprimand along with the presence of an all-consuming darkness, collapsed any confidence I had left into a ball of puss.

First came nausea. Then a swelling throat. My body was tearing itself apart. Corpses clutching my flesh, desperate screams. Decay. Waste. Total annihilation. Hell, if there ever was one. Suddenly I saw a pack of hyenas eating a baby elephant who was crying out for its mother.

I locked eyes with the elephant, and it pleaded, "Please help me. Please." The pleading was thin and broken, a desperate sound that cut straight through me and hurt in a way I can't explain. I couldn't do anything.

The dark one demanded attention. He rode with a terrifying stillness—upright, regal, predatory. While the court of elders glowed with a gentle radiance, this rider absorbed every trace of light around him. His outline wavered like smoke trying to remember the shape of a man. The horse's eyes burned a deep starlike silver, but the rider's eyes were worse: two polished voids, reflecting nothing, promising nothing but hunger.

He guided the horse to the cliff's edge with the poise of a king returning to his throne.

Then, from beneath the stallion's hooves, a bridge of coal colored stone unfurled across the canyon—smooth, silent, impossibly long. It stretched toward me like a living thing, a diseased tongue tasting the air in desperation.

"Come," the dark spirit said. His voice was velvet dipped in poison. "Ride with me. Cross the bridge. All the riches of the world will be yours. Just get on the horse."

Images detonated in my mind—beautiful, naked women sprawled on silk sheets, penthouse apartments high above glittering cities, luxury yachts cutting through turquoise seas, crowds chanting my name, medals, money, power stacked to the heavens. A life of appetite without consequence. Ambition. Greed.

"Get on the horse," he repeated. "It will all be yours."

Each repetition grew heavier, more hypnotic, like a drumbeat meant to drown out my will. I felt drawn to it. I moved in its direction. Everything in me fought it and I stammered back.

Behind me, the court of elders stirred. Their pearl-colored robes rustled like wind through pristine, old-growth trees. First, they rhythmically chanted something unintelligible. "Shacha! Sha. Sha. Shana!"

Then, it made sense. "Do not listen to him! Stand your balanced ground!" They chanted over and over in one unified voice. "Focus. Have courage. All for one and one for all!"

The dark rider chuckled and tilted his head, amused. The horse pawed at the cliff's edge, sending sparks into the abyss.

"Come," he whispered again. "Everything you've ever wanted. Just get on the horse."

The bridge pulsed beneath me, alive, waiting. The ground began to sink toward the bridge. I held onto a rope-like root on solid ground.

And for the first time that night, I understood the stakes—not cosmic, not symbolic, but deeply human. A choice between self and all. Between greed and meaning. Between the easy path and the true one.

"Hope! Courage! Hold on! Don't let go of the root," the court chanted. "Stay strong!"

“Courage! Hope! Truth! All for one and one for all!” I shouted. I was determined to resist the temptation.

The dark force erupted with a roar that split the air. “It’s not over,” he bellowed—voice cracking like iron under strain. The court cheered.

His horse reared back, towering, its hooves slashing at the sky. A screech tore out of its throat, wild and primeval, as coils of black smoke poured from its nostrils. The smoke curled across the canyon bridge and around us like living shadows, tasting the air, searching for a way in.

“It’s not over… It’s not over…”

The words rolled out of him again and again, each repetition softer, more seductive, as if the threat were slowly turning into an invitation. The echoes stretched across the unseen distance, thinning into whispers, then into breath, then into nothing at all. The black bridge crumbled and fell to the floor of the canyon in an avalanche of sound and dust.

And just as suddenly as the dark one had appeared, the world fell back into stillness—a clear silence that felt less like peace and contentment and more like relief.

A beam of warm, yellow light shot into me and filled my mind and belly.

“Remember the source of the light,” said the court in unison. “Worry not about the dark forces that try to obscure it. No fear. Courage! All for one and one for all!”

Buzz. Pop. Steady hum. Glowing white formulas flashed against the blackness of never-ending space, racing into my mind. Movement everywhere. Mad vibration. I felt as if I were on a space-vessel tearing across an ocean at hyper-speed. The spirit wasn’t with me. I could sense I was headed home alone.

I was back in my room, curled on the floor in the fetal position, braced against the wall. The familiar details told me I'd returned—the carpet, the corner, the air—but my mind hadn't caught up. Awareness felt strangely outside of me, yet shaped by whatever was happening right then, as if it were both mine and not mine at the same time.

From the position of the sun and the warm hue spilling through the window, it looked like late afternoon. The clock confirmed it: 5:55 PM—a confirmation of the impossible more than a simple reading of time. I was gone for exactly twenty-four hours.

Then the alarm clicked on. College radio, FM 89.5. The Grateful Dead. *"Ripple."* Those opening lines—about a song handed down, a voice that isn't yours alone, a ripple with no explanation—echoed around the room. The melody moved like a wave with no visible cause, stirred by forces far beyond my power or understanding. The sound filled every corner. I listened to the whole song and perfectly understood each and every word of the lyrics.

It floored me. I was stunned. The poignant, upbeat tune somehow let me slip from one world of possibility back into the one I thought I knew. In that moment, the song felt like evidence—proof that the trip had touched something real.

I adjusted my eyes, trying to make sense of the room. The light felt too bright and too dim at once, as if my vision hadn't fully returned from wherever I'd been. Edges wavered. Shadows pulsed. Colors seemed slightly off, like the world had been repainted in my absence. I blinked hard, but each blink only reminded me how far behind reality my senses were trailing. The blinking that worked to calm me in the other world was just plain blinking back home. All it did was make my eyes water.

My eyes were wet, but my throat was so dry it hurt to swallow, a deep, parched thirst that felt like it had been there for ages. I had just come off a life-altering experience, and I felt like I'd just finished a thirty-mile hump in the desert—one hundred pounds of gear, ammo, and a weapon on my back, blisters on my feet, and not caring whether I died or who I hurt. A voice inside kept begging for water. *Water. Please—just a drop.*

I rushed to the bathroom and drank straight from the faucet, lapping at it like a wild animal because my hands wouldn't work right. When I finally looked up, the shock hit me.

I didn't recognize the person in the mirror. Sweat soaked my shirt. My hair stuck to my forehead. The face staring back looked like me after being left on the charger too long—overpowered, over-bright, over-heated and slightly unhinged. It was the kind of face that made me want to apologize to it. Seeing it felt like walking in on myself mid-transformation, as if I'd interrupted a version of me that wasn't finished becoming whatever it was becoming. It was like an electronic file in the process of uploading.

A sudden panic pushed me away from the mirror. I ran toward my room, but my legs gave out halfway there. I collapsed on the floor, overwhelmed by a wave of raw, wordless anguish. I just wanted it all to stop. I craved rest the way an addict craves a substance—completely, blindly, with nothing else left in me. My mind ached like the back of a retired professional wrestler.

My whole body vibrated, shaken from the inside out. I felt feverish, like I'd contracted some museum-grade illness—something with a name like "dropsy" that no one's suffered from since the Civil War. I tried to stretch, but a vivid image of the saltwater taffy-pulling machine from the Wildwood boardwalk rose up in my mind and stopped me in my tracks.

I tried to adjust my body but everything I registered lagged. The air smelled of stale beer, the dusty warmth of late-day sun, and the water-logged carpet soaked with the sour remnants of young men who'd indulged too much. The light had that hazy, suspended quality—like the hallway was holding its breath. The walls looked both familiar and foreign, like I was seeing them through someone else's eyes.

I was confused and wobbly, unsure who I was, barely remembering my own name or circumstances. Re-entering didn't feel like waking up. It felt like being lowered back into a smaller world after touching something vast—one foot still planted in that incomprehensible elsewhere; the other struggling to remember how to stand in this more ordinary place.

Eventually, my breath steadied. I focused on it. The feverish heat eased. My body balanced and cooled enough that I could sit up, then stand, then leave the house. I needed uncontaminated air. I longed for it. I felt sure enough to open the front door. The world outside looked completely new—sharper, stranger, impossibly fresh. I felt born again, but without belief, without a savior, without a story to hold onto. I was alone, but new, and I had no idea what to make of it.

I made the mistake of deciding to visit my girlfriend at her job at the mall. I was compelled to walk there, then to run. I couldn't even process the fact that it was eight miles away. Back then I was a serious runner, and something about the movement grounded me.

The world looked magnificent—too sharp, too alive—and the physical effort released whatever chemicals my body could muster to counter the aftershocks of the drugs. I still couldn't grasp that I had eight miles ahead of me; my legs had already made the decision. All I could do was follow them.

I arrived soaked in sweat, shirtless, barefoot, and wearing only my Marine desert fatigues—looking less like a boyfriend and more like a broken recruit on Parris Island who'd finally snapped and tried to escape through the swamp. I knew it was a mistake the moment I saw her expression. She looked torn between hugging me and alerting mall security. Her white-collar boss at the jewelry store made the choice for her. I knew right then and there that she was sleeping with him. She leaned in and whispered, "He's calling security. Run." She cared enough to warn me, even as she kept her distance.

A few hours later she pulled up to my house in her old Chevy Corsica. When we sat down and I told her what had happened, it was the beginning of the end. I asked if she was sleeping with her boss. She looked scared. She said my eyes looked too wild to meet—like something in me had cracked open beyond her reach. She tried to understand, but it was too much. She thought I'd been swallowed again by the trauma I carried like a bulging ILBE pack (Improved Load Bearing Equipment) on my back. She drove away after only a couple of minutes and never looked back.

After that, I grew my hair, changed my major to philosophy and moved into a remote cabin near the Cornplanter State Forest. Past gone. Present new. Future forever altered—all because of four microscopic grains of invisible fungus. I don't recommend hallucinogens to anyone.

EXPERIENCE TWO (*My Miami Family*)

I hadn't gone to Miami Beach looking for anything profound. If anything, it felt like the last place anyone would find peace—all neon shine, sculpted bodies, loud music, and restless display. I was just visiting a friend, filling my days while she worked.

Each day I wandered the streets with nothing to do but pay attention, and in that simple, aimless drifting, something in me came alive.

I moved through the city like a child again—unguarded and curious—letting the colors, scents, voices, and salty, ocean-warmed air move through me. The more I noticed, the less I needed to be "someone." I felt myself thinning into the wider hum of life around me—not disappearing, but joining.

For a few days, the boundary between "me" and the world softened. I wasn't the center of anything. I was part of everything.

The city's hustle and bustle, with its hurried people and palpable stress, vibrated through me. I felt for them, their nervous systems handling so much. Some reminded me of another local resident, the whaling seagulls, unpredictable and untamed.

On the first day, I encountered a homeless woman sitting on a cardboard box. Her weathered appearance and strange mumbling drew my attention. She was wrapped in layers of mismatched clothing, each piece stiff with old rain and street dust, and her eyes flickered with a kind of inward lightning, as if she were arguing with storms only she could see. Premature wrinkles cut sharply across her face, and her cracked skin looked as if it had been left out in too many seasons. As she convulsed, I hesitated, fearing my curiosity might cause her more distress.

The next day, I witnessed a picture-perfect family: a young boy holding his mother's hand, a small girl clinging to her father's. They were not dressed in trendy clothes, took their time, and seemed free. They looked happy to be together, as if nothing else in the world mattered. As a divorced man with two children, I savored the completeness of it all. They took a selfie in front of the Martin Luther King statue, and it melted my heart. It must've been a good one. One that they would all cherish for a long time to come. The father explained something poignant to the children who were attentively listening. Perhaps a few personal reflections on MLK.

I focused on the family, trying to keep my distance. I felt like one of them. It was a good, pure vibe. I hoped they didn't think I was following them.

Finally, we reached a familiar corner. The homeless woman from the day before stood up and said, "Your family is beautiful. Please cherish these moments forever."

The tourists were startled and quickly crossed the street to protect the children.

My experience was different. The woman glowed and smiled. Her posture changed. She looked like a noble angel. She was clean, like an innocent girl.

I realized she had probably lost her family and children due to her illness and trauma. In a magnificent moment, she passed on a priceless lesson: "Cherish these moments forever."

She sat down, hunched over, shook, and mumbled more. I wanted to talk to her, but there was no space or stability for communication. I wanted to hug and tell her I loved her, but it was impossible.

The next morning, I was walking with my friend to breakfast. The woman was still on the shabby box.

"I'm buying her what we're having and bringing it to her," I said.

"She's a junkie. Why waste money on her?" my friend responded.

"Yesterday, I was here with my kids. She saw us and was happy. She was normal. She told me to cherish the moment. I appreciated it. She cleaned herself up."

Confused, my friend said, "Your children have never been here, and you weren't in Miami Beach with them yesterday. She's a dirtbag. Maybe that crazy lady is rubbing off on you?"

Then it hit me again.

There was no separation between me, the family, and the homeless lady. I directly saw our true, unified nature. That experience floored me, you know? Where had I gone?

EXPERIENCE THREE (*The Devil's Embrace*)

He was so violent, so deeply demonic in presence, that one state paid another simply to take him off their hands. Legend has it he even rattled the Governor—sent a chill through a man who claimed to be a white knight on a crusade to conquer evil. The story followed MW like a shadow.

MW's cell neighbor, a death row student of mine named WD, was worried about him. He told me he'd seen things—moments that convinced him MW's black-magic persona wasn't just talk. He said MW chanted in strange languages at night. WD was legitimately freaked out, maybe even a little scared, though he couldn't admit that to himself without cracking something in his own psyche.

He asked if I would try to guide MW in a different direction. He saw something in him, a small spark he hoped might be redirected with the right kind of attention. He told me MW was all alone in the world, that he'd never had someone stable and kind like me to guide him. Praise like that reaches even the humblest among us.

WD's compassion moved me, and I agreed to take on the task. So, I reached out to MW through the corrections system. We exchanged emails and then talked on the phone. The relationship began poorly. He tried to intimidate me immediately. Somehow, he knew the gender and ages of my children and threatened to possess them.

"Great," I responded. "Child possession is a big seller. And two at the same time no less. I'll write a book about it and make a fortune."

He let out a low, guttural laugh and whispered, "I'm not kidding."

I felt nothing. His power seemed real, but I wasn't afraid. The whole exchange slipped out of my mind—until two in the morning the next night, when something in my sleep opened like a trapdoor.

They arrived without sound: the devil and two demons, forming themselves out of darkness the way storms gather on a horizon. They weren't bodies so much as shapes—clouds with eyes, drifting and collapsing into symbols I couldn't read. Everything felt both impossible and utterly real, the way only dreams insist on their own truth.

Lucifer stood in the middle of the two demons. He introduced them. Their names shook me to the core. I couldn't utter these names even if I remembered them. I'd be too afraid to release them into the world.

When I looked into the face that called itself Satan, dread rose through me like lava. It wasn't panic. It was older than that—something earth-deep, something that seemed to recognize me. My legs gave out. I felt myself kneeling without choosing to. The devil forced reverence.

A sour, rotting smell seeped into the air, as if the dream itself were decaying. And yet, even inside the terror, a small part of me watched from a distance, trying to understand what my mind was revealing and why.

Then the lucid dream turned violent. I buckled with a burning sickness like I had ingested acid. A puke brown substance rushed out of my pours and pooled into a boiling sweat on top of my head. Patterns, formulas, screams, strange languages, and fractured images rushed through me. It felt as if the collective suffering of the world had been shot straight into my skull. A piercing pain exploded behind my eyes, and for a moment it felt as though my mind shattered into little pieces.

I woke up choking, my head pounding, seized by a fear I hadn't felt since that life-altering, twenty-four-hour, acid trip back in '95. The hours that followed dragged on without mercy. I couldn't lie still. I squirmed and twisted in the night like some de-earthed creature caught in a rare desert rainstorm—alive, exposed, and desperate for conditions to go back to normal. By the time morning finally came, I felt scraped raw from the inside out.

I had an important assignment at work. It didn't feel so important anymore, but if I wanted to keep my job, I had to go in. I tried to focus. I made it look good. I didn't say a word to any of my co-workers, but they sensed it anyway. They kept asking if I was alright. They said I looked pale, as though something had drained the color from me overnight. They told me to make sure I wasn't sick before coming back in.

I was relieved I had an excuse to take off the rest of the week. My mind couldn't have been further from work—it was still caught somewhere else entirely, suspended in another dimension, hovering at the edge of something I couldn't push away.

That night, exhausted, I did everything I could to stay awake. Even copious amounts of caffeine and a Marine's will-power couldn't fight sleep. The devil and his demons returned quickly. But this time something in me caught itself. I came back to my breath, went still and silent, and realized my fear was giving them power. My meditation training surfaced.

I stared Satan in the face, endured the barrage of darkness, and pushed through it. Then, in the middle of the nightmare, I did the most unexpected thing: I offered him a gentle hug. I told him I was there if he ever needed to talk.

The evil forces quietly recoiled. The entire scene collapsed into a pin-point silence. There was nothing. It felt peaceful, warm and even older than the devil himself. I woke up feeling strangely strong and clear, as if I had reclaimed something I didn't know I'd lost.

It wasn't long until MW reached out. He snickered, "So how's your sleep been?"

I started to tell him about the dream, but he cut me off mid-sentence.

"Dude, I know. I was there."

I believed him. He said he was the demon who stood to Satan's left. He even gave me the demon's name, and it sounded familiar. It carried a kind of darkness that didn't leap at you, but waited for you to notice it already living inside. He joked that he didn't blame me for failing to say hello. He admired my courage. He told me the devil had scolded him for assuming I was weak, and that the dark one genuinely thought I was "A cool dude."

He finished by saying, "You really are a Bodhi Bobo the Clown," which sounded like a compliment, though I had no idea what he meant.

It was a breakthrough. Something in his fractured mind softened. For the first time, MW showed me respect. In that moment, I saw how simple kindness and skillful means could pacify even the most primordial darkness. I hugged the devil and that shifted everything.

EXPERIENCE FOUR (*Blue Light Son*)

Years ago, I received a call from a Kung Fu master inviting me to use his studio for meditation sessions. He wanted his active students to learn to sit still. That's a wise man. I committed to a year, each Wednesday at noon. Every other week, there was an open session where we invited the public. They were usually attended but sometimes I was alone. Initially, it bothered me to be alone, but I soon preferred it. The studio was beautiful, with hardwood floors, Asian decor, old bonsai trees, good lighting, and a large window facing the parking lot.

The studio was in a strip mall, next to a flooring supply store and a nail salon. People would gaze in, seeing me sitting still. I enjoyed their bewilderment. Most were customers drifting between errands—women with freshly lacquered nails, men carrying samples of laminate under their arms, all of them wearing the distracted, half-present look of people moving through a day they didn't choose. They paused at the window as if they'd stumbled onto something out of place, unsure whether to be curious or unsettled. Some looked as if they'd seen an alien and rushed away.

Other people came to meditate. Many arrived late, draped in loose clothes and clutching their mats like they were boarding a flight. They stared down at their phones, fidgeting like stillness was something that might bite. They'd see me through the glass—a motionless figure in a room meant for movement—and immediately turn around. I didn't stop them. I rang the starting bell at noon, whether the room was full or completely empty. Maybe I should've been more inviting, but the bell never seemed to care.

I always showed up a half hour early to meditate. One day, a radiant blue light from a truck window caught my attention. Usually, I fix my gaze to nothing, but it demanded my focus. Suddenly, a woman entered. It took me about thirty seconds to transition from the light to the woman. She saw that I was occupied, noticed my neatly placed shoes and carefully set hers next to mine. I thought, "She's paying attention."

We exchanged pleasantries. She introduced herself as W and said she had come to meditate. She wanted to sit like me, so I helped her settle into the kneeling position on my mat. She was well into her senior years, and I was surprised by how easily she assumed the position. Her posture was perfect, as if her body had been waiting for this shape all along. I asked how long she'd be comfortable sitting like that, and she said, "As long as it takes." There was no pride in her voice—just a calm certainty that made my own confidence feel a little forced by comparison.

W asked what I'd been staring at in the parking lot. I pointed out the blue light reflecting off the truck window. It was still there. At first she squinted, unable to catch it, but then her eyes widened as the color finally revealed itself. I told her I'd been dancing with the light when she walked in.

“Oh my God in heaven! You were dancing with it? Of course you were!” She burst into tears, unguarded, and I reached out to comfort her, unsure what I’d just opened. After a moment she gathered herself, wiped her face, and began to tell me her story.

W’s husband had dementia, and she couldn’t manage him alone. Her days were already stretched thin. Then her son passed away unexpectedly at fifty, leaving behind a wife and two children. She was devastated.

One evening, while drinking wine with her girlfriends, she told them her son had always said she should try meditation. Later, she told her husband’s nurse the same thing. The nurse encouraged her to go and mentioned that I offered free sessions every Wednesday. The nurse, she said, reminded her of a childhood friend in Chicago who had eventually become a nun—steady, gentle, and impossible to ignore.

Before leaving the house, she gave the nurse the address of the studio and texted her girlfriends where she was going. She told them to call the police if she didn’t return. She confessed she’d imagined a cult leader, but after meeting me, she realized I was just a regular old guy.

W was crying because her son’s favorite color was blue. At his funeral, she released a hundred blue balloons, even though she knew it wasn’t good for the birds or the sky. She said she couldn’t help it—blue was the only way she knew to send him off. As the balloons lifted, the overcast sky suddenly broke open. Sunlight poured through the clouds and caught the drifting blue shapes, turning them into small, glowing lanterns. For a moment, the whole crowd stood in that light. No one denied it was him.

Blue had been woven through his entire life—his clothes, his car, his shoes, everything. Even his nickname was Blue. It was the color he carried, the color he gave away, the color he left behind. And now here it was again, flickering on a truck window in a parking lot, waiting for her to see it.

When she saw the light with me, she knew it was him. It was the same light she saw at his funeral. Blue was there next to us.

As she told me the story, a warm chill moved through me—heat and cold braided together, rising from a place I didn't know how to name. My eyes filled before I understood why. I cried, and W gently patted my back, comforting me even as she carried a grief that could have swallowed her whole.

What struck me wasn't just her story. It was the way she came toward her suffering, not away from it. She didn't hide, or harden, or protect herself. She reached out—fragile, honest, trembling—and somehow still found room to care for me. That was the moment I understood something I had only ever repeated as an idea: compassion isn't a concept or a catchphrase. It isn't a virtue you try to perform. It's a living spirit that moves through people when they're honest and hurting and brave enough to stay open. It was in her voice, in her tears, in the way she touched my back without hesitation. It was presence—real, breathing, unmistakable.

We meditated for thirty minutes afterward, both of us quieter, steadier. She settled into stillness like she'd been doing it her whole life. I felt almost giddy. It made me putting myself out there to help people meditate all worth it.

When we finished, the room felt different. Softer. Brighter. And so did we.

In the months that followed, W didn't disappear into her grief. She started sitting groups for grieving mothers and wives. She formed a support group for spouses caring for partners with dementia. She built community out of the very things that had broken her.

I credit her for all of it. She credits me. And she and I both credit Blue. That's balance.

What she passed to me—the compassionate, resilient spirit she carried—remains. Zen Buddhists talk a lot about transmission, but it isn't mystical or ceremonial. A teacher may pick who to give it to, but sometimes Zen itself does the picking. It's natural. It's in the air, like oxygen and hydrogen—unseen, but present, waiting for the right conditions to combine. It's a subtle thing that moves from one person to another when the moment is honest enough. That's what happened between us. She didn't teach me anything or pick me. She transmitted something that can't be given in a ceremony or title.

I don't know what happened to W. We lost touch. That's life, time, and change. People cross your path, open something in you, and then move on. But what she gave me stays. I know I'm doing what I'm meant to do even when others doubt me.

Such experiences are commonplace now. They're no big deal. They don't make me special or more aware. If you pay attention, you'll notice them in your own life too. Forget enlightenment. Just pay attention and catch yourself when you lose sight of the bigger picture.

That's why a practice like meditation matters. It takes all the complexity, mysticism, and noise and reduces it to a single point you can rely on. A place to return to.

I'm not interested in analyzing every transmission or out of this world experience I've ever had. I don't claim to know how any of it works. I focus on what's right here in front of me (X). I don't look for answers or signs outside of myself, but sometimes they find me.

I'm an ordinary man—into my family, practice, plants, exercise, sports, and music. I just stare at the wall. You might be tempted to dismiss me because I don't claim any special authority or awareness, but the truth is simpler:

I am just a regular dude, and I'll do whatever it takes to make sure that stays clear.

I am also a happy tourist family, smiling into a camera.

I am a disheveled homeless woman whispering secrets into her palms.

I am you, appearing for a moment as if you'd always been here.

I am a mass murderer and Death Row inmate.

I am a man with dementia searching for a memory that keeps slipping through his fingers.

I am the stressed-out people of Miami Beach rushing past in desperation.

I am even my heartless former friend who thought I was crazy.

And then—something shifts. The veil thins.

I am high-priced pastries lined up behind glass like tiny, edible lies.

I am a stained couch sagging under the weight of forgotten nights, its fabric still holding the ghosts of choices I barely remember making.

I am a brilliant blue light flickering through a window, pulsing like a heartbeat.

I am Satan and his demons.

I am the hallucinogenic fungus blooming in impossible colors, its spores drifting like tiny balloons through the dim corners of memory.

I am the court of ancient beings watching from their thrones of drifting stone, their faces shaped from starlight and non-judgment, as if they see everything and condemn nothing.

I am the dark lord rising among them like a wound in the fabric of the scene. "Get on the horse."

I am the black horse rearing back, hooves slashing at the sky, smoke pouring from its nostrils like a living shadow.

I am the planet turning below—ocean blue, breathing, impossibly alive.

I am the Spirit beside me, pointing down with a gesture so simple it feels like a revelation.

I am a bridge to greed crumbling to nothing.

Of course, I can't forget that I am myself. That wouldn't be a good idea.

Chapter Twenty-Three

Raw Acceptance

Raw acceptance begins with taking life as it is, not as we wish it to be. That's the hard part, and the liberating part. Meditation helps us assume the form of our balanced nature in our little pocket of life in the endless universe. When we settle into the posture and listen, we signal to God or the universe that we're ready to grow into something new. If our efforts are genuine, we can set aside our usual fears, judgments, and expectations for a while. We can act like seeds that quietly grow into refreshing fruit, nourishing a hungry world. Magically, staring at a wall may help us unify. The pain we face in meditation brings us back to what matters before it's too late. Once our practice fills our bodies, minds, and homes, it naturally feeds those around us. We don't need to follow anyone else.

We didn't choose where our parents planted us, so we came out kicking and screaming. If a baby is born silent and calm, something's wrong. That simple fact reveals something essential about our nature. Raw acceptance doesn't mean liking everything; it means acknowledging the conditions we were born into. It doesn't mean we stop trying to fix what can be fixed. It simply lets us release what we can't.

We might not like the world—its demands, tragedies, ideological battles, exploitation, violence, and judgments. We need things like money and air, and we can only act with enough of them. We can live happily with almost nothing, but life and practice are impossible without air and money. Raw acceptance includes accepting these basic facts. It might not be fair, but it's the way it is.

For some people, their first practice is figuring out how to make enough money to survive. For others, it's going to the doctor, a mental health professional, or a dentist. It might be finding reliable childcare. Sometimes our practice is simply cleaning up. Other times, it's apologizing. We need a degree of stability to meditate. The posture itself is stable. When we get into it, we become that stability.

We can lose our ability to discern what's real. We can become rigid in our beliefs. Practice itself can turn into a wall—something we hide behind instead of something that helps us let life in. Nature has two sides, and meditation isn't all balance and harmony. We can follow a self-absorbed guide, develop anxiety-driven aerophagia, or injure our knees through fixation. That's not raw acceptance; that's self-inflicted trouble.

We can complicate our situation and overthink it. The point of staring at a wall is to simplify, accept our conditions, and take better care of ourselves and those around us. It's better to have no point at all. To just do it. I meditate with no preconceived notions and watch myself change and grow in a world that evolves alongside me.

A seed never doubts itself. It doesn't worry about what it's not. It accepts itself as it is—pure raw acceptance. It follows an intuitive force we call God's design (if we believe) or genetics (if we don't). Everything in nature shares the same potential, from the smallest particle to the largest system. A seed can't act in a self-defeating way like we can. It may land in the wrong place and die, but it can't intentionally destroy itself.

The meditation posture sets the conditions for us to grow into a more receptive, less fixed understanding of ourselves and the world. It helps us live more naturally, like a simple seed. A seed grows through each stage without confusion. So do we, when we allow it.

We're unusual in that we can direct nature's ways. We can convince ourselves we exist for any reason under the sun. We can even believe we don't deserve to live. What we do depends on our conditions and our intentions. Raw acceptance brings those two into alignment, so we can act in a way that feels natural, not distorted.

All seeds have one intent; we have many, often in conflict. While nature's individuals tend to work together unless forced to compete, we can work alone against ourselves and everything else. We can invent problems, judge strangers, feel separate from nature, and act on beliefs that reinforce that separation. We can use symbols and words to change the direction of change itself.

Some people write books to help us destroy each other; others make millions telling us how to save ourselves. I wrote this book to encourage you to accept life as it is, to stare at a wall, and to appreciate the balance it takes simply to be until being is no more.

Wall meditation helps me feel at home in the world—that's all. I know my place and feel free. It's simple, but not so simple. I may need to write another hundred pages for you to believe I'm encouraging you to do nothing.

You might not be ready for empty words, but whatever you believe cannot be threatened by doing nothing. Meditation isn't a belief; it's a stable action. It's a way of life—a tool, if you like—that helps us stay afloat in the choppiest seas. It's a silent prayer. We listen to God in stillness instead of telling Him what we prefer, deserve, or need.

Meditation may help us sense the interconnections that make us who we are, but it doesn't interfere with our beliefs or traditions. Our monotheistic traditions already hold that God is one and all things are connected. Meditation doesn't touch the how, who, or why of creation. That's up to us.

Things begin to change when we commit to practice. Things are changing anyway; meditation helps us stop and witness it. The wall helps us examine our circumstances, beliefs, thoughts, feelings, sensations, words, and actions in the most balanced and inclusive ways possible. It helps us appreciate our limited time and realize when it's time to pivot.

When I bring something new into the universe, it's a big deal. The ingredients were here long before I turned on the flame, but I can rearrange them however I like. I can cook with total disregard for the ingredients, but will it taste good? *(54)*

When our intent becomes a simple posture that honors the original balance of nature, we become more seed-like, more natural. We merge the consequences of our limited understanding with an ageless reality beyond our reach. That merging—that willingness to let things be as they are—is raw acceptance.

All I want out of this is for you to sit down, quiet and still, and stare at a wall. I'm trying to convince you to do nothing, to accept yourself exactly as you are. Raw acceptance begins with stopping the habit of bullying yourself like a troubled kid in the schoolyard. Kids are the way they are for a reason. So are you.

Once we trust the posture, everything else falls into place. Nature or God takes over. We make good decisions based on circumstances rather than fixed ideas. We fulfill our obligations. We grow confident and warm. Less conflict drives itself into us. We have a lot of fun. I'm more than satisfied with whatever I do or don't have, and because of that, I have more than enough to share. We can't share what we don't have.

When we meditate, we align our intentions with our conditions, without expecting future gain or reward. What could a wall possibly do for us? That's not something to ponder. It's something to experience. You might be curious about meditation because you want enlightenment, solutions, peace, or the ability to help others. Whatever brought you here matters. Your intent is beyond my judgment.

But for the seed to grow freely, I had to step out of the way and let it do its thing. That's raw acceptance in practice. A seed takes care of the rest if we don't interfere. Usually, we think we need to push or pull something along, or that we need a force larger than life to carry us. Meditation is the opposite. I meditate so I'm ready to run into the road and remove obstacles without hesitation. If it helps others, great. If not, that's fine too.

I'm like the neighbor with the chainsaw clearing the road after a hurricane. People drive past without thanking me. After a storm, everyone's stunned by the force of nature. I don't expect praise. I'm just doing my job. I need a clear road, too. The old-timers say, "It ain't work if you love what you're doing." If you love God or the pulse of life, you work smarter, not harder, and you enjoy the flow.

I'm far from a well-oiled robot. I have obligations, a full life, and plenty of moments where I get pissed off and do stupid things. I need perspective to shake off the negative feelings. I need to reboot. I rely on the turning words of my practice friends. *(55)* Without them, I'm a frozen screen. My mind is a computer: when I meditate, I click "shut down." You won't lose anything by shutting down. Everything is still there, but now you're in a better position to choose what to open when you start back up.

Ironically, rebooting the part of my mind that plans and organizes helps me determine what's most appropriate once I stand up and move into my busy day. I still judge others falsely, but now I notice when I'm doing it. A big part of practice is catching ourselves—being aware of what we think, feel, and say. It's an internal fact-checker that doesn't let us get away with nonsense.

It's a cosmic irony that silent meditation mimics the singularity—the emergence of the universe from nothing. How could a timeless "nothing" help me make better decisions here and now? I don't get stuck on big questions. How does a single acorn become an oak? Regardless of who or what created life, it's good to let the universe settle occasionally. That's all meditation is: waiting for the water to clear so we can see what's swimming around. And it's all swimming in our minds. That's not an easy thing to realize, no less practice in real life.

We pause the creative expansion of life to prepare ourselves for the heated action that begins the moment we move again. Doing nothing to do everything else is perfectly simple and balanced. We let the big questions go for a while and listen to things like walls. Our walls sit silent, flexible, and strong, watching everything come and go.

"Just do it," said my most cherished Zen Master Suzuki Roshi. Sit there. Observe yourself doing nothing, with minimal expectations and judgments, and go with the natural flow of an expanding, perpetually changing universe. If you need to ask what Zen is, you probably won't know. The key is to stop studying it and start doing it.

When you stare at the wall long enough in the prescribed zazen position, you don't need answers. Then you may be free enough to help others *do* their own answers. We don't find answers or provide them. We do them. We practice answers to see if they truly are.

Allow yourself to be yourself. You might not realize it, but you are the universe itself. I know it, and I'm no better or different from you. Everyone is enlightened already. We share the same potential. The trick is realizing it without getting carried away. That's the heart of raw acceptance. It's OK to know you're enlightened. It's not OK to stop working at *being* enlightened. Enlightenment is knowing we're humans and everything else at the same time. Self and everything are two sides of the wall.

We get carried away when we think we know something others don't, or when we separate ourselves from our unified nature with our discriminating minds. Those are the real walls. Raw acceptance means refusing to build walls to separate ourselves from anyone else.

I'll say it again: if someone claims to be enlightened or more aware, run away from them. If someone tells you someone else is enlightened, run even faster. If you pay attention, you'll see the delusion in their eyes. They usually look stoned or mentally unwell. If they say you don't represent their tradition, it's not your tradition. Get lost and forget it. It's not for you.

Be aware of this much: you can't teach meditation. All you can do is show people how to teach themselves. And you can't do even that unless you've spent enough time staring at a wall to know that balance is everything, and you are merely a tiny pocket of it in endless space. The real deal isn't someone polished or perfect. It's a flawed human being who shows their vulnerability and makes it perfectly clear that it's a privilege to practice.

An enlightened person couldn't conceive of their enlightenment because it's just their ordinary life. In a trillion, trillion kalpas (periods of transition), they'd never allow anyone to think they were anything other than human. They'd make mistakes on purpose to reinforce it.

Enlightenment shows up in every state—high and low, pleasant and unpleasant. It's suffering, joy, and hard work. It's a red-tailed hawk gliding through thin air, a dew drop catching a ray of light, pond scum and sewage, the sun and the moon, gravity and the Earth spinning on its axis.

Enlightenment is hard drugs and pornography. It's sober living and our bodies as temples. It's a shot of whiskey and a smack filled needle. It's the bubbling stew of everything in the universe. It's not serious until it is. It's fun until it's not. It's balance, imbalance, and the return to balance. It's nature's way.

At the time of death, we may realize our enlightenment, but by then it's too late to do anything with it. God or the universe balances the ledger one way or another. When we balance our own ledger, we balance everything else. The universe learns from us as much as we learn from it. Our balance has bigger implications than we can imagine, but that doesn't make us special. We don't sit around pondering it.

Later today, I'll sit still in traffic while picking my daughter up from school. Then we'll see how balanced I am.

Now and then, in the middle of life's traffic, we find a clear lane. The clear lane is in our minds — in how we perceive and feel about our situation. We can sit in traffic and make the most of it: listen to an audiobook, jam to music, or catch up with an old friend. But if we always feel like we're running late, we'll be too stressed to enjoy anything that gets in the way. We'll complain, and nobody likes a complainer—especially when the complainer is the voice in our own head.

Our stories are often the problem. Who doesn't love a good, embellished story?

A couple of months ago, I stepped into the shower and nothing came out. I was freezing. My mind went wild: "Did I forget to pay the bill? Did a pipe burst? That'll cost a fortune! Does insurance cover it? Oh shit—is it terrorists? Or that damn neighbor shutting off the water to do half-assed work without a permit?"

Pissed off, afraid, and shaking like a wet skunk in December, I learned the utility company had shut off the water to clean the lines. My internal bitching was unnecessary and unpleasant. I had released a storm of negative energy for no reason. I laughed at my own stupidity. Enlightenment is ordinary. It's the moment you catch yourself, laugh and let it go.

If we intend to stare at the wall and get out of its way so that what it plants can grow within us, we have the potential to bear fruit. But we need to stay on solid ground and not get ahead of ourselves. If we dig too deeply in the wrong place, we get into trouble. We don't put all our tomatoes in one basket when they're still seeds. We wait until they're ripe. Seeds grow one step at a time. This is nature's way of teaching patience and wisdom—and the beauty of raw acceptance.

Chapter Twenty-Four

Forget Words. It's Time to Meditate!

(Interactive Photos/Video Available at: https://stareatthewall.org/)

We teach ourselves to meditate through years of trial and error. At first, we do it at home with whatever's handy. If we do it to join an exclusive social club, or stand out, it will only let us down. Alone, in front of the wall, we single ourselves "in" not "out." We experiment with everything from sitting positions to posture and breathing techniques. It's an intimate thing, not a show. We observe our bodies and minds without expectation or judgment. We teach ourselves how to do that by practicing it. We take a realistic, compassionate approach to our pain. We become intimate with it. On our own, we find what works naturally. Practice is not one-size-fits-all. There's no right or wrong way to begin. Start with just five minutes a day for two weeks without missing a day. It's a manageable way to cultivate simple balance. Last is a reminder that at some point, we must forget the words, books and discussions and actually sit. After we sit for a few years without missing a day, it's time to bring it Further into the rest of our lives.

Think of the following instructions as a fruit-seed packet. Before opening a pack of seeds, we read the back for basic information. It tells us when, where, and how to plant. The rest is up to us. The instructions say very little. If we're patient and skillful enough to harvest fruit from seed, it's through trial and error, awareness of conditions, and focus.

We watch seeds grow repeatedly and work closely with them. We listen without getting in the way. They tell us what they need and don't need. Like any successful relationship, it's a collaborative effort.

Discussions about seeds are irrelevant until we plant them. Fruit results from balanced conditions. What's the point of discussing fruit when it's still a seed? It needs to mature and tell us, "Harvest me. I'm ready." Trees bloom before they bear fruit.

If we don't grow, we have nothing to talk about. We can't call ourselves farmers if the only farming we've done is theoretical. We need to get our hands dirty. The more seeds we grow and care for, the less talking and reading we do—and the more fruit we enjoy. Forget the words. It's time to meditate.

When practicing the balanced position, we are like seeds ready to grow. We signal to our original nature that we're ready. Ready for what? Maybe to help others, appreciate life, or reach our full potential. Intent changes over time. Meditation teaches us to be ready for anything.

We need to remember who we work for. We follow the lead of nature. God or the universe is the big boss. We are the little boss. We direct some things, but control very little. When we get in trouble with the boss, we only hurt ourselves. Once trust is lost, everything becomes unnecessarily complicated. Everyone loves to mess around sometimes—so don't be too serious. The boss will understand.

If we pay attention, we directly experience ourselves as a seed moving through its growth stages. Once we love, trust, and appreciate this transformative process, we no longer need experts, instructions, labels, descriptions, or explanations. That's when the chapter title becomes literal: Forget the words. It's time to meditate.

The Prerequisite

You plant the seed of meditation by simplifying your mind. Just do it—no expectations, no dramatic inner negotiations. Follow these simple instructions at first, and then, once you get the hang of it, toss them in the compost and follow your own. That's how practice works: start with a little patch of ground, before getting ahead of yourself. My job is to give you the best chance of getting the first seed in the ground. The book instructions also include twenty photos. Hi-res photos are available on the *Book Page* of my website *(https://stareatthewall.org/book/)*.

There's a how-to video on the *Home Page* of the site as well *(https://stareatthewall.org/home/)*, if you learn better by watching. I'm a visual learner. You might learn differently. I wanted to make sure everyone was covered. It mattered to me that no one felt shut out or confused. Practice opens doors, not closes them. That's why I offer different ways in.

Find your own way of learning. The little things matter. Pay attention. Are you listening? If not, put this down and come back. Whatever your point is, there's no point without focus. Meditation helps with that. It takes all the complexity and noise and reduces it to something steady you can return to again and again.

Sit for five minutes, two weeks straight without missing a day. If you miss a day, start back at day one. If you need to start over, you're not a failure. If you meditate for the rest of your life, returning to the beginning is what you'll do every day.

The only way to fail in meditation is to stop doing it. Pay special attention to **day nine**. For whatever reason, very few people make it past that day.

We work under the Harvard honor code. *(56)* Once you've meditated in the prescribed way for two weeks straight without missing a day, email me at *blacknellzen@gmail.com* and maybe we can grow together. If I don't answer, keep trying. If not me, I'll refer you to a qualified guide. Please respect my privacy and personal space.

Keep your email short and be aware of your intent. Remember, what you say matters. I'm a lazy nothing who doesn't let people waste my time. I waste enough of my own.

Of the thousands I've introduced or reintroduced to meditation, only a few have completed the prerequisite. That's because staring at the wall, even briefly, is infinitely more complicated than it appears. It's complicated in the mind, not on the mat. On that mat, it's simple. We just do it.

Preparation

These instructions are mine alone. They don't represent my sangha, teacher, lineage, the Soto Zen tradition, Zen Buddhism, or Buddhism in general. They are not a guided meditation. They're the basics to get you started at home without me or anyone else. Don't take them literally. Listen to the Coach's voice within. Let Coach develop a rapport. You already know what you need to do. If you show up, Coach will show up.

Meditation is intimate. At first, sharing your experiences may not help. Still and silent in the position, you are in an enlightened state. We don't talk there. We listen. We may find peace in the warmth that assures us there's nothing to achieve. If we are patient and sincere, achievement achieves us. Nature expresses itself through us. We sit balanced and it rubs off on the rest of our lives.

Once meditation feels like a good friend, we'll naturally find other wallflowers with similar interests. We don't stare at the wall to gain access to an exclusive club. We do it to practice raw acceptance and to honor the balance of nature. Our reward is the relaxed feeling of home we may be privileged enough to carry everywhere. We will appreciate the balance of life and do our best to stay out of its way.

Genuine meditators could make a real difference, not by forming a movement, but by standing quietly in their own clarity. If they ever “band together,” it’s only in the sense that constellations do—each one holding its own place, each one true to the causeless balance that shapes all things. I don’t know what such a group would look like or what it would do. If you have any ideas, let's talk.

But first things first. We must concentrate on planting our own seed. To meditate, sit on a chair or the ground with a mat, pillow, or whatever’s handy. Face a blank wall.

If lying down, face the ceiling with your back on the mat or floor. Position pillows as needed. Make sure the wall or ceiling is clear of distractions. If possible, set the room temperature just right.

Wear solid-colored, dark, loose-fitting clothes. Remove shoes and jewelry. Empty your pockets and your mind may follow. Smile! It's not so serious.

[INSTRUCTIONAL PHOTO #1]

(Go to: *https://stareatthewall.org/book* for hi-res image)

My wall is smooth and plain white. My cushion and pillow are black. We stare at a blank wall to minimize distractions and put ourselves in the most natural position for growth.

[INSTRUCTIONAL PHOTO #2]

(Go to: *https://stareatthewall.org/book* for hi-res image)

If you are traveling away from home, outside or homeless, use whatever's available. Our practice teaches us to adapt to and accept our relative conditions.

Your meditation posture doesn't need to look good. There's no right or wrong way to begin. Grace is not always required so long as we know the steps. These are the steps. Don't worry about other people on the dance floor. Just dance.

I took my first practice step on an old exercise mat with a couple of pillows from the couch. Use whatever's available. During my lunch breaks, I also sat on park benches and stared at trees.

I wish my parents were there to video my first steps into meditation. I can't imagine what it looked like; maybe a big baby, stumbling around, learning to find his balance?

Choose a Mat and Cushion

If you are a beginner, I wouldn't buy costly meditation equipment. If you quit, it won't feel so good to see it lying there. Its presence might make things worse. There's no need to invest in your practice until you invest in it. Have you ever bought the latest fad exercise equipment?

Our walls and clothes are blank and plain. So are our mat and cushion. Black is the preferred color of our meditation kit, but any light, solid color will work. Most dark browns, greens, and blues are OK.

I like a thinner mat and a large pillow because that's what I started on, but it's up to you. I'm loyal to my kit. It never fails me. Some habits are worth keeping. Some aren't.

Use anything handy at first, like a throw rug, a thick beach towel, a folded blanket, a yoga mat, a large pet bed, or household pillows, if it doesn't distract or stimulate your senses.

[INSTRUCTIONAL PHOTO #3]

(Go to: *https://stareatthewall.org/book* for hi-res image)

Create a Practice Space

For those in populated areas, noise is a factor we can't wish away. I don't recommend earplugs. We practice in the real world and appreciate pockets of silence when they show up, not when we demand them. If you have kids and responsibilities, they come first. Our practice isn't more important than the people who rely on us. Our practice is them.

If the dog barks or the kids interrupt you while they're playing, work with the irritation. Don't stop and tell them to shut up. Tell yourself to shut up and work with it. That's practice. Anyone can be peaceful in a monastery. Try doing it in a living room in the middle of a city with a two-year-old and a Labrador.

My whole life is in relative silence. I live right next to a busy road but experience it that way. I'm privileged. I'm only opening my big mouth to share the subtle practice that helped me find stability, but talking about silence is a crock. Doing it is real. We do silence in silence. We become it. Alone.

Can you hear a pin drop? If there's a jackhammer outside your door, chances are, you can't. I'm here to tell you that we can hear pins drop even when hammers are jacking. Quiet is within. You'll still hear the hammer, but it won't irritate you or consume your attention.

Putting your meditation kit out of the way if space is an issue is fine. Whenever possible, however, leave it ready for action. If you have a furry friend, like Porkchop, they may appreciate it.

[INSTRUCTIONAL PHOTO #4]

(Go to: *https://stareatthewall.org/book* for hi-res image)

Some people create an altar next to their practice space. Mine is made from cheap attachable plastic and includes photos of close relatives and teachers in my lineage. I also put important books and items with sentimental value on my altar.

We work with what's readily available. What we have is enough. We can look at "enough is enough" in many ways. In this case, enough is enough; really, it is enough.

The only statue on my altar is a statue of nothing.

[INSTRUCTIONAL PHOTO #5]

(Go to: https://stareatthewall.org/book for hi-res image)

I place fresh flowers on my altar when they are in season. The plumeria bush in front of my house blooms twice per year for several months each time. The flowers are vivid yellow and smell like spring. They look like the sun. Sometimes when I see light reflecting off something, I see plumerias. They drop while they are still alive and well. I pick up the flowers only after they fall.

Every flower that drops goes on the altar. I never cut them. When they're still connected to the bush, they have more important work to do. I don't disturb the balance of nature for my altar. I thank the plumeria even when it isn't blooming. The bush itself is an altar. It died in a rare winter frost, and now it's out there withering to nothing. It reminds me of my own skin as I get older.

During COVID, I homeschooled my kids. They loved to play on my meditation kit. At first it bothered me. Then it became beautiful. Hint!

[INSTRUCTIONAL PHOTO #6]

(Go to: https://stareatthewall.org/book for hi-res image)

Sometimes, I light incense and say a silent prayer for a particular person, a problem in the world, or myself. Occasionally, I also light sage and bathe myself quickly in its smoke. These types of practices are optional. All habits that encourage us to sit in front of the wall are good and relevant. You can get as creative or stay as simple as you wish.

Brush Away the Past

If your pillow is on top of your mat, place it gently to the side. First, we brush the dust off, no matter what we use as a mat. We remove the remnants of the past.

[INSTRUCTIONAL PHOTO #7]

(Go to: https://stareatthewall.org/book for hi-res image)

Pay attention. Addressing the past to focus on the present is not a precursor to meditation; it is the first act. We bring our minds to (X) or what we are doing here and now.

Wipe off any dirt that has accumulated since yesterday. You may be surprised. Where did all this grime come from? Take your time. Consider the gravity of what you are doing and why.

I found it best for my busy lifestyle to buy large, black laundry bags and use them as covers for my mat and pillow. That way, I can take the covers off and wash them quickly and easily.

Place the Pillow on the Mat

Now, take your pillow and put it on the mat. Leave room for your legs and feet. If a part of your body is off the mat and on a hard surface, you'll pay for it later.

Like a driver adjusting the mirrors and seats in a new car, each meditation rider naturally adjusts their pillows. To take off safely, we make sure everything's in order.

Fluff the pillow(s) on four sides by pushing down as if you were doing CPR. Rotate the pillow and push. You will thank yourself later. Eventually, you will feel like you are pumping life back into yourself.

Each day you stop to meditate, you will revitalize yourself. I push the pillow down on four different sides to accept all directions. Whichever way I go, it's cool. Even when we're lost, we're learning the way.

[INSTRUCTIONAL PHOTO #8]

(Go to: https://stareatthewall.org/book for hi-res image)

Don't be shy. Your practice is yours. Feel free to design a unique routine. Whatever gets you consistently still and balanced is just right.

You are gently leading yourself home by the hand. We tend to shut off when people try to force their way on us. Only you can lead you home. Try a gentle approach. Be kind to yourself, and the rest of the world may follow.

If using a household or bed pillow, you may want to use more than one or fold it over. It will be easier on your back and legs.

If you intend to lie down, clean the mat or floor and fluff your pillow(s) as best you can.

If you intend to sit in a chair, brush it off and adjust your pillow(s) as instructed.

Now is the time to sit or lie down.

Choose a Position

In Asian cultures, people sit on the ground until their funerals. In mine, babies and children do, but big people don't.

Some sit in full or half lotus, cross-legged with the feet resting on the thighs, but if you can do that, the chances are you don't need instructions.

If you are flexible, search "Zazen position" or something similar. Be careful of the source. I don't sit in lotus and don't know much about it.

When I first started meditating, I looked around. Those who seemed to know what they were doing were in a lotus. I thought it was mandatory. My assumptions did not help.

I hurt myself trying to sit like that. I learned the hard way that the point is to be still and balanced enough to pay attention. Once I got into the groove, the Coach within helped me feel perfectly fine sitting however possible.

An eighty-five-year-old Japanese lady taught me that sitting on the ground is not necessary.

Our preferences and personalities do have a place in practice. Like everything else, they are perfectly natural. If we listen to them too much, they turn us into gluttons. If we don't listen to them enough, they turn us into gluttons of pain.

Walking meditation is also part of my practice, as is meditating in nature, but today, we stay put inside. We stay put to limit sensory stimulation and observe the subtle dance of body and mind with as few distractions as possible.

If our daily practice is outside, what do we do if the weather is inhospitable? Our mother might be pissed off and not want us out there practicing. If we walk to meditate, what happens when our legs refuse to do what we tell them?

If you're homeless, all bets are off. Do whatever it takes to sit. It will help you navigate the mean streets. Once, I showed a homeless woman with three children how to meditate. It clicked for her. I worked with her. Her life is not perfect, but she's not homeless anymore. The point of meditation is to simplify and accept our conditions at home or without a home, as they are, not as we wish them to be.

When I stop for thirty minutes and assume the still and silent position, it whispers a week's worth of good advice. I give God or the universe an opening to speak. I signal stability. I plant myself on fertile ground and grow. God shows us love directly when we meet in the middle. Balance is the fundamental principle of good, sustainable things in life.

One way or another, I remember the power of simple practice. Especially if you're your own worst enemy like me, it's better to get back to basics before big trouble forces little you back. I try to become as pure and aware as I can. Some people wouldn't call my version of "pure and aware" anything close to that. But I know what it feels like from the inside, and I trust it.

Sometimes, I clap like thunder during a meditation session. People get startled and scowl. They glare around with a "What should I do next?" or "What's your problem, buddy?" look on their faces.

Those who stay still and quiet, no matter what I do or don't do, probably have a strong practice. These focused souls know someone else's noise is not theirs. Why get upset or distracted by noises we don't control?

Once we accept our conditions, we can finally start working with them. For example, if we're homeless because of an addiction, the first practice isn't meditation—it's addressing the addiction that put us in that situation. That's the real work. We might even try to get help with the same determination we waste our lives using to get the substance. It's the same drive, just pointed in a direction that doesn't destroy us. It's the direction of forgiveness.

I kneel to meditate because it feels most tolerable and natural to me. At first, I didn't see anyone else doing it and thought I was doing something wrong. I worried about what I should call it. Eventually, I accepted that my position was mine alone. I call it kneeling. Experiment to find yours. Call it what you will. Just stare at the wall.

Kneeling

If kneeling, straddle your pillow and keep your knees pointing down toward the mat. Let gravity do its thing. The position of your legs and feet is not that important. Whatever's tolerable works.

[INSTRUCTIONAL PHOTO #9]

(Go to: *https://stareatthewall.org/book* for hi-res image)

Use this photo #9 to establish your base. Notice chin down a little, back of the head up, shoulders back, spine as straight as possible, stomach in, and eyes open, relaxed, and fixed slightly downward. My posture isn't perfect, so I'm always working on it. I don't beat myself up.

Cross-legged

Many people are comfortable sitting cross-legged. If this is your choice, make sure a pillow or cushion is under your butt and your knees are facing down. The elevation will help you stay balanced longer.

[INSTRUCTIONAL PHOTO #10]

(Go to: *https://stareatthewall.org/book* for hi-res image)

Some people like to sit on the floor with their backs to the wall for support. While that could be an option, for this meditation, it's better to sit in a chair facing the wall.

Turning our backs to the wall is symbolic. We face the wall and ourselves.

Chair

If sitting in a chair, you can use pillows or a small cushion to support your back. An armless chair with a back is best. One of the disadvantages of sitting in a chair is that you won't experience deep pain in your legs. I feel it's a disadvantage because the pain I have experienced in my legs while sitting has taught me how privileged I am to be able to get up and walk away.

[INSTRUCTIONAL PHOTO #11]

(Go to: ***https://stareatthewall.org/book*** for hi-res image)

Put your feet shoulder-width apart and point them directly away from your body. Make sure your spine is straight. The back of the chair makes it easier.

[INSTRUCTIONAL PHOTO #12]

(Go to: *https://stareatthewall.org/book* for hi-res image)

If your chair seat is long, use pillows to support your back. Sit up straight so your knees hang over the edge.

[INSTRUCTIONAL PHOTO #13]

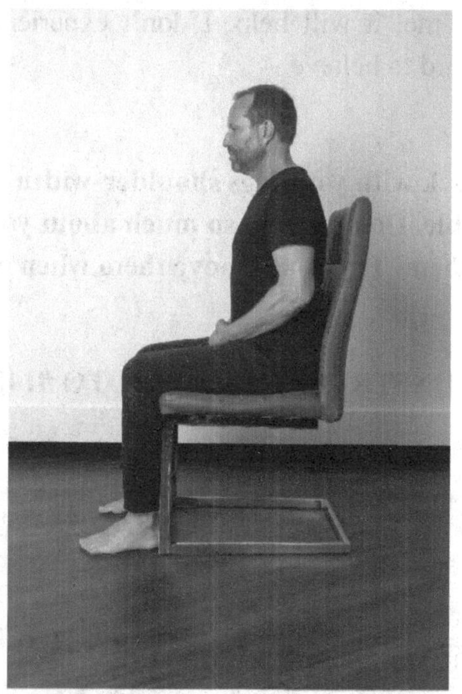

(Go to: *https://stareatthewall.org/book* for hi-res image)

Lying Down

If you're lying down, use the mat to support your body. Lie on your back and stare at the ceiling like you're waiting for instructions from above. You might not need a mat if you have carpet, but at least make sure the space is clean before assuming the position. Running a vacuum to tidy up your meditation area feels like a perfectly modern way to bring real life into practice. It's a merging of the modern with the ancient—household chores and timeless stillness sharing the same room.

You can use pillows to support your head, legs, or other body parts. Unless bedridden, do not meditate in bed. If bed it is, bed it is. Wherever you stop and focus, even if it's not ideal, is the perfect place. That's balanced thinking. Once you establish your practice, you will likely meditate without trying as soon as you get into bed. If you are like me, it will help. I don't experience sleep issues anymore. It's hard to believe.

Lie on your back with your legs shoulder-width apart and your feet comfortable. Don't worry so much about your feet, but be aware of them. Try not to move them when meditating.

[INSTRUCTIONAL PHOTO #14]

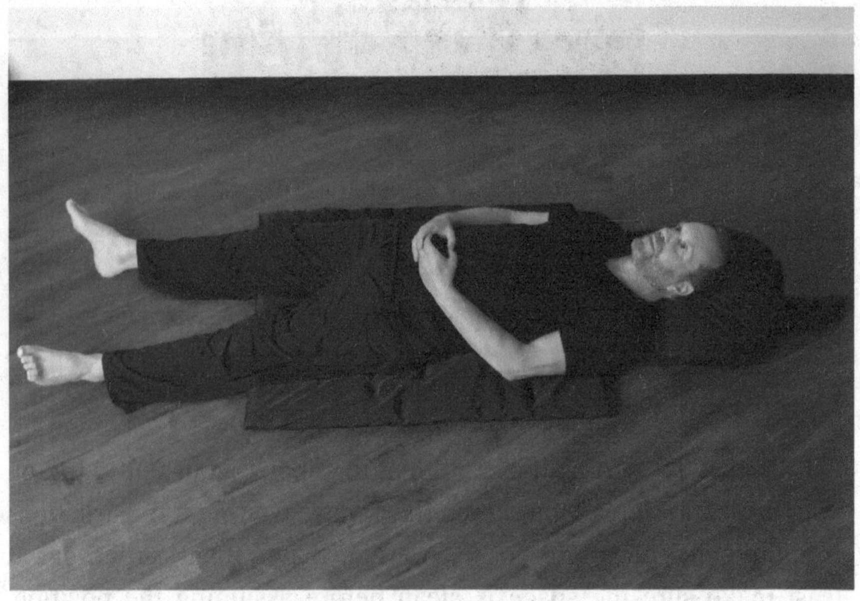

(Go to: *https://stareatthewall.org/book* for hi-res image)

Maintaining the hand position may be more difficult when lying down. In the lying position, gravity can demand quite a bit from your hands.

If you find it too hard to keep your thumbs together in a heart shape by your naval, try bringing the heart up to the ribcage *(see hand position in INSTRUCTIONAL PHOTOS #15, #16, and #17)*. Put your arms and hands to your sides, palms up, as a last resort. In yoga, this is called the Corpse pose. It's far harder for me to meditate lying down than sitting up.

Do not close your eyes. Stare at the ceiling.

Eyes Open

We keep our eyes open in meditation at first. How can we stare at a wall or ceiling with our eyes closed? I fell asleep and hit my head on the wall. That's when I learned it is best to keep my eyes open when practicing.

Over the years, I have learned that people naturally want to close their eyes when meditating. Those who have dabbled in practice before are often determined to keep their eyes closed.

I keep my eyes open because they are closed when I sleep, and practice is about being fully awake. When out and about in the hustle and bustle of the world, I want to be prepared. If my practice is to close my eyes, I might do so in the worst possible situation. I might crash my car to remain calm in rush-hour traffic.

If you are stuck on whether to keep your eyes open or closed in meditation, it's a good idea to try both. How does open feel? How does closed feel? The balanced approach is to keep our eyes open and closed, which is why, at first, I recommend keeping your eyes open when meditating.

You'll naturally want to close your eyes, so be aware of them and do your best to keep them open. That's all. We do wall practice to accept change and try a different way of balancing ourselves.

We gaze slightly down at the wall, but not so far that our neck bends or our head tilts down. Some beginners say their eyes hurt. Pay attention to the distance between you and the wall. Experiment. Move closer one day and then further away the next. You will find a distance that is just right for you if you stop and pay attention! The Coach will help you along.

We live with our eyes both open and closed, but we meditate with them open. Our eyes aren't wide open. They are relaxed. If they start to close, just be aware and open them. That's good practice. The same goes for your hands, feet, and other body parts. Be aware if they are moving and bring them back to stillness.

Once you firmly establish a meditation routine, you may experiment with your eyes closed.

How long does it take to establish a practice? For today's purposes, at least seven days a week or more, twenty to forty minutes per day, for one year. How can we practice more than seven days a week?

If our first practice is to sit for two weeks straight, five minutes per session, does it count toward establishing our practice? Yes, it counts.

Especially if we have previous meditation experience, why not do longer sessions upfront to speed up the process? These types of questions don't help.

Just stare at the wall for five minutes each time for two weeks straight without missing. In the beginning, that's more than enough.

Our practice is to always be a beginner. I remind myself often. I tend to be stubborn.

The Hands

Put your hands in front of your face, about chest high, like two little shark fins, thumbs up, facing each other. Your eyes need to be open to do this.

[INSTRUCTIONAL PHOTO #15]

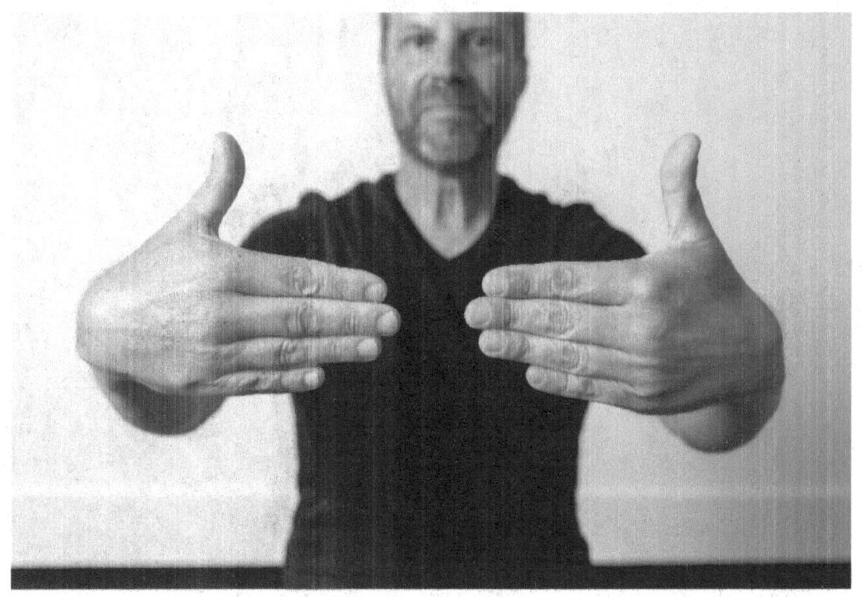

(Go to: *https://stareatthewall.org/book* for hi-res image)

Now make the two little sharks swim toward each other. If you are right-handed, slap your right hand over your left. Put your left hand over your right if your left is dominant. Make it snap! That's the sound of success.

[INSTRUCTIONAL PHOTO #16]

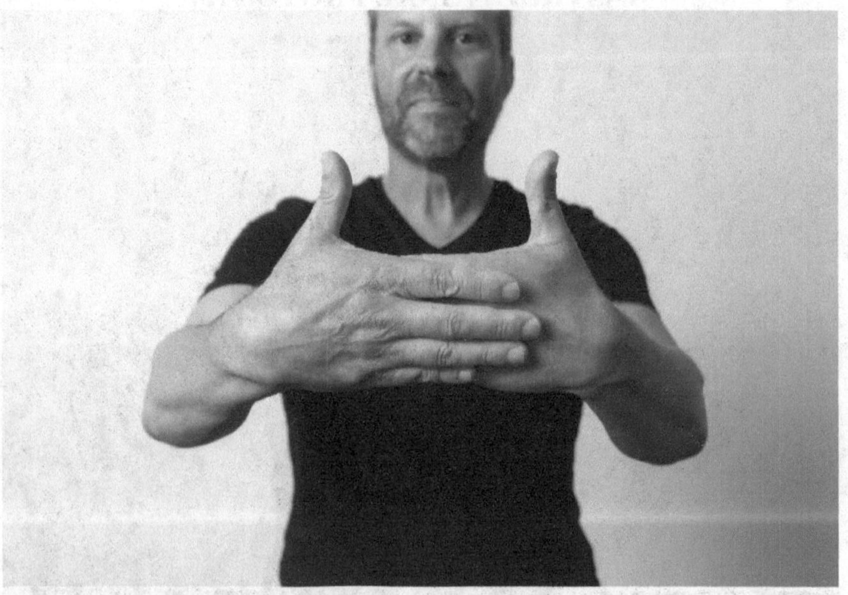

(Go to: *https://stareatthewall.org/book* for hi-res image)

Now, bring your thumbs together. To the best of your abilities, form a heart with your thumbs. Even if your hands don't look like a heart, they can create a heart. To someone else, they may look like an oval, but to you, they are a heart. Such a simple exercise reveals how we perceive the world.

[INSTRUCTIONAL PHOTO #17]

(Go to: *https://stareatthewall.org/book* for hi-res image)

People with long nails or physical issues may have trouble forming the heart. Do your best, but pay attention to your hands when meditating. They are often the first outward display of our inner distraction.

The heart represents your love and appreciation for the entire universe. More simply put, it shows your respect for yourself, life, and your practice. Try to keep it whole.

Now, drop your hands to your lap. Let them drop. Gravity knows what it's doing. Don't resist. Let them sit there.

Be aware of any tension in your arms, hands, and shoulders. It may feel awkward at first. If you stick with it, it won't.

You may notice something interesting when you look down after dropping your hands. Your less dominant hand is now facing up toward you. It's a direct example of balance. If you don't believe you are already balanced, maybe your own hands will convince you.

[INSTRUCTIONAL PHOTO #18]

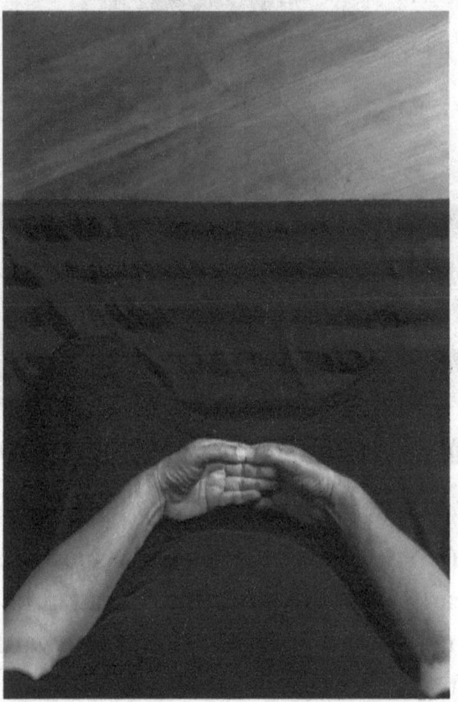

(Go to: *https://stareatthewall.org/book* for hi-res image)

The Chin

Facing the wall, point your chin downward, but not too far down. Tuck it in a little. Just double-check that it's not up. Take the time to focus and experiment. Our practice includes many subtle movements and non-movements.

Pull the back of your head up to help your chin find its way. A practice like this helps us be our natural or original selves.

Pay attention to your chin and head while meditating. Try to keep them perfectly straight. When they go crooked, please don't beat yourself up. If you are aware of it, you are paying attention.

The Stomach

The stomach is key. It's where a lot of our emotions are stored. If you are anxious by nature like me, you probably know all about this. My stomach talks to me in a strange language. I feel its words.

Suck your stomach in a little at first with your chest out. Now, try to relax in that position. Find what's natural. Don't be afraid to experiment. Practice is a long-term study of the self. At the very least, it's a lifelong commitment.

Pay attention to your stomach while meditating. Notice your breath coming in and out. Follow it in and out of your darkest, foulest bowels.

Long-term meditators sometimes experience "Buddha belly." There's a reason why we sometimes depict Buddha with a nice, round belly. It isn't because of his bad eating habits! Or is it?

We get out of shape if we sit too much without moving! Even too much meditation isn't good. "Everything in moderation" applies to practice as much as anything else. It is the practice.

If we are in the flow for many years, our stomachs may become so relaxed that they are full of themselves. Leave that pride to the stomach. Pride in the mind is extra.

From my standpoint, "Buddha Belly" is a perfect balance. It doesn't look good, but it sure feels good!

I had many stomach issues. I do not anymore. Meditation and medication together relieve my suffering. We address our perceived problems to address them. We address them with our minds in stillness. Then, we find out if they're real or perceived.

If our problems are real, we use calm and quiet time to decide how to address them. An appropriate course of action will come to us. We don't force it or go into meditation looking to work out specific problems. Answers come to us when we're ready for them and open to them. We have the answers, but we need to develop the discipline to hear and do what we already know.

The Shoulders

Many of us hold tension in our shoulders. Once in the meditation position, relax your shoulders as much as possible. Shoulders slightly back, proud like a peacock, I always say.

At first, especially if we come to practice with low self-esteem, it is good to fake confidence. "Practice makes imperfection as perfect as possible," says the Coach.

Try to feel your way into making both shoulders equal, and pay attention to them while meditating. Go into them with your mind and let nature do its thing. Observe them.

The Neck

Every neck is unique. I don't really have a neck. I joke that I'm neckless. It isn't easy to explain how to relax a neck, but it becomes self-evident once we routinely focus on it. Adjust it. Pull the back of the head up. Chin down a little. How does it feel?

We tuck our chin down a little with our head straight to keep our neck that way. Experiment with your neck. You may want to spend a session focused only on your neck. If we stick with meditation, these are the kinds of subtle practices we might get into.

A lot of my physical pain is in the neck. Life can be a pain in the neck. I still have neck pain, but I accept its role in my practice. First, I made sure that nothing was physically wrong with me. I went to a qualified medical doctor. With those worries out of the way, I was free to get to the root of my emotional pains in the neck.

The Back and Spine

Like the neck and shoulders, the back takes a lot of stress. If you have a bad back, you'd be better off sitting in a chair or lying down to meditate. In practice, we keep our spine as straight as possible. It was helpful to check my position in a mirror when I first started meditating, but I didn't make it a habit. The point isn't to criticize our physical appearance. We tend to do enough of that already.

[INSTRUCTIONAL PHOTO #19]

(Go to: *https://stareatthewall.org/book* for hi-res image)

Our spine is more important than we may realize. All kinds of signals, impulses, and messages flow through it. Some call it the "spinal telephone," insinuating that it receives messages from nature and the universe. I'm not sure who originally coined the term, but they talk to us if we pay close attention to our spines.

Coach talks to me through my spine. He says things like, "Don't give up. Just stop! Before doesn't matter. Start fresh. Clean. It's never too late. Straighten up. Hydrate. Careful. Apologize. Eat right. Go to the dentist! Get a colonoscopy! Just keep going."

Some say the entire universe moves through our spines. I don't know about all that, but sometimes I sense it's true. Depending on where we are in life, a big idea like that and five dollars might get us a little cup of bad coffee. In other words, most of our big ideas produce nothing worthwhile. Think little to think big, I always say.

Breathing

Many folks focus on their breath to reach a calm, meditative state. Just breathe naturally and notice it. Simply directing our minds to our breath is a powerful practice.

If we expect too much of our breath, we may be disappointed. It's better to keep our expectations and assumptions to a minimum.

Sometimes, at the start of a meditation session or during a long one, it feels good to take a deep breath or two or three (you get the picture).

When I do it, it sounds like a sigh. It releases tension and brings me back to (X). There's a reason why professional footballers always take deep breaths when lined up for big kicks.

Some people go in through the nose and out the mouth. Some, the other way around. I tend to breathe in and out through my nose.

The point isn't how you breathe. It's essential to pay attention to it. Follow it with your mind. Breathe naturally and notice it. How do you typically breathe? Do you find it changes depending on the situation? If you don't know, find out.

Breathe in through the body, to your stomach, and out. The flow looks and feels different for each of us. Depending on our state of mind, it varies.

I try not to complicate or overanalyze breathing. If you can't focus on your breath, let it go. If you keep trying, you will appreciate it someday. It's like learning to surf. Once it's second nature, it sure feels free.

At first, it may be helpful to count your breaths until ten. Never go past ten. When we keep counting, we tend to measure. We might think, "I focused on my breaths to one hundred yesterday, but today, I can't get past three." Discouraging feelings usually follow. Counting breaths is funny because when I did it, I would catch myself at six hundred and thirty-four when I was supposed to stop at ten. That's a good laugh.

Focusing on our breath is effective, but it's another one of those subtle things that's so obvious it's hard to believe. How could focusing on the invisible air that's everywhere do anything good for me? That's the wrong question. Just do it and see. Air will show you its primordial wisdom.

Adjustment Time

When you first sit or lie down, adjust as long as it takes to settle. Settling in is not an afterthought. It's part of the practice. If you can slow down and pay attention before you even get started, you've already started.

Once locked in, start your timer or hit a bell three times. After the third chime, or when the timer begins, try not to move.

[INSTRUCTIONAL PHOTO #20]

(Go to: *https://stareatthewall.org/book* for hi-res image)

I have turned bell ringing into a practice. After about a year, I finally realized that my bell had a little arrow engraved on the side, showing the ideal place to hit it. I hit it gently now. Before, I was loud and half-cocked.

My hands generally tremble a bit, but I steady myself as much as possible and prepare to hit the bell by paying attention to my breathing. I try to hit it precisely the same way all three rings, which is an arduous practice. I rarely succeed. My inability to consistently ring the bell keeps me humble. It reminds me that I'm far from perfect.

I don't need a timer anymore. When meditation does what it needs to do, I get up and move. It's a feeling. I don't reflect on it.

Even when leading groups, I don't use a timer. I see people squirm. "When is he going to hit the bell?" They don't know that the bell rings us. We don't ring it.

When we first start our practice, we might have anxiety anticipating the finish bell. We may long for it like a cold drink on a humid summer day.

"My back hurts!" It may feel like forever. If we have a timer and are meditating alone, we'll likely watch the clock. That's an easy habit to fall into. How slowly the seconds ticked when I first got down in front of the wall.

Now, when I sit, time is gone. I realized that while sitting. It doesn't matter if it's a forty-minute sit or ten minutes, a weeklong retreat or just a couple of rounds. It's an experience, an inner voice, a pivot in thinking that diverts my mind away from any lazy ways out.

It's like driving a car after a few years. Our feet and hands know when to press, turn, and adjust. We don't need to think, but we'd be foolish to lose focus on the road.

When I practice, I practice "no time." I had to let go of time to practice it. There's no more, "How much time do we have left?" Or "My leg hurts so bad, I think I'll just give up."

Yet, I am still subject to time. To focus on one side of time is not a realistic experience. If I need to be at work at nine o'clock and tell my boss time doesn't exist, she will not be very pleased.

When I go to work, I'm doing "work time." Time is what we are doing. If we are doing nothing or restraining ourselves and not doing something, like drinking alcohol, it's "no" time.

When we have a responsibility or realize we are getting older and changing, it's "yes" time. Time matters, and if we stop and sense how precious it is each day, we are wise.

So there "is and isn't time" depending on the circumstances. This kind of thinking is the result of many years in the balanced position. The position rubs off on the mind. We think, act, and eventually even feel as if we sit. We learn to sit with our pain and irritations, redirecting, learning from, and accepting them.

The Mind in Pain

In conclusion, I want to focus on pain because it's so important. Pain in the body is in the mind. To be aware and alive is to feel it. Suffering is a fundamental condition of life. For that reason, it belongs.

Pain is simple to me; it's obvious, but it may not be so easy for you. Simplifying or authenticating it doesn't make a painful experience more pleasant. Persistent physical or emotional pain can be a living hell.

I don't look forward to pain or impose it on myself. That's not what practice is all about. Enduring pain is not a test. It's life at its rawest. Our mothers suffered to bring us into the world.

When meditation is uncomfortable, I see it as an opportunity to sit still and quiet through pain without hurting myself. We are creating a warm, safe, and reliable space within ourselves that isn't dependent on external factors. It's so simple, but not so at first. Like anything else, we need to practice.

When we consider pain our teacher, we learn. When pain keeps us focused on what matters, it becomes worth more than diamonds.

It is perfectly natural in the beginning to think, "This is so boring. What's the point of sitting in pain like this? How could all this effort lead to anything worthwhile?" Just keep doing it and experience the point directly. The abstract will become self-evident.

A seed doesn't know that if conditions are balanced, someday it will experience life as a tall, strong, well-rooted, fruit-bearing tree. Be like a tree. *(57)*

Like me, you may find value in what appears as boredom. When life shakes us to the core and we are in pain or facing grave danger, we all want our boring lives back.

If you are bored, it may mean you are relatively stable. It might also mean you need to get off your lazy ass and try something new. When we get into the balanced position before the wall, we take our boredom somewhere new. Our boredom doesn't seem so boring. The word "boring" becomes something else altogether. Personally, I never use the word. I don't know what it means anymore. Boring is now banal.

After my military service, I began to notice a sinking feeling in my stomach. When I felt it, I knew I was depressed. It dreaded what I considered my boring life as a civilian. I thought I needed action. If I wasn't moving, something was always wrong. I stared at a loaded nine-millimeter for two years. Now that I stare at walls instead of deadly weapons, I get the same sinking sense, but don't feel depressed. I don't need to move. It doesn't bring me down. It grounds me.

I think, "Oh, there's the sinking feeling. I don't miss those years of depression," and move on. My body doesn't need to move, in order for my mind to. I don't push it away. I stop and acknowledge it. But at the same time, I don't identify with it. I let go. I do the opposite of what I used to tell myself. I tried something different over and over again until it became routine. Different is now the norm.

Neck and shoulder pain accompany the experience. I have them right now. Those pains are symptoms of my anxiety. Sometimes I get them, but they don't get in the way. Technically, I still have anxiety, but anxiety doesn't have me.

Most of my stress sits in my neck and upper back. It pulls on my throat, making it feel swollen. I used to get dizzy. Doctors labeled my dizziness and swollen throat "panic attacks." My throat occasionally feels swollen, but I don't panic. I acknowledge it and move on calmly. Except when I first sit down in the morning, I don't feel dizzy anymore. Over the years, my dizziness has soaked into my meditation mat.

Before my meditation practice took hold, I was constantly massaging my neck and shoulders and using a TENS machine under my clothes. I took a lot of over-the-counter painkillers. I tried portable massagers, heating pads and cold presses. I had trouble sleeping. I'd lie awake, tossing and turning and sweating. When I did fall asleep, I'd wake up from terrible dreams.

The only thing that offered temporary relief was passing out from alcohol, but my symptoms came back worse after a binge. I went to the emergency room several times because I thought I was having a heart attack. My mouth ticked and contorted. My health issues took a lot of my focus. I didn't have much room to care about anyone else.

These symptoms come back from time to time, and I think, "Wow. I don't miss pain like that. How did I manage to move past it?" It's a rhetorical question. I know how. I focused on my issues for a long time, and my mind and body worked them out. Now, I don't interrupt nature's work. I trust the process. If given the right conditions to grow, a seed will bear fruit.

Before meditation could holistically treat me, I had to reach relative stability. I had to own up to my problems and seek professional help. First, a trained medical doctor poked, prodded, and x-rayed my head, neck, shoulders, and back for physical issues. They didn't find anything too serious. With the relief and emotional space created by negative medical conclusions, I reached out to available networks for mental health help. In my case, it was the Veterans Administration.

My pain used to scare the hell out of me, but once it was out in the open, I was in a better position to address it. Psychologists diagnosed me. At first, I identified with their labels. I announced my conditions to strangers.

Now, I talk about my struggles to let you know we are equal. If I can do it, you can.

Finding the right meds and getting over social stigmas associated with mental illness is a hard practice. It wasn't easy to participate in long-term counseling and buy into it. It took a lot of courage and self-compassion. All of my old, self-defeating voices tried to get in the way. I saw through their little games. I needed to be patient and trust the process. Modern medicine works within its own set of unique limitations. I didn't expect too much. Cures are always collaborative combinations. I got creative.

My practice took over once my treatment helped me become relatively stable. Now, I use all available tools without stigma or reservation. Sometimes, the best thing I can do is get back to basics. The worst thing I could do is think I'm so stable I can quit my meds cold turkey. I've seen well-intended people who feel great about their new meditation routine make that mistake one too many times, and it's ugly.

Balance means not getting too excited about our new practice. If our practice works so well that we make bad decisions, it isn't working at all.

Sitting is often uncomfortable, yet we maintain a stable position. Think of the discomfort as all the shitty stuff that happened in your life. What happened is not necessarily what's happening. We tend to keep connections that are no longer useful.

Despite sometimes being miserably uncomfortable, if you can consistently sit still and quiet without caving into distractions or doubts, you are well on your way.

Do not identify with your current state of mind when possible and appropriate. Let all states come and go. Don't ignore your experience, just double check that it's coming from a balanced place. If the dog barks or kids laugh and scream while you are sitting in silence, don't shush them. Stay upright and still while studying how the irritation feels.

Sometimes, we need to identify with our current state of mind. We have responsibilities and people who depend on us. Even if we feel spiritual, they deserve our attention. Remember, there is no difference between spiritual and real life.

Our preferences and habits are perfectly natural. They are not bad. Try to watch them without judging them. It's not easy. It takes patience, compassion, and practice to see what's necessary and what's not. In time, we may see our bad habits as funny little friends meant to brighten up our day.

You are exactly where you are supposed to be. You are already here as a spiritual person, but might not know it. My job is to help you know it. Know what? It! It = (X).

All effects have causes. Everything now is a culmination of everything then. For me, writing these instructions in the present is it. It all comes together. Sometimes we like what's coming together, sometimes we don't, but it all makes sense to me, even when it doesn't. Mysteriously, meditation brings the entirety of the spinning universe to a stable point in my head. It's a focus and warm feeling more than anything else.

So long as we're not hurting ourselves physically, the more meditation hurts, the better. Each time, we build our tolerance for letting things come and go in a stable position. We can become rock solid no matter what (X) feels like. That's easier said than done. I fail less than I succeed. I call that progress.

Direct your mind toward the pain. Acknowledge it. Go toward it. Don't judge it.

Breathe through distractions (like itches, aches, and troubling thoughts) and bring your mind to them. Then let them go. Acknowledge and try to accept them. Stay still. See what happens.

Try to watch it all come and go. What? Everything. Anything. Other than paying attention to your body, breathing, hands, etc., just let come what comes and go what goes. Our aim is not to focus on only one thing. It's too see the bigger picture. If we completely focus on our rear-view mirror when driving and lose track of everything else, we'll crash.

There's no need to note the patterns you discover or intentionally scan your body. Go into daily meditation fresh without a goal in mind. Let all things reveal and plant themselves in you. Stay out of the way.

Sit in the cat-bird seat or the best position to watch things come and go. If something interesting passes by, spring into action!

If something troubling keeps coming up, pay attention. If it's a physical pain that doesn't come and go, address it. If possible, make it your practice to find a qualified doctor.

Our loved ones need us. Our planet and God are counting on us. It's time for us to get our collective shit together. If not now, when? If not you, who?

There's no pressure to do the right thing, but make the wrong things count. Keep your posture upright through it all. Return to the still, composed position at the wall. Go back to being careful and simple.

If life is spinning out of control, plant yourself in stillness. It won't let you down. You will find your balance. Sometimes, if we're headed in the wrong direction, we should do the opposite of what we tell ourselves to turn around. Be careful who you listen to and that also applies to your own voices. Don't believe what you tell yourself until you believe in yourself. No matter how much you trust yourself, don't take yourself at face value.

Let your Coach introduce themselves to you. Don't go looking for them.

Find some good practice friends that you trust. It's easy to know who's genuine and who's not. If they act naturally, trust them. If they name-drop or regurgitate terms or practices, be wary. If they try to sell, convert, condemn, or convince you, walk away. If they promote prophets or enlightened leaders, run as fast as you can.

Try not to get caught up in exotic customs, rumors, hierarchies, or the politics of spiritual practice. If there's a lot of drama or people aggressively protecting tradition, step out of the group for a while. Lean on your wall. It's strong enough to support you. Just do it. When you're balanced and humble, the entire spinning universe has your back. Even when you're alone, you'll know you're not. Then, everything might begin to come together in your mind.

It's already coming together. You might realize that what appears to be imbalanced is still perfectly balanced.

I wish you lots of love and congratulate you on your meditation practice! If you are doing it, it has come together! Let it emerge from a limitless nothing. Don't get in the way.

Remember, if it goes well, don't get too excited. Give yourself a chance to grow. Act naturally. Wisdom is about balance, love, and nature's flow, not forcing your way through the earth to get ahead.

If you offer people nourishing fruit before it's grown, you may turn them into hungry ghosts. You may hurt them. We can't give what we don't already have. Birds might live off seeds, but not people. The seeds that feed us are meant to grow. All we can do is provide the best conditions for them to transform into nutritious fruit.

Everything you ever want and need is here (X) at home. Place no head above your own. *(58)*

Fertile ground is under you. The Earth is balanced. You don't need to be anywhere else to grow. Know that the sky will send light and rain to nourish you. God and nature won't deny you.

Be patient and silent like a seed. Let growth come to you. Sit there doing nothing. Then get up and pay attention to what you're doing. It's no big secret. You don't need anyone else to teach it to you. It's simplification at the molecular level. It's raw acceptance. It's you being your original self.

Know that boredom in balance is a privilege. Acknowledge your problems as they arise and address them. Seek professional help if necessary. Don't feel ashamed. That won't help.

Not trusting modern medicine has nothing to do with spirituality. Trusting it too much doesn't either.

Feel your way through your practice. Eat and move when it's time. Address real problems as they arise. Don't invent them. Focus on those who rely on you, but don't feel guilty when you let them down. Sit in a stable position. Once you're stable, the whole universe is.

Nothing extra is not extra. What's extra is extra in the mind first. Let go of what's extra. Simplify your mind.

Your body and mind already know what to do. Let them do their jobs together. Fruit will come.

Don't worry about fruit. Pay attention to the seed, one growth stage at a time. Take my hand. Together, we will plant ourselves in front of the wall.

What if you sincerely and consistently practice with great focus and do not feel the difference? In that case, trust your nature or God. Don't give up! Ever! I assure you, whether you see it or not, everything is unfolding as it should. In support of life and diversity, "should" = balance.

I'm pretty sure if you meditate long enough, someone else will notice the difference long before you do. They'll say something like, "Dude, you look good. What are you doing differently?" They're sensing the early surface signs of a shift that runs much deeper than looking rested or less haunted. It's the same shift that matters when everything is on the line.

When we sit still and quietly in meditation, the conditions are stable enough for the seed of practice to grow. If my practice is balanced at death, whatever comes next will flow naturally. The seed knows what to do as it moves from one stage to another.

Balance prepares us for almost anything, and I'm speaking from experience. I've been in some wild situations. I've stared down Mr. Death more times than is healthy. He's not the gentle, poetic type. He wants the whole bundle—body, mind, and soul—and he wants it with this little twinkle of *I told you so* satisfaction, like he's been waiting for me to mess up just enough to make his job easy.

When I close my eyes for the final slumber, what will I see? Will it be me? What will I be? I feel some insight arise, a glimpse of the afterlife, but I let go and focus on now because I will be no more. I feared birth but had no choice. As a man, I do not fear. My nature will embrace me. I am not foolish enough to claim to know how the fruit of my faith will feel and taste in the end.

I'm not sure I'll be able to maintain perfect composure when it counts, so I don't count. Will I be brave enough to look death in the eye and welcome it? Will I show those loved ones present how to die the expansive way? Will it come quickly and render such talk meaningless?

I'm not a karma pollinator or soothsayer. I don't fly in the face of God and bother him with bold, sweeping predictions that have nothing to do with reality. I try not to get in the way. I try to buzz past God without him, her, or it, noticing. Maybe that's freedom?

Until my last breath, I'll try to pay attention to the light, flowing air in a balanced position. That much I'm sure of.

Together in our meditation practice, we are already making a big difference in small ways. Please don't trust me. Trust yourself.

Look at something beautiful each day. Appreciate yourself as a manifestation of universal love and passion. Even if your parents are/were pieces of work, you are a "miracle masterpiece."

If your own people make/made you feel little, trust the awareness of the BIG, limitless universe or God. Even when we don't, it knows what it's doing. It always has and always will. It loves all children equally and unconditionally.

Be aware of any feelings of superiority or specialness. They aren't helpful. We are all the same but different.

Seasons change for good reason. Life is a family. Celebrate life. No matter how unstable, depreciated, or dark the world looks in our tired eyes, fall is still fall. A falling leaf from a tree is still a falling leaf from a tree. That's why it is called fall. God is still God. The universe is still the universe. The planet and sun are still the planet and sun. A child is still a child. You are still you. I am still me. And, finally, our practice is still our practice.

Do we wholeheartedly believe that the endless universe is perfectly sacred, balanced, and unified? How strong is our faith? It's crunch time. As the wise and holy women say to the smooth-talking players who promise them the world, "It's time to put up or shut up, buddy." *(59)*

We hear the word of God or our original nature when we humble ourselves and acknowledge that our problems, feelings, and opinions are infinitely limited. We listen. Putting pressure on ourselves and one another does no good. Try the gentle approach. Come on home.

Compassion can evolve alongside our technology. If our tools grow sharper while our hearts stay dull, we end up building instruments of war and exploitation instead of instruments of peace. Every advance we make—in medicine, communication, energy, transportation or exploration—needs compassion woven into its design. Without it, progress becomes reckless. With it, progress becomes sustainable.

Kindness is the one adaptation that keeps our inventions from turning against us, and keeps us from turning against each other. This is not a grand theory. It is simple. If we want a livable future, it must be the fundamental aspect of the blueprint.

It has to guide how we build, how we solve problems, and how we treat the people and the planet around us. Technology without love accelerates harm. Technology with love repairs it. And the only way compassion survives into the future is if we practice it now, in small, ordinary ways, until it becomes the natural direction of our lives. We can't always be kind and welcoming, but we can do our best and care.

History has brought us to this crucial point. Do we go further into chaos, or turn toward love? The worst thing we can do, the absolute worst, is nothing. The best thing we can do is commit ourselves to cultivating compassion, at home, right now. This is where evolution actually happens—not in governments or institutions, but in the daily choices of ordinary people.

If kindness becomes our focus, it can spread. It doesn't spread through picket signs, violence, or loud speeches. We plant and nurture it like seeds on every corner of the earth, discreetly without raising the eyebrows of the authorities or offending anyone. Every generation has faced a turning point. This one is ours, and it begins with the smallest possible step: choosing compassion in the moment we are in. It's starts with being kind to ourselves.

People have tried to unite across borders before: the socialist movements rose to stop the exploitation of labor, and the democratic nations formed to unite people around personal liberty. Each was an attempt to bring humanity together under a shared purpose.

But the real leaders, the real innovators, have always been the compassionate ones of all religions and cultures—the people who move others toward cooperation instead of conflict, toward sustainability instead of exhaustion. They are the ones who build trust, repair harm, and make progress possible. If anything deserves to unite us now, it is compassion itself.

Compassionate people of the world, unite—not in anger, patriotism or ideology, but in the steady, human work of keeping us alive and well and moving in a meaningful direction.

Do we practice the word of God or the cosmic consciousness, or regurgitate it like a bird vomits into the mouths of hungry chicks? CHIRP! CHIRP! CHIRP! Finally, as one, let's bow our heads in silence to appreciate the miracle of our lives—no more chirping. Just stare at the wall.

Time is still time. Even a minute of life is still life. (*60*)

REMEMBER!

DON'T FORGET.

IT'S NOT TOO LATE!

Mark Blacknell, Spring, 2026

THE END

NOTES & CITATIONS

1. "The Murder Case of the Wife of Suzuki Roshi (Shunryu)." *Cuke.com.* https://www.cuke.com/Cucumber-Project/interviews/masaji-letter.html.
2. Tolkien, J. R. R. *The Fellowship of the Ring*. London: Allen & Unwin, 1954.
3. Descartes, René. *Meditations on First Philosophy.* Translated by Michael Moriarty. Oxford: Oxford University Press, 2008.
4. Hanh, Thich Nhat, and Sherab Chödzin Kohn. *You Are Here: Discovering the Magic of the Present Moment.* Boston: Shambhala Publications, 2012.
5. Coyote, Peter. www.petercoyote.com.
6. Sheindlin, Judy. www.judyjustice.tv.
7. Nilsson, Harry. *The Point*. Murakami-Wolf Productions / Nilsson House Music Inc., 1971.
8. "Pelican Landing Assisted Living Home." www.thepelicanlanding.com/assisted-living/arts-music-culture/. Sebastian, FL.
9. Chadwick, David. www.cuke.com.
10. Schneider, David. *Street Zen: The Life and Work of Issan Dorsey*. Cambridge, MA: Da Capo Press, 2000.
11. Glenville, Peter, dir. *Becket*. Paramount Pictures, 1964.
12. Kesey, Ken. www.furthurdowntheroad.org.
13. Suzuki, Shunryu. *Zen Mind, Beginner's Mind.* Boston: Shambhala Publications, 2010.
14. *Maui, Hawaii, Upper Kula.* 1427 Poli Poli Rd. Old farmhouse next door to the Thompson Ranch. If you stop by, say hello to Scotty and Woody, my old next-door neighbors.

15. Suzuki, Shunryu. "Sandokai Lecture V." June 6, 1970. www.shunryusuzuki.com/suzuki/transcripts-pdf/ezt-1-pdf/70-06-10.pdf.
16. "Transmission Lineage." Shunryu Suzuki of San Francisco Zen Center → Lew Richmond of Vimala Sangha → Peter Coyote of Wild Dog Sangha → me of Nothing.
17. "The Sea of Galilee, or Kinneret in Hebrew." The monk was Greek Orthodox.
18. Zahavi, Amotz. Personal recollection. "Before his passing, Professor Zahavi worked tirelessly to save the Arabian Babbler species from extinction. I met him through Professor Yossi Leshem… who I met through Jim Brett (R.I.P.)… who I met through Rick Carlson, who took a chance on a young cocky punk (me)."
19. *Bible Hub.* www.biblehub.com/catholic/luke/12-27.htm.
20. "Ecstatic Dance." www.ecstaticdance.org; Melanie Fisher, *Star Born Agency*, www.starbornagency.com. Asheville, NC.
21. Senauke, Alan. "No Gaining Idea." *Berkeley Zen Center*, February 2022. www.berkeleyzencenter.org/2022/02/28/no-gaining-idea/.
22. Hoffer, Eric. *The True Believer: Thoughts on the Nature of Mass Movements*. New York: Harper Perennial Modern Classics, 2019.
23. Kubrick, Stanley, dir. *The Shining*. Warner Bros., 1980.
24. Sugar, Rebecca, creator. *Steven Universe*. Cartoon Network, 2013–2019.
25. Plato. *Apology 22d.* Translated by Harold North Fowler. Cambridge: Harvard University Press, 1966.
26. Pearl Jam. "Nothingman." *Vitalogy*. Epic–Legacy, 1994.
27. Kerouac, Jack. *On the Road*. New York: Penguin Books, 2011.
28. "Pai-chang's Fox." *T'ien-Sheng Kuang-teng Lu*, ca. 1036.

29. Reagan, Ronald. "Address to the United Nations General Assembly." New York City, September 21, 1987.
30. Malcolm X, with Alex Haley. *The Autobiography of Malcolm X.* New York: Grove Press, 1965.
31. *Airplane!* Directed by Jim Abrahams, David Zucker, and Jerry Zucker. Paramount Pictures, 1980.
32. Global Citizen. "The Richest 1%." January 2023. https://www.globalcitizen.org/en/content/wealth-inequality-oxfam-billionaires-elon-musk/.
33. Nietzsche, Friedrich Wilhelm. *Thus Spoke Zarathustra: A Book for All and None*. Cambridge: Cambridge University Press, 2006.
34. "Darby, Pennsylvania." www.darbyborough.com.
35. Pope, Alexander. *The Poems of Alexander Pope*. Edited by John Butt. New Haven: Yale University Press, 1963.
36. Wesley, John. Letter to Alexander Clark, August 10, 1772.
37. "Consumer Spending Drives the Economy." *Foundation for Economic Education.* www.fee.org/articles/consumer-spending-drives-the-economy/.
38. Berry, Thomas. *The Great Work: Our Way into the Future.* New York: Harmony/Bell Tower, 1999. See also www.thomasberry.org; and Mary Evelyn Tucker, "Journey of the Universe," www.journeyoftheuniverse.org/bios/mary-evelyn-tucker.
39. *The Holy Bible: Matthew 4.* United States Conference of Catholic Bishops. https://www.biblegateway.com/passage/?search=Matthew%204&version=NIV.
40. *The Holy Bible: Genesis 18:2.* www.chabad.org/kabbalah/article_cdo/aid/379749/jewish/Abrahams-Hospitality.htm.
41. *The Quran*, 96:1–5. www.theprophetofislam.org/en/muhammad-and-divine-revelation.html.

42. Suzuki, Shunryu. Lecture at San Francisco Zen Center, June 11, 1967. www.chzc.org/SR4.htm.
43. Suzuki, Shunryu. *Zen Mind, Beginner's Mind.* Boston: Shambhala Publications, 2008.
44. Vedder, Eddie, and Nusrat Fateh Ali Khan. "The Long Road." Columbia Records, 1996. www.youtube.com/watch?v=FmzT_wb6Dlo.
45. Smither, Chris. "Cave Man." *More from the Levee.* Signature Sounds, 2020. https://www.youtube.com/watch?v=E5mqq31Jz-U
46. Suzuki, Shunryu. "Lotus Sutra No. 6." Lecture, Zen Mountain Center, February 1968.
47. Killgrove, Kristina. "New Analysis of Hitler's Teeth Confirms Nazi Leader's Vegetarianism." *Forbes,* May 21, 2018. www.forbes.com/sites/kristinakillgrove/2018/05/21/new-analysis-of-hitlers-teeth-confirms-nazi-leaders-vegetarianism/.
48. Author's note: "As an extension of my practice, I teach meditation to Florida Death Row inmates. I was once locked up on a serious felony charge. Though the charges were dropped, it was an eye-opening experience that drew me back inside to help."
49. Author's note: "Perfectly sober, I once saw the body of Bodhidharma in a shimmer of light on my pond."
50. Dylan, Bob. "Blowin' in the Wind." *The Freewheelin' Bob Dylan.* Columbia Records, 1963.
51. Dylan, Bob. "Ballad of a Thin Man." *Highway 61 Revisited.* Columbia Records, 1965.
52. Brazier, David. *The Feeling Buddha.* New York: St. Martin's Griffin, 1997.
53. Byrne, Rhonda. *The Secret.* New York: Atria Books, 2006. (Not a fan.)

54. Brown, Edward. *The Tassajara Recipe Book.* Boston: Shambhala Publications, 2000.
55. Wild Dog Sangha; Clearwater Zen Center; Marin County Zen Group (Steve Stucky's old group); Florida Death Row Sangha; Vero Beach Buddhist Sangha; Paul Shippee Non-Violent Communication (RIP); Pelican Landing Assisted Living Home Sangha.
56. Levingston, Ivan B. K. "Five Questions About the Honor Code Answered." *Harvard Crimson,* September 2015. www.thecrimson.com/flyby/article/2015/9/8/5-questions-about-honor-code/.
57. Passiflora. "Like a Tree: Noches en Vela." *Grabado en La Nave,* 2012. www.youtube.com/watch?v=hffrzFZPo-Q.
58. Suzuki, Shunryu. "Wherever You Go, You Will See Yourself." Lecture, San Francisco Zen Center, 1971. https://www.shunryusuzuki.com/suzuki/transcripts-pdf/ezt-1-pdf/71-02-07.pdf
59. Moore, Christy. "Wise and Holy Woman." *Live in Dublin,* 2006. https://www.youtube.com/watch?v=P_WbrccVeE8
60. Keneally, Thomas. *Schindler's Ark.* London: Hodder and Stoughton, 1982.

www.ingramcontent.com/pod-product-compliance
Lightning Source LLC
LaVergne TN
LVHW040215110826
845146LV00005B/1296

* 9 7 9 8 9 9 5 7 6 7 0 0 8 *